The
VALLIAN TRILOGY
An Inventive Life
Part III: The Geometer

THE
VALLIAN TRILOGY
An Inventive Life

Part III: The Geometer

ooooo

SHARON C. WAHL

2017

River Sanctuary

PUBLISHING

The Vallian Trilogy: An Inventive Life Part III: The Geometer
Copyright © 2017 by Sharon C. Wahl

Cover Illustrations by Larry E. Wahl
Cover Design by River Sanctuary Graphic Arts

ISBN 978-1-935914-74-7

Also by Sharon and Larry Wahl:
The Vallian Trilogy: An Inventive Life. Part I: The Engineer
The Vallian Trilogy: An Inventive Life. Part II: The Learner
The Tesseract: The Path Through Optical Illusions
The Elephant in the Room/Chasing the Tesseract: History of the Vallian Coordinate System

Printed in the United States of America

To order additional copies please visit:
www.riversanctuarypublishing.com

RIVER SANCTUARY PUBLISHING
P.O Box 1561
Felton, CA 95018
www.riversanctuarypublishing.com
Dedicated to the awakening of the New Earth

Do Not Stand by My Grave and Weep

Mary Elizabeth Frye

Do not stand at my grave and weep

I am not there; I do not sleep.

I am a thousand winds that blow,

I am the diamond glints on snow,

I am the sun on ripened grain,

I am the gentle autumn rain.

When you awaken in the morning's hush

I am the swift uplifting rush

Of quiet birds in circled flight

I am the soft stars that shine at night.

Do not stand at my grave and cry,

I am not there; I did not die.

Acknowledgements

How can I begin to thank all of the friends who have walked with me on the difficult road to writing this book after the loss of Larry? I can't. So to all of you—and you know who you are—I dedicate this book, with much love and gratitude.

And I wish to extend loving thanks to my Creative Expressions writing class at Avenidas; their critiques and suggestions resulted in much improvement of this book.

SCW 2016

CONTENTS

Prologue

The pain now is part of the happiness then.
That's the deal.

—C. S. Lewis

Let me began by pointing out that this is the third book of the Vallian Trilogy—the life and times of Larry E. Wahl. But, unlike the first two that were written by Larry and edited by me, I am writing this book as a narrator that will continue his life story, but also will include some of Larry's essays, poems, and writings regarding his invention and new geometry: the Vallian Geometric Hexagon Opting Symbolic Tesseract (Wahl Patent #5982374). Larry felt that I might put a softer touch on some of what may prove to be unpalatable material. We both felt very strongly that this part of the story needs airing as much as the earlier, formative events of his life. However, the Cosmic Intelligence has Its own plan for Its inhabitants, so due to his untimely, but not unexpected death, I will have to carry on without his input. We had been a team for so long that I have a pretty good idea of what he would want to be in this last book of the series. And I have, at hand, literally hundreds of pages of written material and drawings to guide me and to quote. I only hope I can do him and his work justice.

We had been married for 53 years, and even we, as well as our friends, wondered how that happened! To say that those years were *all* wonderful or peaceful would be an outright lie, and yet they *were* wonderful and had some special peaceful periods. But also they were exciting, energizing, full of life, and, most importantly, growth-producing. Upon learning that we were planning to celebrate our 50th, a young woman asked, "What is your secret?" Larry and I responded simultaneously: Larry—"fight," me—"a sense of humor!" Can you see how we, and others, might be puzzled by our longevity?

So, while we were different in many ways, including, unfortunately, how we thought and how we communicated, we persisted because (1) we loved each other and (2) we shared values. I think that says it all! (But of course, there is the fighting and sense of humor ...)

EULOGY

Larry Eugene Wahl
Aka Lewis X. Vallian (LXV)
1927—2013

Larry Wahl had 85 years of dynamic and exciting living before he passed from this existence in a peaceful and dignified manner on February 27, 2013, in Menlo Park, California. He leaves behind Sharon, his wife of 53 years, son Eric Wahl of Eugene, Oregon, daughter Jill Grove and her husband, Tim of Colorado Springs, Colorado, and sister Anna Mae Tichy of Portland, Oregon. Larry and Sharon lived in Menlo Park for 32 years. Prior to moving to the Bay Area in 1980, they resided in the Portland Oregon Metropolitan area.

For his wife's web page, Larry described himself as a survivor, a former CIA agent without a paper trail, not an aficionado of formal organizations, religious or otherwise—they become locked-in and rigid over time—and perceived himself as a bear in a world full of coyotes. He was an inventor, a geometer, an artist, a scientist, an engineer, a writer, a generalist, and had held so many different jobs he had trouble counting them! Recently, he did portraiture with coffee as his paint, tried a variety of drawing techniques, and was exploring watercolors.

Larry was of Polish/German/British Isles heritage, a Libra with a Capricorn moon and Leo ascendant—the Leo was much more present—a Leprechaun sense of humor, a Myers-Briggs type preference of INTP, and spiritual preferences for Zen Buddhism and the Kabbalah. His hobbies included reading detective novels with his wife, exploring used-book stores, taking short and long road trips in the Prius, and watching the NASA TV station. He contends that his peer group were historical figures: George Bernard Shaw, Sherlock Holmes, Kraft-Ebbing, Diogenes, Tail-Spin-Tommy, and Mandrake the Magician. But more important were his heroes and the "giants" he stood on: Buckminster Fuller, Einstein, Socrates, Buddha, and many, many others.

Even though he had spent the last 15 years studying the Kabbalah and the Tree of Life, he respected all faiths and was willing to argue with any of them! Larry used the concepts of the Kabbalah to heal his spiritual self, making his final years much more peaceful and fulfilling. He did not believe in an omniscient, omnipotent god who tended to each individual's needs and concerns—or to a football team's, for that matter. But he did believe in a Cosmic Intelligence and the Akashic Records that provide knowledge and direction to each person's Inner Guide. In his first book, he wrote, *I had tripped into the Akashic Records, a million times more powerful than the Library at Alexandria; Akashic Records are fire and age-proof! There is no "now or then," no "here or there"—there is only eternally "The Moment." Heaven does not exist as a place, a clothes closet for the religious to hang their unworn faith. Rather, it is an ideal, a plan, a scheme, and a map to and for the un-named and un-knowable. I had found pure mysticism; I ceased to be a Catholic at that moment.* (Wahl 2011, p 97)

Larry spent many years writing his autobiography, with two books completed and published: The Vallian Trilogy: An Inventive Life. Part I: The Engineer and Part II: The Learner. Part III: The Geometer will be completed by his wife and editor. Comments about his books include "funny"; "well written"; "inspiring"; "courageous for sharing his tortured early life and later frailties."

Larry used his artistic talent to share his love of ships and sailing and to advance his understanding and appreciation of people.

Finally, as a geometer, he wrote and received a patent on the tesseract, having a unique view of mathematics and geometry. His seminal work will probably be appreciated in the future as he failed in the present to spark the imagination of the mathematical or computer community. As physicist Brian Green (2013) noted when discussing the discovery of the Higgs-boson, "Mathematical equations can sometimes tell such a convincing tale, they can seemingly radiate reality so strongly that they become the vernacular of working physicists, even before there is data to confirm them." (p.27) Unfortunately, Larry had the data, but lacked the all-pervasive mathematics. But, the data are published (the patent & An Elephant in the Room) and no doubt will someday find a home.

Addendum

Thoughts About Loss in the Middle of a Sleepless Night

For almost 53 years we fought and fought and laughed and laughed and cried and cried. There were good times and very good times, and bad times and very bad times, but through it all we loved each other, almost to the exclusion of others, including our children. And we were cruel to each other and we were tender with each other and we never stopped saying "I love you!"

There were times earlier in our life together when I considered that he loved me more than I did him—maybe so. But later on our love for and care of each other was very well balanced—the secret of our longevity. Larry used to say, "I really love you!" in such a way that it sounded like he was surprised, but his surprise was not at loving me, but that he loved. With a life together like that, I can accept the pain of loss.

SCW 2013

Never More Will the Wind
By H.D.

Never more will the wind
Cherish you again
Never more will the rain.

Never more
Shall we find you bright
In the snow and wind

The snow is melted,
The snow is gone,
And you are flown.

Like a bird out of our hand,
Like a light out of our heart,
You are gone.

In This House

In this house are four creatures. One of these creatures is a small, longhaired cat; three of these creatures are members of the genus Homo sapiens. All of these creatures live together in a dynamic, changing, growing environment. The cat is busy in the normal course of events, trying, with no noticeable success, to train the humans. The humans, for their part, try to civilize the cat, with a similar lack of success.

No day for these creatures is uneventful, embedded as each day is with various seen, or invisible, matrices. There are rich and multiplex dramas played in each of their lives against the strong linear-based fabric on the loom of life. Every single day, each of these creatures chooses a piece of yarn and sends the shuttlecock skimming across the separated strands of each day.

Some days the color is rich, vibrant, red, and strong in the tints and tones of vitality and passion. Some days the shuttlecock pulls a dark and sober thread, one of muted sadness, eerie loneliness, and lost dreams. Sometimes there is a green of hope and growth; sometimes the rusts and browns of rest and sleep. Often one sees yellows and yellow-oranges of momentary change. Regardless of the day's addition, by planning or accident, each day's entry at the loom is forever present. The loom has no "cancel," and if no color is chosen, the white of nothingness will automatically be added. Is it not strange how often the white of forget-fulness (nothingness) will follow the black threads of despair?

In the end, one can only surmise how God—be It a He, a She, or perhaps even a They—may respond to our final efforts. Will we tremble as They cut the threads that hold the tapestry of our lives safely in the loom of life? And as They look upon it, perhaps They will find it adequate.

Perhaps not.

We must weave. Maybe we must work without good instructions. Maybe we must work without adequate plans. Perhaps the pattern is loose, varied, disorganized. But ready or not, weave we must, and hope and pray our God, whoever and whatever we conceive It to be, will find our garment worthy.

But perhaps we are not weaving it for the Gods? Suppose it is for another. Perhaps we are only weaving our own next garment for a day that has not yet dawned. May we weave well, then, that the weaving we must do will be done well and true ... that the suit may really fit, honor, and justify the tailor.

Louis X. Vallian (Larry Wahl)
For his wife and daughter
Mothers' Day, May 9, 1981

Chapter One

What Has Gone Before ...

I have measured out my life with coffee spoons
—*T. S. Eliot*

To help you make sense of Book III, I am offering a summary of the previous episodes in Larry's life. His first 20 years (Book I: The Engineer) might well be characterized as intense and lonely.

The Engineer

His beingness started in the small town of Goble, Oregon with his birth parents, Ira Mescher and Gertrude Pflieger. While this should have been a pleasant growing and learning time for Larry, it was marred by frequent, bitter marital fights. He did grow and did learn from his gentle, loving father, but that didn't last. His mother thought she was made for better things than being a farmer's wife, so when the first good-looking, but dangerous man came along, she bid an un-fond farewell to the farm and Ira. Unfortunately, she took Larry with her.

The next stage unfolded when he was a toddler, and they lived a sordid, gangster-infested existence with the likes of Al Capone, Chicago mobster, and his many associates, and where Gertrude served as entertainment and an accountant. Larry continued to learn, but these lessons were harsh and cruel mementos to impose on a young, fragile mind. After his hated stepfather, Tony, shot and killed Larry's only friend in that cesspool (the friend was an important mob member; the stepfather was just a lackey), the banished family was relocated to a ghetto in Portland, Oregon, where they lived for approximately the next four years and where Larry's half-sister was born.

An accident (perhaps it really wasn't) swept Larry into a hospital and away from Tony and the ghetto life of malnutrition and neglect. After his mother surrendered him, Larry became a ward of the Catholic Church and was domiciled first in an orphanage in Portland and then in a Catholic boarding school (Providence Academy) in Vancouver, Washington. While the nuns attempted to tame him, Larry explored his new environment, read many books, and depended upon himself to sort out his existence and manage his loneliness. His mother visited one last, painful time

Just as he was becoming accustomed to the Academy, he was catapulted from a known situation into the chaos of an adoptive family. This family came with many new faces and behaviors: relatives and friends. Larry felt as though he was being shown off as a new pet! But, by now, he had learned to safely submerge himself in his psychological submarine; the new folks just became part of his ocean. He lived with the Wahl family (which now included his half-sister) for eight years, but never became of them. Fortunately, after writing this first book of the trilogy, he was able to experience the extraordinary person his adopted father, Gene, had been; his adopted mother, Masie, didn't fare so well.

While Larry never accepted the gifts and socialization of his family, he continued to grow, explore, learn, and survive. A large component of his survival was his gang, which he termed as "a bunch of misfits, like me." Another important aspect of this portion of his life was his extreme thirst for learning everything about everything. That learning offset some of the effects of the sexual abuse he endured from a "beloved" priest and from his adopted aunties.

The last two years of high school were precious to him, primarily because of some special teachers who went out of their way to encourage his intellectual gifts. Also, Larry was mentored by Rodney Strong (yes, the wineries by the same name in California belonged to the adult Rodney), who encouraged his theatrical interest. But as soon as he graduated, he was, proverbially, "out of there," putting forth a great effort to join the Navy: he lied about his impaired vision and flat feet! It was June 1945 so there wasn't much war left, but Larry managed to find his own brand of battle, an outlet for his submerged rage. This first book was called "The Engineer" because so much of his learning was about how things worked, though people got short shrift. This early learning would serve him well for the rest of his life.

The Learner

Book II finds Larry cast adrift from family and school, trying to find a place for himself in a noxious world. Even though he never "belonged," they still provided anchors. Unbeknownst to him, when he was washed out of the Navy as being mentally unstable, he was recruited by the Office of Special Services (OSS)—later to become the Central Intelligence Agency (CIA)—as a telepath and assassin.

Between missions for the OSS (he recovered the knowledge of only a few of them, some 25 years later), Larry supported himself by means of a large variety of occupations, the most favorite was as a merchant seaman. As he worked in different fields, he honed his engineering and observation talents: as police security for Westinghouse and North American Aviation; as a sign painter assistant for several different firms; as a designer and scenery painter; as a manager in theaters; and later as an orderly in hospitals and ambulances. In between and among his jobs, he got married ... 3 times. And had children, including a lovely, but neurologically damaged daughter that he tried to nurse back to a limited but functional life. Unfortunately it was not to be, and Larry ended up in a mental institution for a short stay. Most of these episodes took place in California: Los Angeles and the San Francisco Bay Area. Despite all that he lived through (never mind the effect on his so-called significant others), he maintained a degree of integrity and spirituality.

In the mid to late 50's, he established residency in Portland, Oregon, acquired employment in health care, and pursued a place as a designer and artist in this new environment. It was while working in the hospital that he found me and secured me as his 4th wife. Yes, I know, you probably have considered that my elevator didn't go all the way to the top, but I saw in him the beautiful soul that emerged many years later. I was patient.

The rest of Book II examines our first seven years together, and his struggle to confirm his place in the art domain. At the same time, he dealt with another damaged child—Aspergers syndrome—and was successful in assisting this child to become a vital and productive citizen. While his CIA experiences were mostly underneath his day-to-day consciousness, behaviors reminiscent of those intervals occasionally emerged, including an episode that was interpreted as "they were trying to get me back!"

Now, the narrative will continue with his life as he becomes a geometer and inventor, with bits and pieces of the rest of our 46 years together. Since the first two books of this trilogy were focused on his growing up and his many jobs and marriages, I feel it is important, in this third book, to present Larry in the context of his life as a member of a stable (well, mostly) family.

Musing 101 by Larry

Pearls of My Life

To know that which before us lies in daily life
is the prime wisdom
John Milton

I don't believe I ever intended to make it a life's goal to see how many jobs I could find, lose, screw up, get fired from, get injured on, or how many of them would be difficult if not impossible to explain, much less to do. It was not a function of my being especially difficult, although many of my employers would say that was exactly the problem. No, it was that damn track I was set upon. That track was invisible, just as a real railroad track is invisible for long stretches. When you are on a trestle and the track is straight ahead, you find that you are simply moving forward. The car you are in is following the one in front of it, as is the car behind following the one you are in. There is no sense of the rails, only a feeling of being pulled along towards some invisible future station.

The track was invisible to me most of the time, and although each of the jobs seemed properly portioned in the state and the flow of things, the life expectancy of any job I was on was strictly curtailed by the forced direction of those steel rails. Those rails were completely invisible to the bosses I worked for and were mostly invisible to me as well. I never had the sense that anything in my life was liable to be finished, until ... three quarters of my life had passed by me. Only then, with great heaps of repeated experiences, did I realize that the only job worth doing and staying with until you had finished was the job that you were doing on *yourself.* On any job, I was completely reliable and honest and trustworthy, right up until the moment I fell completely out of grace, competence, security...and employment.

I seemed to project a life force that would make even otherwise intelligent people believe that I could be trusted, and this was always the truth, right up to the finish line. But whenever that line appeared ready to cross, something would come up that would completely change my course. Sometimes that thing would be tragic, sometimes it would be comic, and sometimes it would be dangerous, lethal, or just plain stupid. There was never a time that an experience was forgotten and never a time that it was not grist for the mill. Every incident that had any importance to me was remembered in such detail and perfection that it could be played like a CD over and over again, with no diminishment in detail, clarity, or point. In every case, these items were not embellished; nothing was added to nor taken away from.

What took some years to comprehend was that a time connection line between these events was the thing that was missing. Each experience was like individual pearls, perfect and beautiful, but there was no string of serial events connecting them. It was years before I realized that the reason for this was that each event was a separate and individual lesson supposed to be exactly what, where, and when it was. Life was waiting for the brilliant but foolish person who was having them to put them together. That time arrived only when I came upon them years later and then strung them together. That took wit and wisdom, two things that were acquired only after the very, very long passage of time.

LXV

Chapter 2

Studios: The Artist

The artist, like the God of the creation,
remains within or behind or beyond or above his handiwork,
invisible, refined out of existence, indifferent, paring his fingernails.

—James Joyce

When we began working on Book III, Larry was quite ill, but his mind was still sharp and creative as it ever had been. He wanted to start right out with his geometric theory, an expansion of what was in his patent. During the previous few months, he had been diligently trying to find the right formula to describe his "tesseract." He had done hundreds of illustrative drawings, but felt the mathematicians would never take him seriously if he didn't have formulas. In his theory writings, he talks of his disdain for "formulas," while later admitting he couldn't write formulas because of his dyslexia. However, as will be apparent, his spatial drawings were obviously enough to grant him a patent.

While I understood his urgency to complete this task, I knew that when his ideas were appreciated, perhaps by a later generation, he had enough written descriptive material that others would do the formulae for him. And he had a beta-type computer program of the graphics application, just needing a programmer to translate it into modern code. Thus, I suggested that instead of theory, his readers might benefit from knowing more about how he came to "invent the 4th dimension," and about his art career and his studios that were important factors in evolving the new geometry. And so he agreed. The following is what he wrote until his energy waned.

The Studios as Identified by Larry

All my art started with confusion and the necessary studios were as ad hoc as casually meeting a stranger on a street corner. As I thought about what was actually my very first studio, I ran into two possibilities, only one of which could be correct. I remember working with Don Douglas down at the beach, just after I had married Dorothy and moved up from California. Don and I were working together, with him doing the drawing and me doing the continuity, or story lines. As I watched him work, I realized that I was learning about cartooning. So, was this the first studio?

Andrew Loomis

Shortly after my 18th birthday while sailing in the Merchant Marine for various shipping companies, I became interested in carving in balsa wood on my off duty hours. I became proficient at this hobby, and for the first time in my life, concluded that I was an artist. The State of California's employment agency soon disabused me of this idea. I had purchased a book by Andrew Loomis (1943), called *Figure Drawing for All It's Worth*, and decided, "I can do that!" There is much time between sailing jobs, and I figured I could get art jobs while waiting for a ship; if the time between assignments became extended, I would be able to collect unemployment benefits from the State.

The lady at the agency viewed me with jaundiced eyes and informed me that I couldn't just walk in off the street and announce that I was an artist, sit back and receive compensation. She explained that the agency had a battery of seven tests that had been given to various professional artists. The results of the tests would indicate if there were minimum skills in the seven areas that would allow the State to consider the individual a professional. Most normal people simply decided that they were proficient in some other field and didn't even shame themselves by taking the elaborate four-hour test, but not me! After the tests, including many involving spatial ability, were completed, the grinning employee—with an I-told-you-so look—gave me the news. In all seven areas, I had rated below 40 where 90 was passing on a 0 to 120 scale. As far as being an artist, based on their tests, I might have made a good plumber.

Before I was married, I spent several months working on Guam (among other things), and, after the testing fiasco, what really seemed to be the beginning of my art career came from reading Loomis from cover to cover, in my non-existent spare time. Apparently, I learned more and I learned faster than I realized at the time since so many other things were going on simultaneously. Someplace along the line, I began seriously drawing and, in spite of the nightly sessions at Halsey Hill where I was learning to be a first class assassin, I was actually doing figure work.

Some of the guys in my hut saw my work and asked if I could put bodies on their girls' portraits. I found a sheet of packing material, some kind of composition matte, and on that I did my first nude, putting what the horny customer wanted his naked girl's body to look like, attached to the face in a snapshot he had provided. I was amazed to discover that I could do this quickly and competently; there were no complaints about the finished products.

Nude in Ink and Pencil

At the time, there was so much going on that this performance seemed neither strange nor unusual. I don't remember ever thinking about the space in which I did this artwork. Since I haunted the galleys at night after work, a table was no problem, and the book provided all the additional information I needed. That table actually provided me with my very first, sort-of studio.

Our contract was completed early, finishing on Guam in only three months; we were given the option of staying on or going home. If we stayed, we would have been in competition with the even lower-paid help from the Philippines. By this time, I knew I could draw, paint, cartoon, and carve, so I went back to the lady at the agency. She pulled up my former results, and explained patiently to me that the tests were scientifically designed to check the natural parameters of artistic ability. She explained that they represented inherent abilities, or the lack thereof, that would not change in a lifetime. I listened carefully as she explained all this to me in a manner that one would assume in talking to a person with seriously damaged mental facilities. After she was all done, I insisted on taking the battery of tests once more. She said, hoping to discourage me, that there would be a fee for taking it a second time. I assured her that that was fine with me.

Hours later she came back and admitted, somewhat sheepishly, that had she not observed all testing herself, she would never have believed it. I had passed two of the tests at the 120 rating, and had passed all then rest above 100. We sat down, and I described some of the finger exercises I had developed, showed her some of my work, and finally left her office with a signed certificate that said, in effect, "Yes, by God, this weird guy actually is an artist." I simply left with my dignity and my future. I never did use the unemployment insurance.

The Geometer

I do not remember making a conscious decision to become a geometer, it just sort of happened, but not as a result of what I was supposed to learn in school: I actually flunked geometry in high school—me and

Einstein! Regular math, as taught in Providence grade school, had been full-scale torture, and so it was with some relief that I realized I had, instead, a natural feel for the geometry. In the intervening years, I have met mathematicians of all kinds and stripes. Some I can connect with, but not with the most pragmatic—those with the unwavering opinion that all *real math* must be performed only with the rigors of tight and essentially formula-driven formats. I found these entrenched beliefs impossible to deal with. My anger and frustration was absolutely met by the same from them. Later, when I tried to explain the possibilities of my Vallian Geometric System to businessmen, the first thing they would do was introduce me to one of these absolute monarchs of math who would immediately shoot me down with neither grace nor mercy.

Interval with Toby

Back to my studios. When I completed my contract and flew from Guam to the United States, the plane landed on the tarmac at a remote point at the Moffett Field Naval Station in Mountain View. The plane crew had taken on many quarts of booze at Hawaii; it was a wonder that they managed to find and successfully land anywhere near the North American continent. The whole motley crew debarked after pouring the awesomely stiff and terminally hung-over crew chief into a jeep specifically located several hundred yards from the assigned parking area in order to keep his unconscious body off report or out of the brig. I, on the other hand, was sober as a judge and came to the conclusion that Sunnyvale was as good a city to be stuck in as any other.

The just started art career took a back seat to getting some kind of a job. I had a pretty good payout from working on Guam, so I spent a few days checking out the grounds of the Rosicrucian Park before I moved to Los Angeles where I met Toby Marshall. Still not painting or drawing, I became great friends with Toby who treated me like an adopted son.

I suppose the reason I liked Toby instantly and so deeply was that he was just an older version of me. Toby was married and in love with

Faye, having been married for over twenty years. However, Toby was exactly like me—in this period of time—in that he had never really been married to a single woman, no matter what the marriage license said; he was incapable of being true to one woman because he was in love with all of womanhood. This is what drove him. Toby and I never delved into his past—or mine either for that matter! I didn't know anything about his nuclear family or anything about him growing up. As I now look at his life and his talents, as well as his experience in the war and with the Red Cross, I see the confusing and dissolute trail of my own life, so apparently without intermediate goals, much less any endpoint. But he taught me a great deal about writing and researching for a movie he had a contract to write. Unfortunately that project fell through, as did my job with him.

By this time I was routinely drawing almost everyday for two or three hours. It was mostly cartoons, but gradually I spent more and more time working in bars and taverns. I suppose that originally I was just trying to pick up the girls who would watch me drawing. But gradually I started to resent the interruptions and arrived at the point where I was drawing for myself and using the bar and tavern patrons only for models, all the while utilizing the human energy glowing in the place. Very quickly the drawings became professional. In a few strokes, I could get the subject nailed. It was more satisfying than the figure work done on Guam and demanded more of me under the almost human tutelage I got from Andrew Loomis. I have not had another book in my possession that has been more valuable, with the possible exception of the works of Vesalius.

During this wayward time of my life, studios became not a matter of place but a matter of mind. It was like flying by the seat of your pants. But when I got into murals, and my whole perspective changed, I found that I really needed someplace to have the tools, as well as the canvas and supports necessary to do large paintings or wall murals.

2ⁿᵈ, 3ʳᵈ, 4ᵗʰ Studios

Thus, I now realize that what I was actually doing at the beach with Don was specifically watching him for cartooning technique, which in any case is very different from so-called "fine art." As we sent batches of cartoons to the New York market, rejections followed—some fast, some slow—in return mail, but I got a better idea of both the validity of Don's drawings and the strength of my joke writing. No one in New York ever agreed with us on either point, so eventually it was necessary to move on and get off the Long Beach, Washington Peninsula before we all starved to death. Therefore, Long Beach was my second studio.

One time we interviewed with the Art and Display Director at Meier and Frank department store, looking for a job. Being familiar with Don's "shooting from the hip," I exhorted him to let me do all the talking. Don's work was excellent, and I was talking a good plan. I explained that I was married, and that Don and I had worked together for sometime. I then paused to give the manager—whose name I have forgotten—time to investigate the drawings. It was a good presentation, and we looked like what we were: a couple of good guys, ready and willing to do a good day's work. Suddenly, not being able to stand the silence, Don leaned forward and opined, "Oh, yeah, and we would work for nothing to start!"

My shock was evident, and the art director looked at me with ill-disguised pity. Needless to say, that was the end of the interview. He was not looking for idiots willing to work for nothing.

When Don decided to take "French Leave" from our apartment in Vanport, Oregon, I confiscated his drawing equipment in lieu of rent. Thus Vanport, and then Vancouver, Washington became my third and fourth studios, as Dorothy and I strived to make a living. Dorothy had started working for the U.S. Forestry department. By this time I actually had a professional drawing board, t-square, associated angles, and other drawing paraphernalia.

Dorothy and Cartooning

I decided that, since I had picked up the cartooning trade from Don and was now quite good myself, I would submit completed drawings under my own name. But what I didn't understand was that Dorothy was the perfect North Dakota wife, which meant that she was the last living person on earth an artist should have been married to. Dorothy could go for hours without saying a word, just adoring me from afar. She loved our sex, but in fact, we had little else. As I got into the meat of the creative process involved with conceptualizing cartoons, I realized I had a serious (read terminal) problem in trying to work around Dorothy.

In retrospect, I describe her as the perfect wife: she worked at a good job, cooked well, loved sex, took care of each of the children as they came, and worked feverishly to make me into a North Dakota farmer, or at least a good North Dakota businessman. Although I worked eight hours at a theatre and did well on admittedly low pay, when I came home, I looked forward to two or three hours of cartooning work … but, that was never going to happen.

Cartooning all happens in the mind. I mean it literally takes place inside your head. When you are in the clutches of the muse, you hear nothing, see nothing, and actually wrestle with the gargantuan idea of what would get the attention of some unseen executive in New York, the Mecca for cartooning in the United States. Your tool is not the drawing table in front of you, nor the blank sheet of paper, the pens, pencils, or other equipment; it is just some twisted thought that has to make it all the way from the depths of your fevered imagination into the deadly serious land of humor.

Your key tool, besides any imagined genius you might have, is a "silence" so rapt, so deep, and so religiously pure that it has no name. This silence comes with atmospherics in the form of an impenetrable miasma, a fog so thick that, though it comes from nothing, it goes on forever. The clock stops in mid tick, your head weighs a thousand pounds. Then every once in a while, as you peer blindly into that fog, it appears to change … a little less dense here and there … and then the vague appearance of a random thought. Is it an idea? You do not know, but you try to make it out. A fuzzy outline appears. Is it an idea? Oh, God, I don't know, but I think so. "There were these two virgins and a Rabbi ... "

"Did I tell you what Shirley said to me at the office yesterday?" This breaks through the again-forming fog, the words emblazoned in neon lights, blinking on and off!!

"What the hell are you talking about?" I scream as I will the fog not to return, never mind the two virgins ... they are gone!

Dorothy appears only a foot away from me, a vacuous smile on her lips.

My heart turns wicked and evil, and I stare at her. I remember telling her not to do this. She who can keep silent for hours at a time under ordinary conditions, but cannot seem to keep her mouth shut for the twenty actual minutes it takes to construct a cartoon nucleus. I do not love her. I want to kill her ...

"A guy is married to this dumb, loud-mouthed red-head an ... "

A Change of Venue

Larry eventually left Dorothy and gave up on having his own studio for a number of years. During those years, he worked for a variety of businesses that enriched his understanding of engineering and design. He even had the opportunity to utilize his cartooning when trying to get his point across about the severely dangerous conditions at the Westinghouse plant where he was employed as a safety guard. This cartoon included a demeaning illustration of the safety chief with his feet on his desk, surrounded by empty beer bottles and his favorite guns. Larry left that position shortly thereafter.

Larry moved back to Portland in the mid 1950's where he found—not yet studios—jobs where he could practice and further develop his artistic skills. At Allied Arts, he learned the facility of designing and painting theatrical flats as well as the complications of setting up displays for advertising events. With Ron Spear, an imaginative craftsman, he assisted in the experimentation with a variety of plants and weeds for decorative creations. But even these positions, which usually fell through due to lethal interactions with his bosses, did not provide the milieus Larry envisioned, what he needed to exhibit his artistic talents, especially for wall murals. So, with a third marriage failing and a brief, but unsuccessful attempt at a college education, he focused his energies on the medical field as a valued orderly and ambulance attendant. He continued on this pathway until he found and married me, and I began the long journey of taming him while supporting the genius that lay within. Thus, with a loan from my parents to settle his outstanding debts (he never could manage money—he just spent it), we embarked on our lives and the rest of his studios. But he had one more sort-of studio he loved writing about, so even though it is out of the timeline, I'll include it here.

Charlie's

Well into my career, I had the opportunity to work at a huge downtown restaurant called Charlie's Broiler. It had been a former whorehouse in the old days, where the entire two floors upstairs were full of cribs for "the girls" and their customers. On the first floor there was a huge bar with an accompanying restaurant; massive freeze boxes were located in the basement. I loved the place! Early on I discovered that the world is full of idiots and that some of these loved to destroy things just because they could. Fortunately I have not had too many pictures destroyed, but in the early days of tavern paintings, I found out where people put out their cigarettes—they preferred the nudes.

Months before I started working at Charlie's, I encountered the wonderful qualities of wrong-sided Masonite paneling. When this stuff is created, it is a kind of wood and paper paste that is extruded and spread out on a sheet of screened material, much like a porch screen, where it is formed into many homogenous layers and then dried. The good side, a shiny, almost indestructible surface, is what is used in homes, but for my purposes, the back (screened) side was just perfect. It had a natural pattern of crossed lines, much like the weave and warp of canvas. It was dark brown when untreated and dry, capable of being spread with the white material called gesso that then made a perfect base for any kind of oil or plastic painting material. When I used plastic paints almost exclusively, any technique was feasible, and once on the board, even with acrylic bases of different types, the painting was practically impervious to any type of attack, cigarette or otherwise.

I loved the acrylics because of their durability, and with the techniques that I used, they were very fast. I could finish some fairly straightforward abstracts in as little as two or three hours for a 4 by 4 foot, or even 4 by 8 foot panel. In short order, there were people watching a painting being created while they were having dinner and drinks. The owners were thrilled with the cost—nothing—and I was thrilled with the exclusive use of the place. I loved working with people around, and it tested my ability to work under any circumstances, even when I was being heckled. While this was going on, especially in a tavern ambiance, I simply filled in necessary spaces that were not too technically difficult and concentrated on handling the competition. I gave as good as I got and sometimes even better. It was fun for me and fun for the customers, but some of the finer work had to wait until I had the place all to myself.

Of the twenty or so paintings I did for Charlie's, as well as owners who came after, only two or three survived in my possession. In the process of all the redecorating and messing around involved with several different owners, the rest of the paintings disappeared one way or another. I take it as a mark of distinction that someone thought enough of my work to steal it, especially in the larger editions, many of which were temporarily—I thought—stored upstairs. Perhaps the ghosts of some of those hundreds of prostitutes that lived in early Portland took them ... 30.

Carrying On In Number Five

This ended Larry's writing about his studios. I was more or less present for the remainder of the studios; in fact, several took the place of what a young bride called a living room! However, the first studio I encountered was an attic in Edna's house, when we were just going together.

Larry was recently divorced from Jan, his 3rd wife, and had rented this attic apartment in Edna's (he didn't remember her last name) large, old Victorian house near downtown Portland, primarily because it was cheap, and, oh yes, it had north light as well as a hot plate to make coffee! What more could an artist want …. Larry told me how he would be drinking hot coffee, and then the next sip would be ice cold—he had no idea that he had been painting for hours. And sometimes he abruptly noted the colors of a painting he was working on were all wrong, only to become aware that he had started in the cool, yellow light of morning, and now it was the soft oranges of sunset.

These stories, and subsequent events, should have alerted me to what I was getting into; I think I did know, but it didn't matter. One day when I was visiting him in the apartment, he asked me to get something out of the closet. To my astonishment, the entire floor was covered with used Jockey shorts. When I asked him what that was all about, his reply was, "When I need clean ones, I just go buy some." I did laundry that night, as I was to do the rest of my life. This man needed a caretaker!

Edna's room provided him with silence—even though he wasn't cartooning—and his 5th studio, but who's counting. The silence was good; it was the solitude that allowed him the ability to concentrate.

Larry, A Crazy Artist?

About this time in our relationship, he took me to a movie called *The Horse's Mouth*, which was about the crazy artist, Gully Jimson, whose art took priority over other people's money, property, and time. I was a little jolted by that, especially since it was seen by my fellow student nurses who didn't approve of my going with Larry—a thrice-married man, ten years my senior, and a fallen-away Catholic! But, what my friends didn't know was that I believed, and rightly so, that Larry and I were very much a match, that we were soul mates. He learned how to manage me by practicing on the previous three wives. And given that neither of us emotionally bonded with parents, we would spend many years mothering and fathering each other.

The Notorious Airbrush

Since I didn't learn with the Gully Jimson movie episode, I was soon to experience another reason perhaps why I should have run like an antelope, away from this crazy man while I had the chance. Unfortunately, when this next notable Larry event occurred, I was already 8+ months pregnant with our first, Eric. Too late!

Larry had bought an airbrush, using it for delicate work. Since an airbrush needs an airflow to push the spray of paint onto the canvas, he bought a small "melon" of compressed air from a local dealer, who also supplied hospitals and related agencies with large and small tanks of oxygen. Larry was happy as a cat with a bowl of ice cream—he even had the Cheshire grin. Because Larry used the airbrush for some rather large paintings, it was necessary to frequently get his melon recharged. And herein lies the catastrophe.

It was on a cold December Portland night that Larry left the Jolly Joan's restaurant to come pick me up at the hospital where I worked the evening shift (yes, I was still working). Earlier that day, he had gone to the compressed air company to get a refill. When he went to pick it up, the clerk commented, "Wow! Your container almost exploded when we filled it, but it seems OK now."

"What was the problem?" Larry inquired, not really concerned.

"Don't know. It blew off the gauge, and we had to replace it. But, as I said, it's OK."

Larry acknowledged the expert's reassurance and went on his way. It was 4:30 in the afternoon.

Larry was having his second cup of coffee in the cafeteria at St. Vincent's while he waited for me to finish work. Unexpectedly, an explosion was heard from somewhere outside. An orderly coming though the breezeway, which was between the main hospital and the cafeteria, was saying, "Gee, they must be blowing up the Oregonian trucks close by."

Larry thought that was probably so: a nasty strike was in progress at the local newspaper. But he decided to go take a look. "My car is out there," he commented to the orderly.

But the best was yet to come. As Larry walked into the breezeway, a snowstorm of business cards came fluttering down: *"Larry E. Wahl **Worlds Greatest Artist!!** Well ... Would you believe one of the best in Scapoose"* was their message. Larry felt faint.

With minimal hope in his heart, he went to see about the 1954 Chevy sedan that he had parked just outside the cafeteria. Please note: this was *my* car; his was a 1937 Chrysler. Anyway, the pretty little car was now junk. The back seats were blown into the front seats, the front seats pushed out the windshield, and the trunk lid was nowhere to be found. The offending melon was on the other side of the parking lot, its gauge still intact, but side blown open. Larry had a pretty good idea what had happened, why the gauge was blown off at the shop, but also why he was still alive when it finally ruptured. We won't mention guardian angels.

Concerned that someone might have told me and I would be scared that he had been damaged or killed, he went up to my floor to explain the situation to me. I was glad he was OK, but devastated about the car. Later, I wanted to kill him, but that's not important to the story. Since home was across town, both of us, still in shock, decided to take a bus home—a very long, very uncomfortable ride for this very pregnant lady. Neither of us had the sense to take a taxi and charge it to the insurance company, and they sure didn't offer. On the way home, Larry gave me his theory of why the accident happened.

He posited that the company had erroneously filled the small melon as though it were a full size oxygen tank; that was why the gauge blew off first time. But they recharged it, still with an excessive amount for that small melon, and cinched down the gauge with a few extra twists; Larry was literally carrying a bomb in the trunk. Why did it not blow up while he was driving to get me? Again just a theory, but Larry felt the inevitable was delayed because of the cold temperature, somewhere around freezing. But then there is always that guardian angel!

I don't remember us getting any money for the totaled car, and while Larry gave ample evidence for the State Farm agent to assign blame to the compressed air company, I don't remember that we ever got any payoff from that either. We got precious little help from the insurance company and were too dumb to know our rights to sue. We cancelled State Farm, and Larry hung up his airbrush

... for good!

Math Rears Its Ugly Head

Before he acquired his next, and actually (in my opinion) his first, bone fide art studio, he was painting wall murals in bars at night. I would accompany him and sit on the floor or in a comfy chair while he would describe what he was doing. On this one occasion, he suddenly looked at me, startled, and exclaimed, "I'll be damned!"

What he had discovered, he went on to say, was that Sister Ursula (a 2nd grade, hated math teacher) was right: you did need math! He pointed out to me how, as he was drawing the figure on the wall, several times life-size, his mind automatically adjusted the proportions so that the mural would look merely normal (in proportion) and human-sized to the tavern patrons, at least those sitting at the tables. Since I was often sitting at a table, I could attest to that notion. "So," he concluded, "all of that math, and especially geometry and trig I didn't want to learn, actually did find its way into my painting brain. Good job, Sister!"

In his first book of the trilogy, Larry described the accident that killed Sister Ursula while he was still a student at Providence Academy. He felt so guilty: he thought he had caused it because he had such negative thoughts about her and her math. He now found her, and himself, redeemed.

The "Closet"

On February 20th 1960, Larry signed a lease on 1621 N.W. 23rd Avenue—studio #6. If I had thought Edna's was weird, it didn't come close to this one: it was a long narrow, dark dingy closet. He brought his drawing table from Edna's. All he needed then to work were several flood lights (the only window was in the front door) and a 30 cup coffee pot, which he made all 30 cups-worth at the beginning of the week and drank all week long. There were no microwaves in those days, so the pot was on 24 hours a day. By the end of the week, since it was—as sailors say—so thick you could eat it with a spoon, I wouldn't touch it. The only way he escaped caffeine poisoning was Quality Pie Coffee Shop, a restaurant three blocks away. Other advantages of his domain were the rent—39 dollars a month—and the quiet. But there was one drawback: he had no running water to fill his coffee pot or wash his brushes. He brought those home for rejuvenation.

One afternoon, he got the idea of asking the next door neighbor—also in a long narrow, dark dingy closet, except it had running water—if he could tap into the neighbor's water supply and pay half the water bill. For an unknown reason, the little man adamantly said, "No, no, no!"

Thinking the man had just had a bad day, Larry decided to try again the next day, and got the same response, "No, no, no," with the added insult of, "Get out of my shop!"

Larry saw red. As he described it (much better than I can), "I found myself leaping and screaming around this poor little man—he was terrified; I was twice his size.

"Finally the little guy yelled at me, 'Take the water, take the whole shop, take anything you want!' and ran out. I never saw him again. I never did get my water. Why I didn't just go over there and help myself, I don't know. I was very embarrassed at my behavior, scaring a poor little man."

Our First Home and His Next Studio

Eventually that studio became a liability after we got married and lived miles across town in Northeast Portland. The next stop studio was 3134 NE 75th, the "Little Pink House" he rented and presented to me as a wedding present. If he had consulted me, I would have encouraged him to get at least two bedrooms (I was thinking ahead and it was a good thing because Eric was born nine months and two days after we were married) instead of this tiny one bedroom home. But he saw the advantages: a basement in which to paint, dark but he had all those floodlights. We might have stayed after the two-year lease was up, but the landlord sold it to a woman who planned to live there.

Electrical Fuses And The Kegger

Larry had a favorite story he liked to tell about the Pink House and me. We had just brought Eric and me home from the hospital; because Larry had been "baching" in the house for the week I was in hospital, there was little food. After Eric was fed and settled, I decided to feed us some fried eggs, cooked in my new electric fry pan. The kitchen was as tiny as was to be expected and had only one electrical outlet, not in a location that would reach the fry pan. At a previous time, I had strung an extension cord from the outlet behind the sink, to the part of the counter that was big enough to hold the fry pan. I had not used it, though.

I had just started cooking the eggs when poof, the electricity went out. Larry replaced the fuses, and I was back in business, but only for a few minutes. Poof again! As the eggs languished in the pan, and our hunger exacerbated, Larry tried to figure out what was wrong. Suddenly I had a brainstorm: a friend from nursing school had married an electrician. I called her, explaining our problem, and she affirmed they would be right over. They did come, but they brought their party—a keg of beer and my ex-boyfriend, Kenny, also an electrician. The three guys buried their heads in the fuse box, while I worried about the possibility of electrocution, given their inebriated state. Frustrated with not finding a solution, or even the problem, they had just retired to our couch with candles and the beer keg, when Kenny, on a hunch, directed his flashlight toward my extension cord; there he discovered the source of the problem. I had nailed it up on the wall, putting the nails between the two insulated wires, thus shorting out the current. He removed the offending cord, re-replaced the fuses, and voilá, the lights went on. We finished the evening and the keg while everyone had a good laugh ... at my expense. We never did eat our eggs!

A Different Seattle

I tended to be a source of much humor for Larry in these early days of our relationship. I credit my sheltered, disjointed childhood as the foundation of my innate stupidity, though Larry was inclined to let me off the hook by calling it innocence, but "a rose by any other name ... " While Larry was basically kind to me, occasionally he would singe me by telling others of my "misunderstandings." But, to be honest, Larry's kidding me about my "innocent incidents" helped me to unlock a much-needed sense of humor, one that had been battened down by that same sheltered upbringing.

One of Larry's favorites—maybe even more than the-nail-through-the-extension-cord or my putting my head in his stomach, attempting to push him out of *my kitchen*—took place on a much anticipated (by me) trip to Seattle to attend a nursing conference. I was about five months pregnant and still working at the hospital. For the conference, I was professionally dressed in a newly purchased, blue linen "pregnant" suit.

When we arrived at the conference hotel, we were told that the nursing conference had been moved to a community center—no accommodations—and our reservations had to be cancelled to make way for their big political convention (it was 1960). They offered to find us a room in another hotel, but the city was full-up and the only available rooms were in a small hotel in southwest Seattle. That seemed all right to me. My experience with

Seattle consisted of train stations, ferry slips, and, oh yes, a tour of all the Catholics churches guided by my grandmother when I was staying with her post-meningitis. No problem with Seattle. Larry looked dubious, but he went along with the plan because he knew how much I wanted to attend "my first professional conference."

We parked the car in the underground lot of the pleasant-looking Holiday Inn and took the elevator to the lobby to check in, followed soon after by another elevator to our room. The nice-looking young man who operated the elevator was super friendly. I assumed it was because of how I looked in my new suit; I even flirted a little.

After we unloaded our minimal luggage, we decided to find someplace for dinner. Larry wanted to go back downtown; he suggested that I wouldn't be too pleased with the food in this neighborhood. "Nonsense," I said. I had seen a cute café just a block away, and besides he needn't worry about me, I was street savvy, having spent considerable amount of my childhood on fishing boats and in logging camps. I didn't know my supposed sophistication had gaps. Larry knew when I set my mind on something, I was not easily deterred, so once again, and this time with a slight aura of amusement, he went along.

Now I will let the story be told in Larry's words, as I remember them—I did hear it retold many times!

"I tried to steer Sherry elsewhere, but she literally led me by the hand into a busy, bustling Mom and Pop style café, attracted, I think, by all the couples enjoying themselves. As was her norm in those days, she settled herself elegantly in the booth facing all the activity, leaving me to either look at her or out the window. 'This is going to be good,' I thought. I looked at her.

"For a few minutes, after she adjusted her clothing and smoothed her hair, she smilingly surveyed the café scene, the laughing, attractive young men and women. But gradually her smile contorted into a questioning grimace as she refocused on my face. I nodded assent and confirmed that there were no girls or women in that café."

I don't remember what *I* thought. I knew there was such a thing as homosexuality, but I had never, to my limited knowledge, known anyone of that persuasion, and I had no idea about transvestites—my parents had tried to shield me from most things sexual; everything I knew I learned in kindergarten! I don't remember anything about the conference; I think I was too taken up with trying to digest this new knowledge. And then there was the friendly elevator boy when we returned to our room. I was embarrassed about my earlier behavior as I realized he hadn't been looking at me, Larry was more to his liking. I hung tightly onto Larry, demonstrating my rights of ownership—after all, Larry was gorgeous!

Besides providing fodder for Larry's storytelling, I learned a much-needed lesson from that experience: never assume and always let Larry sit facing the other patrons.

The Insurance Physical

In addition to laughing at me for my "typically female" (I hated that stereotype) peccadilloes, he frequently laughed at himself. Shortly after we moved into the Pink House, Larry decided that since he was now a married man (again!), he would get some life insurance. An agent was contacted and a pre-policy physical scheduled. On the arranged morning, the doorbell rang, and Larry admitted a pleasant-looking young man with a bag. "Just a minute while I take off my clothes," Larry informed him. The young man couldn't get out the front door fast enough. A perplexed Larry watched him go, then shrugged and went back to painting. About an hour later, again the doorbell rang, and again Larry answered it to be greeted by an equally pleasant-looking young man, also with a bag, but this one announced, "Mr. Wahl, I'm the insurance doctor." Larry still wonders if the previous young man ever stopped running. "He must have been an vacuum cleaner salesman, or something," Larry surmised.

Studio on 74th Street

Next up: 3140 N.E. 74th with one bedroom, a very large kitchen (my dream), a full basement with small windows, and a dining room we could use as another bedroom. The proverbial icing on the cake for Larry was a large garage where he could paint regular and black-light murals. The basement served for those functions as well … for a while, anyway. This house we stayed in for about four years also had a large cement front porch where Larry spent many an evening, just thinking or playing his guitar. A lot happened in that house until we were again forced out by a sale. Those happenings are documented with some humor in *The Vallian Trilogy (2013) Book II (Chapter 26, The 74th Street House)*. What I remembered most was how Larry shifted his studio around in the house, basement, and garage.

When we first moved there, we put Eric in the bedroom and we slept in the dining room, but as Eric got more hyperactive and rarely slept, Larry bought a large and expensive, so-called "indestructible" crib and put Eric in the basement, hoping that with less stimuli, he would sleep (Eric would be diagnosed today as high-functioning autism, or Aspergers). That was not to be. Instead Eric worked on the fabric sides of the crib until he managed to create a hole he could crawl through. He spent one night "painting" the basement with Larry's expensive, black-light paints. That was when Larry moved his artwork out to the garage, or the dining room if the weather was inclement.

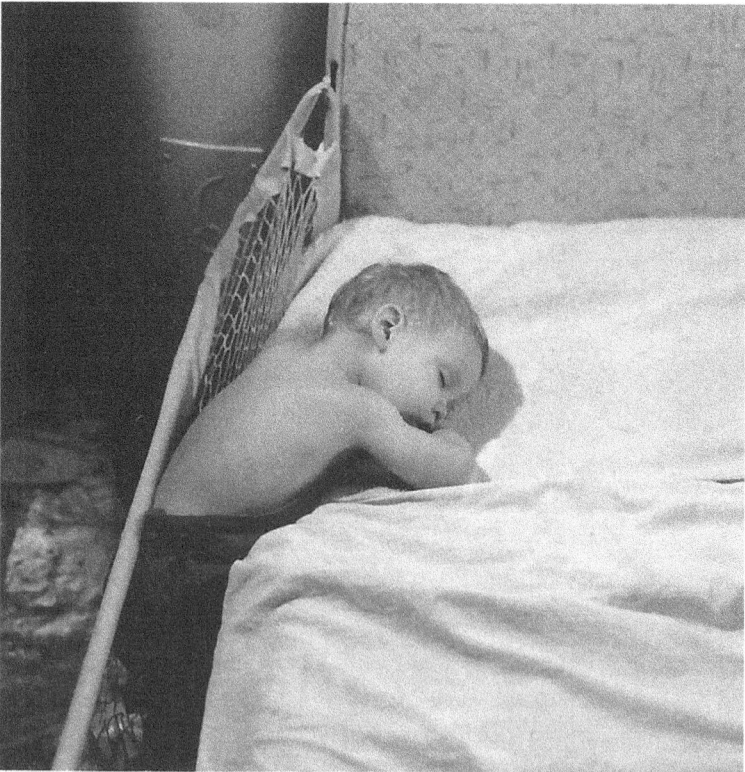

Eric after a long night's work!

Adventures and Disasters with the Volkswagen Bus

Larry bought a used Volkswagen delivery truck from a free-lance janitor; I'll never forget its odor of old wax. However, Larry decided to make it into the equivalent of a SCU (they called them self-contained units then, I think). He built in a platform (removable, so he could transport large paintings) that went from just behind the front seats to the hump (over the engine), at the level of the top of the front seats. A thin mattress covered the platform, so the non-driver could sleep/rest on long trips to the beach. Right behind the driver's seat, he placed a piece of fiber board and attached a shelf to it and the side of the truck for our small camping stove and a coffee pot—also for long trips. Between the "bed" and the hump over the engine, he installed a portion of Eric's destroyed crib rail and padded the area, creating a nice secure travel space for Eric. Eric would ride happily back there, mumbling the names of streets and cities before he even talked (about 4 years old).

We had some good trips to the beach—spent one very stormy night in a parking lot, high above the ocean at Cannon Beach, Oregon. On another trip, when we were coming back from visiting my folks in Crescent City, California (300 miles from home), the engine "blew"—I didn't know what that meant then and still don't. We had only gone a few miles from the folks' house, so we were able cripple back there. My dad took one look and said, "You're going to need a new engine. I have a friend who can get one and put it in for you."

One problem: we were close to broke! But Dad, bless his heart, bailed us out, refusing any payment: the guy owed him one!

A year later, at Christmas time, even though the weather was bad, Dad insisted we come down for the holidays (we owed *him* one!). So we went. But, going home, we got almost to Port Orford, about 100 miles north on the Oregon coast, when we hit "black ice" on a curvy area of Humbug Mountain. I was on the mattress in back, starting to make coffee: we were congratulating ourselves on getting away unscathed (you didn't know my parents!). I was asking him how to turn on the stove, and he was distracted through several signs that said, "Slow to 25, sharp curves." The end result was the bus hit black ice going 40, ran into a steep rock facing when it failed to negotiate the curve, and flipped over onto its passenger side. A rushing creek was a few feet away. Down I went, mattress, unlit heater, and coffee pot full of cold water.

I didn't think I was hurt, but being the scientist, I systematically went about checking all body parts. I could hear Eric: he was OK. Larry got Eric out, all the while calling, "Sherry, are you all right?"

Since I was busy, I quietly said, "I'm OK."

Larry got frantic. I had told him that if I was ever in an accident I would holler and scream; because of my feeble response, he was sure I was nearly dead!

By then cars had stopped to assist and had called the state patrol. With Eric taken care of, an adrenalized Larry kicked in the passenger front window to get to me—I was "buried" on top of the side doors. I finally convinced him that, other than being soaked with cold water (I must have been in some form of shock because I didn't feel cold), I truly was OK. He was able to pull me out after the good Samaritans and police righted the truck. Surprisingly, the engine started and we had a police escort to the closest town. From the police station, I called my folks. Dad brought a board to cover the broken window and one of Mom's robes for me. By 3 AM, we were on our way, once again, up the coast. Eric kept mumbling, "You broke my car!"

There was some damage to something, I don't remember what, so we had to drive slowly, without heat, while it snowed in the higher elevations. A Christmas to remember! My dad never again insisted we come down in inclement weather.

Despite our mishaps resulting in battering it in several areas, Larry loved that truck, decorating it with a scenic mural on both sides. Those paintings were prescient of his future art career.

No Permanent Address

Larry had other art escapades in that time that did not make it into Book II. The following was one of the most bizarre.

This header was noted in the Portland Oregonian newspaper: Police Seek Lost Mural. I've quoted the article directly from the paper (unfortunately, I only saved a piece of the paper and have no specific date):

Sheriff's deputies are investigating the case of the missing mural. Mark Carpenter, 38, owner of the Turquoise Room, 9045 SW Barbur Blvd. reported he paid an artist $200 down and agreed to pay up $100 more on completion of a 20 foot black-light mural in his place. He related he and the artist, Larry Wall, 34, no *permanent address, differed about when the work was to be completed. Monday, Carpenter said, Wall came into his place. When he left, the mural was real gone— the artist had ripped it from the wall and left a kind of post-impressionist hole.*

It is obvious that the reporter was having a good time with this story, but if he were any kind of a first-class reporter, he would have sought out the artist and heard the whole story. As it was, he missed the best part: Carpenter hit Mr. Wall [sic] over the head with a large, heavy cocktail chair, and Mr. Wall [sic] was awarded $7500 in damages! And as Paul Harvey would say, "Now for the rest of the story!"

Larry, the non-businessman, had made a written contract with Mark Carpenter to put a black-light mural over the bar. Larry had asked for, and received, $100 for supplies (canvas, paint, etc.) with $400 due upon completion. But Larry, being the good, non-businessman that he was, put a clause in the contract that if it was not completed by a date specified (Mark wanted it for some anniversary celebration), Larry would forfeit the final payment. Any normal businessman, even I, as a "typical female," would have known better than to do that! The result was inevitable.

Because it was black-light, requiring special lights, and he would have to stand on the bar to paint it, Larry had to have access to the area at night when there were no customers. The colors in the painting and the lighting had to be carefully balanced on site. For a while, Mark would let Larry in after closing, and Larry would work most of the night. But just when it was close to finished, Mark quit coming to let Larry in. As the deadline date approached, Larry finally got the message: Mark was going to prevent him from finishing it so he wouldn't have to pay the final $400. When Mark didn't return several phone calls, Larry went down during the daytime and did indeed remove the painting! Mark came in just as Larry had taken it down and proceeded to hit Larry over the head with a large, heavy cocktail chair, in front of several witnesses. That didn't have the result Mark expected: Larry picked himself up off the floor and muttered, as he walked out with the painting, "That was a stupid thing to do!"

He drove to his attorney Dave Fertig's office where he promptly had a seizure! After a medical exam where it was determined that Larry had no permanent damage, Dave Fertig called Mark and said that Larry wouldn't press charges, but they would be filing a law suit for damages. Mark readily agreed to the $7500 Fertig requested. Larry quipped, "And the insurance doctor said I was in a low risk occupation!"

I do believe Larry learned his lesson on what we called "The Carpenter Incident—no permanent address." In some ways, that was more truth than fiction: In 1966, that part of 74th street was sold to a developer to build condos, and once again we were required to move, a scenario that was to be repeated five times until we were able to realize a permanent home in California.

The Vietnamese

The German house was loved by both of us: me because it had a wonderful kitchen, spacious living areas, and three bedrooms; Larry because it had a huge daylight basement with north and east windows. Larry had room for several easels as well as space for his large, Masonite panel "canvases," some of which ended up as nudes in taverns.

Nude on Masonite

We christened it "The German House" because there were little messages in German taped to cupboards and drawers, such as "über," which, according to daughter Jill, means "above." Located in a quiet neighborhood of NE 22nd and Multnomah, it was to be the first house of the four we lived in that encompassed about a three mile radius, providing us homes for over the next seven years.

It was in this house that Larry did some of his most creative work and a lot of portraiture. I entered his paintings—the smaller ones—in the county fairs and brought home a number of blue and red ribbons. He also met Sam and Cam (I'm not sure how) who owned a bar in southeast Portland and liked displaying the work of local artists. Not only did Sam display Larry's art, he sold a lot of it. Sam was responsible for introducing us to Vincent Guaraldi at the bar and then took us to Vince's first performance of "The Peanut's Suite," as he called it at that time. Needless to say, we were thrilled. I'll never forget the smoky, intimate bar and the delight of hearing this original music being played by its composer for the very first time!

One night, Larry brought up a portrait he had just finished and, shaking his head in wonderment, said, "I don't know who this is, but this character painted himself!" I still get chills when I think about that painting. It was 12 by 18 inches of an intense Asian man with a coolie hat, done in dark oranges and blues, occasionally highlighted with white. Larry called him "The Vietnamese." This was the most powerful painting I had seen Larry do. I had been reading about a juried, modern art show to be held in Seattle at the Seattle Center (site of the World's Fair three years earlier). Within a few days, I had the painting packed up and on its way to Seattle: I *knew* it was a winner.

Three weeks later, the downfall. A kindly letter informed us that our painting had been juried out; it was not in the theme of the exhibit. We were invited to attend the show when we picked up our painting. I wasn't just disappointed, I was furious. These folks didn't know good art when it stared them in the face! Larry adopted a wait-and-see attitude.

We certainly did go to the exhibit, me with trepidation and Larry afraid I would insult the judges. But even he was flabbergasted when we saw what had been juried in: Andy Warhol (we saw his Campbell Soup Can on its premier showing), Lichtenstein, and other lesser-known figures of the Pop Art

School. The display included, in addition to the aforementioned soup can, toilet seats, Marilyn Monroe, even a large "turd" (I kid you not!), and on and on and on. I finally understood. I didn't agree, but I understood. Through the entire exhibit, Larry observed me with amusement, and I didn't insult any of the judges.

We took our lovely painting home and hung it in the living room. Months later, when my rich aunt Wyvonne and her second husband Bill Nordstrom were visiting, she said, "I want that painting!" She didn't offer to pay for it, but we knew it would get displayed lovingly in their beautiful houses, so we acquiesced, rather I did; Larry wasn't as vested in his paintings as I was.

But our German House went the way of the others: the owner decided he wanted to live there, so out we went, sorrowfully, I must say.

The Beloved Mansion

The Mansion must have been about the 9th studio, but it was Larry's favorite. Five chapters in Book II of the Vallian Trilogy are devoted to The Mansion and our life and work there. He wrote, *"In the hills of Portland are very large complexes that would make our mansion look like an outhouse, but to me it was the most beautiful edifice I had ever seen. Though it dominated the corner of the block, it seemed so specifically designed for me that I felt a surprising ease and understanding of the place at first sight. Everything about it was just right... for an artist."* (Wahl, 2012, p. 346). But because it was one of many studios he inhabited, and what he did and produced there is covered so well in Book II, I'll just touch on a few things.

I will be honest: it was not my favorite. The above quote said it all. It was an artist's studio, not a home, and after six years of putting up with paint spatters on the floor and canvasses often stretched through dining room and living room (Larry liked company while he worked, so often didn't use the available basements!), I wanted a home. You know, those places where you relax and leave behind work and just be with family—yeah, sure ... !

The Favorite?

As I reread the first paragraph, I find myself wondering how "The Mansion" could be his favorite when The German House was his favorite, and the 74th

Street house, and even The Pink House were his favorite. And then it came to me: many things were Larry's favorite! We could go to a restaurant, and it was his favorite, even though the one the week before had been his favorite, or we stayed at one of our timeshares, and it was his favorite, as had been the one the year before. Not *one* of his favorites, but his favorite! I believe this occurred because of two quirks of Larry's nature: his utterly unbelievable (by me and most folks) lack of time sense, and his supreme enjoyment of life and his environment. The latter came after many years of depravity and deprivation, so when he did come into his own life, he was in love with it. I'm reminded of my rescued (from the streets) kitty who is content to just sit and stare adoringly at her new environment. Perhaps I am anthropomorphizing here, but I don't think so.

Why Favorite?

I am still perplexed as to why he liked this big, four floor monstrosity, which was hideous to heat and a bitch to keep clean (Sorry, Larry). The basement was dark and damp with few windows and partially underground. He had to haul his 4 by 4 and 4 by 8 foot Masonite panels up ten stairs to even get to the first floor. There was one garage, so one of our cars was left out on the street. But as he said in the quote, "… it was just right." I think it was the concept of it. Larry was a romantic, and while I couldn't see it, something about it inspired him. In the ~ 16 months that we lived there, Larry did an immense amount of creative work, until, that is, I did the unmentionable: I had another baby!

I won't go into it here since it is completely covered in the chapters in Book II. Larry, in addition to loving that house, had big plans for it: *"I could see the studio work, which was the purpose for this monster of a house, slowly receding in a background of diapers and screaming infants."* (Wahl, 2012, p. 350).

The Volkswagen as "Agent"

The Volkswagen truck that had provided us with "adventures" when we lived in the 74th Street house was now mostly a work truck for Larry. I had my own car to get to my job at the hospital, across town; it was an old, green Pontiac sedan with lug nuts in the hubcaps and a hole in the floorboard.

I could see the pavement when I looked down. However, I loved the damn thing. When the last useable part gave out, Larry and I took it to a junkyard so I could have a funeral and bury it properly.

Larry had painted a mural on the side of the truck, and it provided a passport to a painting job, as well as another studio: NEMCO Wahl Galleries. Larry had been working as a security guard to help pay rent and the heating oil bill. In his off time, in the basement, he had painted a large mural of a boat. It was to be advertisement for North American Engine and Marine Works at the Portland Boat Show. Two young men, Del Chandaunet and his partner Louis, offered Larry space in the building on the dock housing their newly bought business, as payment for the mural. Larry was delighted with his good luck (the basement wasn't so delightful after all). However, the luck didn't last: the young men were playboys, more interested in hosting parties then running a business, and before long they went bankrupt. So Larry was back to The Mansion.

One day at a health spa, Larry was approached by a man who had noticed the mural on the Volkswagen and asked if Larry did that professionally. Of course Larry affirmed that he did. The man told him to go see his art director; he needed a mural for behind the bar in a restaurant in Vancouver, Washington (Larry's growing-up home town). Larry went, got the job, received a down payment for supplies, and happily proceeded to work. For the next month, Masonite panels were stretched across the front of the house through the living room and the dining room with newspapers scattered about to cover the hardwood floors.

Honey, I Lost the Car

Larry frequently went downtown, either driving or taking the bus. On one sunny Saturday afternoon, I got this frantic call from him, "Honey, I can't seem to find the car. I'm afraid I might have parked in a tow-away zone. Could you come down and help me?"

I thought for a few minutes before I replied, then realizing reality, I laughed. "Sweetie, the car is here; you took the bus today!"

"Oh," sheepishly, "Could you come get me anyway?"

"Of course."

It was only three days later when, once again, I got a frenzied phone call. "Honey, did I leave the car home again?"

"No."

"Oh, shit. I must have parked in a tow-away zone this time."

"I'll come and get you, and we can straighten it out."

But, by the time I got to our pick-up point, I once again encountered a sheepish Larry. "I found the car. I had been looking for it where I parked last week."

We drove home, separately but happily. When Larry says he doesn't do time, believe him: he doesn't!

Mr. Moon

The Vancouver behind-the-bar mural was a great success, and Larry was feeling very satisfied with the direction his career was taking, that is until Ed Lehey and the puppet show came along. Ed Lehey was a puppeteer who was the voice for Mr. Moon and co-director of The Mr. Moon Show, a children's television hit on KATU TV, which had aired about 10 years previously. Larry had met Ed at that notorious (notorious because it led to no good!) Portland Boat Show. Ed had wanted to resurrect Mr. Moon on KATU, with his former partner, and wanted Larry to help with the presentation by building a stage and three puppets. There was no mention of money, but Larry was "pantingly" eager to put his design and carving skills to use. All he saw was a great opportunity to work for television—a new application for his talents. The idea of potential big bucks wasn't too bad either. But, I began to be concerned when Larry bought all of his supplies out of our meager cash funds and we helped Ed move three times to different apartments.

I think I may be the better judge of people. Larry had a tendency to either be totally suspicious or totally guileless; I tended to like or dislike people at first meeting, but giving them the benefit of a doubt, would withhold judgment. During his time at The Mansion, Larry was mostly guileless and got caught unprepared twice, despite visible clues he later recognized (though his suspicion saved him from being re-recruited by the CIA). The combination of his guilelessness and my wait-and-see approach resulted in my not being able to advise him and head off some disasters—not that he would have listened. Years later, when he was trying to hawk his geometry, I could predict which relationships were going to go down based on his degree of enthusiasm and pronouncement of "this is the one," when he was dealing with possible business partners.

When Ed began to not return phone calls, Larry's suspicious component kicked in and he started asking around. What he learned was not pleasant. Ed Lehey was an alcoholic with little money of his own (Larry had leant him some over the months they were in contact) and he did not even own the rights to The Mr. Moon Show; his ex-wife did. He was trying to get a presentation up in the hopes that the ex-wife would go along with it. When she died suddenly, so did a revived Mr. Moon Show. Larry later heard from a mutual friend that Ed was living a fantasy: it never would have been produced because Ed was persona non grata at KATU. Ed had slept with the KATU owner's wife …

Beginning of the End

Not too long after that, Larry's hopes for The Mansion lost their glow, and Jill's birth finished them off. Larry went back to work at the security company; I stayed off work only about one month after the birth. My dad advised

Larry displaying artwork and painting at the Del Norte County Fair

me how to wean Jill off breast feeding by telling me how they did it with the cows on the farm (why would you want to wean cows ??). In between his security jobs, Larry set up painting demonstrations at J.K. Gills Art Supply store with their new acrylic paints, while I made arrangements for him to do demonstrations at art clubs and galleries up and down the Oregon coast. My mother even set up a booth for him at the Del Norte County Fair in Crescent City, California. And so, we survived The Mansion, but we moved in April.

My Bad

As I am writing this about The Mansion, more than 40 years later, I feel pain for Larry's loss and for all of the opportunities that I missed to support and help him. But I can just hear him saying to me, "Don't be so hard on yourself. We both were young and selfish, and trying to make our way in a world we were totally not prepared for. As Scotty [the engineer in Star Trek] would say, 'I'm givn' it all I got, Cap'n'—and so it is with us." See why I loved the bum!

Next Stop

We signed a lease on a three bedroom house at 1204 N.E. 27th—the Bluff house—on April 20th 1968, and thus the 10th studio was born. This house was old and somewhat decrepit—I had to do a lot of Goodwill decorating to make it *somewhat* homey. But it was spacious (except the kitchen, which resembled Larry's N.W. 23rd Avenue "closet" studio—a real come down from my last three lovely kitchens), had three bedrooms and a sun-porch on the second floor, which Larry tried unsuccessfully to make his studio, and a large living room and dining room. I hung a series of red beads—like in gypsy fortune-telling parlors—between the living room and dining room and got an inexpensive red rug for the living room floor. Come to think of it, it must have looked like a brothel! Larry and I shared the dining room as his studio and my office when I started back to school. The house did have a funky basement, but I don't think it was very useful for much more than storage. The house next door was a mirror-image twin, housing Glen and his wife. We learned a lot about alcoholism from Glen; drunk was the only time he was friendly!

While Larry didn't make the Bluff house his studio for very long, it did have a special meaning for us: the beginning of the space program. Larry had to attend every launch, to make sure they got off safely, so when we knew a launch was eminent, I would put the coffee pot in our bedroom, program it to start perking shortly before launch time, and set the alarm to wake us at some ungodly hour like 3 AM. I often drifted back to sleep, especially when the countdown was on hold, but Larry was there, alert and rooting for their success. Watching the rockets ignite and the whole assembly, slowly and majestically, move into the vastness that is our sky was always a spiritual experience for Larry. This was an activity we shared for the rest of our married life. When Neil Armstrong did the first moonwalk, unfortunately Larry was working an evening shift as a security guard. Whenever he could get to a phone, he would call me, and I would give him an update. Knowing how much he loved the space program, I was so sorry he couldn't see it on the television, but I made my reportage as detailed and accurate as possible.

Larry didn't find this studio very satisfactory, so in about late 1969, after he had saved up some money from his security jobs, he found studio space in an old building that had apartments above and commercial space in the basement (was it always basements?), approximately 15 blocks from our home. This was studio number 11 at 4010 N.E. Hancock, which space he later christened Rose City Art Center Bau Haus. Shortly after he moved there, I received a traineeship to get a master's degree that not only paid my tuition and books but also threw in some money for living expenses. Since I still worked a couple days at the hospital, we were able to help keep his new studio afloat and to buy a couple of lots near the ocean in Long Beach, Washington, where Larry had spent much time as a child. We became avid campers on our bare lots, but were never very good at it.

Gypsies

Larry and I called ourselves gypsies; we came by that naturally since our childhoods were gypsyfied! If we had a workable car, we went somewhere, anywhere, and our housing moves seemed to fall in the same gypsy category. Unfortunately our children had the same tendencies, which had a variety of repercussions. A couple of notable episodes occurred while we were still in the 27th Street house.

Eric walked everywhere. By the time he had reached about 9, we had given up trying to keep up with his travels around the city of Portland. Fortunately, he was not cursed with the spatial dyslexia of his parents, so we were quite sure he wouldn't get lost; however, this one day his adventuresomeness created problems.

It was getting dark, and he had been gone for most of the day, when a police cruiser drove up to the front curb and a battered-looking Eric and a burley policeman got out. "I found this young man walking down the road, just below Rocky Butte. He said he had fallen down a rock quarry and lost his glasses. You need to keep better track of this young man," the policeman scolded.

We assured him we would. Then, we immediately took Eric to the ER (emergency room) at the hospital where I worked. We had some fast explaining to do about the multiple scratches he had down his back; luckily, we had the police report and Eric's coherent explanation. Since he had suffered no serious injury, we took him home after they had treated his scratches, given him a tetanus shot, and provided preventative antibiotics.

After Eric gave us a detailed report of his journey—Rocky Butte was about seven miles from home—Larry asked about his glasses. We had had an ongoing battle with Eric about wearing his glasses—he had severe myopia—including having the last-visited ophthalmologist emphasize the dire consequences of his not wearing them. Eric remembered where he lost them: in the bushes just before he stepped off the quarry cliff. So, armed with flashlights, off we went to find the accursed glasses; it was now quite dark. Eric showed Larry where he fell (I had a funny feeling in my stomach—it really was a dangerous fall), and while Eric and I watched, Larry plowed around in the thick bushes. Finally he gave up, not finding the glasses. Eric would go with him the next day to see if they were locatable in daylight. And indeed they were.

Larry had noted itching on his arms and face a couple days later, but we set off for a scheduled trip to Kahneeta, a favorite high-desert resort on the Warm Springs Indian Reservation. It was later that night when the swelling and blisters appeared. It then dawned on us that the brush he had been plowing through was none other than Poison Oak. As the swelling increased, and

Larry began to have concerns about his throat closing up, he decided that we better get back home and to the often frequented ER. Leaving at midnight, our 100-mile trip back to civilization was a virtual nightmare. More than once that night, I wondered if I would have the courage to perform a tracheotomy with a pocketknife if the swelling finally blocked his airway. But we made it to the Portland hospital in time where Larry received a shot of Cortisone (a corticosteroid to reduce the inflammation) and instructions of how to manage the itching.

End of story? No, while they had found the battered glasses, and Eric got another lecture from the eye doctor, the next related incident happened shortly after Larry's ER visit. I came home from grocery shopping to find Larry in the corner of the bed, curled up in the fetal position with a deer-in-the-headlights look in his eyes—he shrank back when I came towards him. I surmised he was probably having a reaction to the cortisone—I had seen it before in my practice. Moving slowly and gently, I coaxed him off the bed, got him in a coat, and, asking the neighbors to stay with the kids, off we went once again to the hospital. They confirmed my diagnosis and gave him epinephrine and a sedative. That ended the crises, but not the misery: Larry suffered from the intense itching for many more weeks. He vowed that if Eric again lost his glasses, they would stay lost!

The next happening with our gypsy children was surprising for me and distinctly unpleasant for Jill. At 4 years old, she scurried around in our neighborhood on her tricycle, having been instructed not to go past the end of the block. But, being the child of gypsy parents, of course she had to know what was beyond the next hill—or street, as it were. When I saw she wasn't playing with the neighbor kids, I asked them where she went, hoping for the best. They indicated "that way," which lead across a viaduct straight toward the excessively busy Sandy Boulevard. Grabbing a branch, I started up to Sandy and with a hunch, stopped in at a local tavern, fortunately not across the six-lane boulevard. It was really more than a hunch: I saw a familiar-looking tricycle parked neatly by the door. And there she was, holding court and entertaining the delighted patrons who had seated her on the bar. My little princess yelped all the way home from the light switching she got from my branch. I think she was more humiliated than anything else. But ... I said I was not surprised by this activity. Why? Because I had done the exact same thing at about the same age with the same result. However, I wasn't as careful as Jill: I crossed the four-lane Powell Blvd—a major highway in 1942. My mom located me because my tricycle was parked in front of the tavern, just like Jill's. I know I never told Jill about this, that is, not until after *her* trip. Is it in the genes?

Jill Pre-Gypsy Event

I Am

By Larry E. Wahl, 1965

All are in a mountain's sight
Some can see the mountain's height

Some can love the plateau's scene
Some are climbers, or have been

To some a mountain's lower ridges
Build strong lines of paths and bridges

But to a few with questioned aims
Lay the winning of chosen games

Last of all, the very few
Divest the mind of me and you

Take the challenge heard by one
Out of thousands 'neath the sun,

And leave all things to strive and seek
Living in a threat so bleak.

In the terror, the chilling cold,
Slow wet death for life is sold.

For them the danger of deadly plummet
Is fair trade for shining summit

None can live there; none can stay
It's not a goal, but more a way

Of living life in such an air
That death and life become a pair

Like dear old friends you know and trust
That favoring neither is a must

So, through each mountain's toil and wear
You climb and climb because … it's there

And when the summit has been won
The trip down slope again begun

Each climber sees through mystery:
"I am the mountain, and it is me."

Musing 102 by Larry

Fade-in, Fade-out

He who hesitates is not only lost,
but miles from the next exit.
— *Unknown*

Most of the people whom I have met in my various travels about the world have a fairly standard way of keeping track of their life experiences. Generally, if you can consider the various events in their lives as being pearls, these pearls are more or less strung on a strand of time. Thus, if you give them a year, they can usually come up with the information of what was happening to them in that period of time. Conversely, if they are describing the pearl of an experience, they will frequently be able to discuss the time framework in which that experience took place.

Anyone who has been acquainted with me for any period of time knows that my pearls are seldom on any kind of a string! Instead my memories are in a vast box, scattered willy-nilly in great piles, with no special connection to any kind of a timeline. My earliest memory is of being in the womb and becoming intimately familiar with the business end of a twisted metal clothes hanger.

In the years that followed my birth, it was clear, even to me, that I was destined to live a very strange existence. During a routine examination that included an x-ray skull series, the doctor showed me an old lesion, near the corpus collosum and ventral in the right hemisphere, in an area roughly opposite the left hemisphere speech center. It is my contention (which I have no way of proving) that this early injury is the one responsible for this amazing inability to keep any realistic track of normal time.

Whether or not this lack, by some kind of compensatory process, is responsible for my incredible memory, with almost holographic recall of any event I attended, I do not know. There is ample proof I have such a memory for events both common and totally bizarre, but as will become obvious as you read on, such is the unbelievable case. If there is some kind of event of a worldwide nature, then of course, I will have a time notch for that event. And these memories are not just memories, they are experiences: I was there and can be again.

Even though I wasn't there, I know that Hitler started messing around in Europe after World War I; in the late 1920s, he set his maniacal course for World War II. I know that I graduated from Vancouver High School in the Spring of 1945, enlisted in the Navy later the same year, and was on a train back to Portland only three months after that, with a section-8 discharge. However, without documentation, I cannot keep track of my hospitalizations, jobs I have held, sailing trips I have taken, or the exact dates I have served as patrolman, dockworker, scenery painter, artist, teacher, inventor, hospital orderly, sign painter, assassin, or any of a dozen or more trips, jobs, and assignments. President Kennedy's death was an unbelievable shock to me, and I can remember exactly where I was and what was happening around me. But if you threatened me with death unless I came up with the year, I would just have to die.

All this is by way of giving you some idea of why I think I should have called my Vallian Trilogy "Fade-in, Fade-out." During the course of any day, I might find myself working on some specific project. The next day that project might be pushed aside or forgotten and another started. However, my geometry invention appeared to follow a different "life plan." I seemed to suspend time as I thoroughly researched the areas my invention fell under. I was to find out there really was nothing anywhere near it. As a result, I have a patent granted for a Vallian Geometric Hexagon Opting Symbolic Tesseract. Why this project stayed "faded-in," I have no explanation.

Through three patent attempts, hundreds of hours of excruciating work, and thousands of dollars—not to mention seven years—there it sits, a patent on the fourth dimension: Wahl Patent #5,982,374. It is not for light reading, but it sure as hell was a thrill for me and my wife Sherry, without whom I never would have finished the damn thing. She knew of my life-long love of how things worked and of my special talent with spatial objects: the ability to move them around in space—in only my mind. Spatial Intelligence, she called it (Gardner, 1983). She seemed to understand that I would persist with this project. So, she became my timekeeper and filled in for the "Intelligence" I didn't have: perception of time.

LXV (2010)

Chapter 3

4010 N.E. Hancock/RCAC Bau Haus: The Teacher

A teacher affects eternity;
he can never tell when his influence stops.
—Henry Brooks Adams

Taking on a studio at 4010 N.E. Hancock marked a formidable change in Larry's career trajectory. While the artist temporarily retreated, the teacher and geometer emerged.

This location was perfect for a new, away-from-home studio. It was not too far away from the house, yet far enough to allow the feeling of independence. And since Larry often liked to think and draw in the presence of people for whom he had no responsibility, the new studio was just a couple of blocks from Fred Meyers and its coffee counter. As already mentioned, the building was zoned for multi-purpose use, having both a basement for businesses and two upper floors with apartments. Larry shared with me that he had met a Jewish mother who couldn't stop singing the phrases of her piano-playing son. She lived in one of the apartments on the first floor, allowing Larry to hear the prodigy practicing. We had an opportunity to attend a concert from this composer/pianist at San Jose State University, 30 years later. The prodigy's name was Marvin Hamlisch, who played and scored the motion picture sound tracks for *The Sting, The Way We Were,* and *The Entertainer.* Larry and I seemed to have the ability to be in the vicinity where creativity is emerging!

The basement space consisted of two large rooms across the hall from each other at the northeast end of the building. Larry's space embodied one, mostly empty, large room with large corner windows, facing south and east, and a small windowless office in the opposite corner. In the large open space, there resided a mangy couch—I donated a blanket to give it a little class; the office had a desk and a chair. Larry later hired a young woman named Cathy to do his record- keeping in exchange for use of the space for her free-lance bookkeeping business. After he made this a teaching as well as an art and inventing studio, Larry built a small room out of plywood where he set up lighting exhibits to teach his students about color.

The area across the hall was occupied by a printing business run by a husband and wife, Dave and Ester. Larry made their acquaintance quickly; they had a symbiotic relationship for several years, until the couple retired. Dave and Ester printed posters and advertising material for Larry, and he, in return, did design work for some of their customers. Larry was bereft when they left. Their last gift was to me: A beautiful large poster containing the poem *Desiderata* by Max Ehrmann (1927).

A Problem Era

This period of time was a tough one for Larry and me, much like had occurred during our stay at The Mansion. We both needed additional support as we moved into new life areas: Larry into teaching and inventing; me as a Masters of Nursing Education student. But we did earnestly try to help each other. I had Larry get the birthdates of his students (I still have the list) and I did mini-horoscopes of them to help him better understand their individual needs (No, I'm not related to Nancy Reagan, though my mother did introduce me to astrology). And I remember when my very first class was statistics, and I would cry every time I started to read the book's incomprehensible pages and formulas, Larry would sit down and gently read it to me, until I began to understand it a little. Never mind that he didn't understand it much better than I did! And another time, I was writing my first "scholarly" paper (about Split-Brain—cerebral lateralization—studies in humans) and was required to use multiple citations, but had no idea how to include them in the paper. Larry told me to put each of the citations on a 4 by 6 card, line them up in a logical order, and then he would fill in the transition statements between each or each group of citations. Believe it or not, I got a B on that, but I learned how to write a paper, thanks to him.

But many times over the next few years didn't go so well. I remember sitting up on a bluff overlooking the lights of Portland with my clinical instructor, crying because I was losing Larry—not just to his work, but to another woman. Larry had been involved, during our marriage, in several dalliances, but this one seemed more serious. Some time in 1970, he met Julie who became a frequent visitor at his studio. It was she who signed as witness on the Disclosure Document drawings he sent to the patent office in preparation for filing his first patent (he later gave up on it due to lack of financing). Because I was not only going to school, working a couple evenings a week, and keeping the household functional, I had little energy to try to rectify the situation. And Julie (who was also married) did give him the support he needed at that time. But the situation was magically resolved at a New Year's Eve party at Julie's home. It was just moments before midnight when suddenly Larry appeared and started dancing with me. That may sound insignificant to an outsider, but Larry knew how important it was to me to be with the one you loved at midnight, and he made that happen. Later, Julie and I became friends, and we threatened Larry with her moving in with us and he would have to contend with two wives … if he didn't behave! Good thing he wasn't a Mormon.

Part of an ongoing problem I had with Larry was that I did not want him to be an artist. I suppose the Gully Jimson movie may have been residual in my mind, but more importantly, I couldn't participate in Larry's art, and he would be so distant when he was painting: he would "go away." With the teaching, I could help him and understand what he was doing, but when he was painting, his remoteness would leave me feeling very lonely. Now that I'm a writer, I can understand "where he went." I go there a lot myself, especially when I'm developing classes or writing creatively. I wish I had understood that process better then. Larry interpreted my response to his painting as hating the product of that painting, but nothing could be further from the truth: I loved his paintings—they still hang in our home some 40 years later. As I discussed in the last chapter, I had a good eye for quality; I selected the ones that won prizes. I think part of his misinterpretation was due to my impatient nature: I didn't like to sit and watch as he, in practice mode, drew the same figure over and over. That was an ongoing battle until, fortunately for both of us, as we aged together, I grew more interactive with his work, more understanding of art in general, and more accepting of what he did in particular.

Before I Came Here, I Couldn't Even Spell Teetcher

Larry loved having a teaching studio and, with the help of well-placed ads, he ended up with a very diverse collection of students. There was a mix of young and old, male and female, serious artists and some looking for an interesting hobby—no matter, he loved them all. He immediately immersed them in color theory, which they lapped up. Unfortunately, when the next session started and he tried to plunge them into the study of prospective, all but one serious budding artist drifted away. Larry made a few more tries at regular classes, but none of them matched that first group. That wasn't the last of his teaching career, by any means, but by then, he was becoming deeply occupied with geometry and inventing.

Larry describes the reasons for the failure of his art classes, but those reasons provide a hint of the concepts that will be further developed as his work in geometry progresses. In later essays and articles, he incorporates optical illusions into his patented material, based on the experiences with his art students.

The Why

After my studio school at 4010 N.E. Hancock in Portland closed, I hung on for about three more months, working on the Ellipse-ease. Even as I was working on the models, I was still disappointed and constantly thinking of myself as a failed teacher. In all the years since I had taught myself the joys of drawing, sculpting, and painting, I never had occasion to doubt myself in this particular field. It was literally unthinkable. At every junction of my life when I wished to learn any subject, a master in that particular discipline would appear out of nowhere. I could count on this: the master would show up, and I would have the benefit of the brightest and the best (and many would come from the pages of books). I knew that there was something strange and special about me. I came into the world by means of a reluctant mother and, from then on, I proceeded to cheat the grim reaper as a kind of ongoing hobby.

I must announce at the onset that I am a certifiably Freudian, silly-putty kind of psychological basket case. Since I do not intend to run for public office, I can welcome all the ghosts of Christmas and weddings past as a kind of Mardi Gras parade stretched from horizon to horizon. Nothing I had ever determined to do had not worked to my advantage, so I was totally unprepared for what seemed, at the time, an unexpected and unbelievable failure at the heart of my strength.

I believed that 4010 N.E. Hancock and The Rose City Art Center were to be my home for a long time. I had 22 students to teach and learn from—it might have been easier on me if I had been able to identify them earlier as one of my renowned "masters." I had a beautiful classroom in a daylight basement and a reputation as a successful artist and teacher. My students honored me, as I did them. They ran the gamut of ages and types: a nine year old girl (my best student), a half dozen teen-agers, several career-changing adult males, and mature women of an undetermined (and undisclosed) age. I had installed three autotransformers into light boxes so that the effect of varying ambient light could be studied. One wall featured a full Ostwald color 3-D model; moveable charts on anatomy and color wheels were liberally spread around. Special exhibits illustrated color harmony and the relationships of tone, tint, hue, saturation, shadows, and other nomenclature, as well as the intricacies of Munsell, Ostwald, and Hickentheir color. There was a set of full range, original Pantone Color Panels.

The students were subjected to various displays, instruction, and demonstrations. All in all, it was a lively class, meeting religiously two times a week, with additional times set aside for private sessions and remedial training. I kept a small store of paints and other necessary materials on hand, which I sold at cost. Before the lightening struck, I exposed my students to a six-week course in "Color Mastery," as I called it. It was technically challenging and comprehensive. The class mastered the material in about 2/3 of the time allotted. In my spare time, I worked on models of the Ellipse-ease, had an affair with a non-student, and things were humming along. I felt as though I could do no wrong.
  WRONG!!

Since I was on such a roll, I decided to throw in the rules for 1, 2, and 3 point perspective. The entire subject can be covered in three sentences, namely:

There is a horizon line, and a single point on it will be the focus for all lines on the periphery in 1-point perspective.

There is a horizon line, and two points on it will focus two sets of crossing lines, representing the horizontal components of the drawing

There is a horizon line and two points on it; one, either above or below that horizon line, will singularly locate objects with both horizontal and vertical vanishing points, but three points are seldom used because of the increased difficulty.

I was deep into the material that was trivial compared to the color material they had swallowed, whole. However, I was also deep into trouble, but didn't notice until, in less than two weeks, my entire class disappeared. I could not imagine what had happened. It took me almost two years to figure it out.

A short time after my class became a non-happening—to say I was destroyed was a major understatement—my affair ended, money stopped coming in, and a newly widowed "church-lady" moved into the basement apartment adjoining the studio area. My wall murals adorned the basement walls, and occasionally nude models worked nights in life classes. None of this was appreciated by our newcomer; she bought the building! Sadly, it was clear that my time at 4010 was ending.

Ron to the Rescue

Larry had a friend he knew from his days of living in an apartment with three other guys, when he worked at Good Samaritan Hospital in the mid 1950s. Ron Kester was, like Larry, mainly self-educated post high school. Larry didn't particularly like him when they lived together, but when they ran into each other after both had families, they discovered a common interest in discussing "weighty" subjects, including theoretical physics and mysticism. Ron would come to Larry's studio after work, and they would spend half the night in esoteric dialogues. I don't know for sure, but I think Ron may have contributed to Larry's advanced understanding of cubes (the initiator of his later-granted patent). I still have the cube dated 1970 that Larry carved out of balsawood. Ron was also the reason that we moved to the 'burbs in 1972. Larry wanted to live near Ron so they could work together on getting Larry's invention, the Ellipse-ease, produced; Ron lived "near Lake Oswego" (Portlanders know the significance of that!). But I am getting a little ahead of myself.

Another Favorite

Some time in 1972—April, I believe--another landlord decided to sell our 27th Street home, so we went looking again. This time we found a lovely place closer to his studio at 4010, which we christened "The Tile House." We liked to name our houses; it made them seem more like ours, even when they didn't last long. Because he still had the studio, Larry had no need to appropriate space for his work in the house; thus, each kid had a bedroom, and we had a roomy one with a fireplace. At last I had the exclusive use of a living room/ dining room (I did let Larry sit in them!), and a wonderful kitchen that was all colorful tile. We also had a garage for our car—it was now a Buick mini-wagon—and a large Royal Ann cherry tree in the back yard. What it didn't have was a sane landlord! The address was 2833 N.E. Schuyler. We really wanted to buy that house, but when the sensual landlady (also pretty, but in a weird way) wasn't able to seduce either one of us (she wasn't particular), she refused to sell. We stayed until our one year lease was up, then the move to Tigard, southwest of Portland—the 'burbs.

When we were settled in the tile house, Larry continued to work at his RCAC Bau Haus at 4010 N.E. Hancock, now mostly engrossed in his invention of the Ellipse-ease, as well as working on the development of his new geometry based on cubic mechanics. He continued drawing and some commercial design, but didn't do much mural painting after we moved from the 27th Street house (except on the walls of the basement and studio—much to the dismay of that new owner). He did do one black-light underwater scene for friends Ed and Sheila, to decorate the recreation room in their basement. When we went back to visit them after we moved, we discovered they were gone (divorced, the neighbors informed us), and, as far as we knew, so was the painting. Thus, Larry lost track of another of his large works of art.

When I made the decision, after finishing the master's degree, to leave the hospital and go to work teaching at the University of Oregon Health Science Center in the fall of 1972, Eric was in elementary school and Jill enrolled in Holiday-Land kindergarten. The day before the first day at my esteemed new job, Jill broke out with chickenpox and was refused admission at the kindergarten. Desperate, I asked Larry to take her to work with him, which he agreed to do; he and Jill spent the week together, she coloring, he inventing. She didn't seem to absorb many artistic skills, though.

4010 is No More

We might have tried to find another living place in that neighborhood— the schools were great—but shortly after I started the new job, Larry became studio-less again. For some unknown karmic reason, every place we liked, the landlords decided they did too! That secured the decision to make the move out of Portland—the first time in our married life—to Tigard (also good schools) where we found a nice three bedroom home in a new rental tract of similar homes. This had a large double garage and a family room, so the living room became another studio while the garage served as a machine shop. It was here that we started collecting stray cats and stray corporations!

Not Near Lake Oswego

Thus, 1973 found the Wahl Family at 8020 S.W. Thorn Street, near Ron and his family, but not "near Lake Oswego!" We didn't learn until later that we had moved into a suburban ghetto—though I did wonder about the six motorcycles zooming out of the garage next door as we were moving in! Larry had purchased two lathes that facilitated the building of the first—and only—model of the Ellipse-ease. Between 1973 and 1978, two corporations were formed—RCAC Bau Haus, Inc and Unit One, Inc—to finance and produce the Ellipsease.

But before I get into the intricacies of life as a corporation president (he always made me be the president) and editor of his patent materials, I want to talk, in the next chapter, about another studio that was as important to his growth as a geometer and inventor as was RCAC Bau Haus; in fact, perhaps more so.

The Ellipse-ease

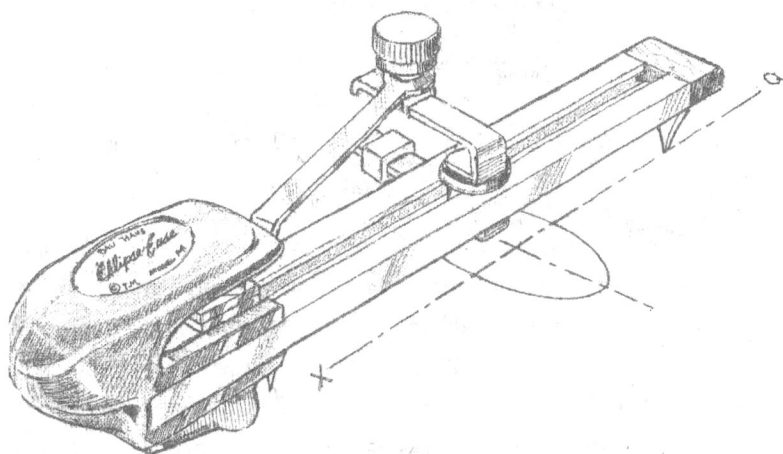

Musing 103 by Larry

About Truth in Art

It is through art and through art alone that we can
realize our perfection; through art and art only
that we can shield ourselves from the
sordid perils of actual existence.
—Oscar Wilde

Keeping your eye on the ball is a simple concept, but it would be meaningless in a ball factory, for which ball should be the ball? The toughest word in the English language for me is "discrimination." Knowing what is the central "ball" in the myriad of plans, goals, objects, and hopes is no small matter. It has been my curse to have understood (I believe) all of Proust that I have read. In a world that is essentially dark and without form until someone shines the light of interest on something present, in that world, nothing much exists. It is because we are given the gift of having so much to look at, look *through*, look *over*, and *overlook* that our lives are as complicated as they are.

In order for my personal life to make any sense, it is necessary for me and for my readers to understand that I have been through the circle of lives so many times and seen so many lies meant to be truth, laws meant to be broken, and dreams meant to be unrealized that most opinions, laws, and rules roll off my back. It is not that all or some of these things are unimportant; I know they often mean the difference between success and failure, happiness and misery, life and death. But if you take the "many lives" point of view, as I must, all these things become colors existing only on a grey scale.

A black and white drawing, when done well, will give me as much enjoyment as a full color painting, equally done well. One can consider the drawing, when done for that purpose, as being the plan for the finished painting. Or if it is be the terminal effort, given it is done with intelligence, wit, and skill, it may well be a classic or a masterpiece on its own. In the writing field, this brevity is exemplified in the preamble to the Constitution where, with a few short words of wisdom—self-evident only after they have been read—we see, feel, and understand great human truths. Such a pithy document is directly opposed to, a three-thousand page government report, from which one would go terminally blind trying to glean any intelligent meaning.

When studying words and their meaning, it is important to make them actually do the explanatory job they were meant for and impart the highly specific meanings they were to convey. The main advantage to literate and illuminative language is to bring forth in the reader some sense of the reality of what is being described by the writer. It does not insist on an agreement with the point of view that even the writer may not espouse, but rather to goad that reader into thinking his own thoughts and considerations on the material presented.

Art, of course, differs in that I consider any valiant effort into legal, religious, political, or sociological breakthrough areas to be akin to abstract art. These efforts are often subversive, daunting, abrasive, and hopefully controversial. The presented descriptions would be true even in what would otherwise be pedestrian but cleverly done family portraits. In some examples that range well beyond the obvious group portraiture, the artist may have cleverly woven in subtle, or perhaps not so subtle, philosophical and psychological information. Often this is done without the observant understanding of the victims/subjects and in a way that would still make their paying for the painting highly likely.

In the old Clay building in downtown San Francisco, a talented portrait painter took on a commission for a large, formal portrait from a spoiled, society daughter. It has always been a surprise to me when painting subjects solicit sexual advances, as though it is a definitive part of an artist doing business. In this case, the subject knew that the artist was married, that he was also a well-known chef, and that he had carefully explained to her that the painting was to be done as the artist wished, but that it would be done professionally, within a given time and not subject to change.

As it turned out, the 26 year old was stunning, with a full figure, beautiful dark hair, shining green/gray eyes, high check bones, and little interest in accepting any change in her desired plans or ideas from anyone. Consequently, she flirted outrageously and tried, in every way she knew, to get the painter into a compromising position. He resisted her for a couple of weeks. During this time, he would steadfastly forbid her from seeing the day's work, keeping the painting covered after every session. The price, agreed upon beforehand, was seven thousand dollars, due at completion.

On the appointed day, while she simpered and batted her eyelashes provocatively, he unveiled the painting. She stood, for the first time completely silent, while a great storm brewed behind her eyes. The painting was done in light chiaroscuro, magnificent in lighting, careful in attention to the subtle skin tones, and nothing that would indicate it was anything but a very good likeness. In fact, that was the problem. My artist friend had painted what passed for this beauty's soul; he had welded his painter's brush like a surgeon's scalpel! Every wicked decision, needless lie, traitorous act, or dishonest, violent, drunken, or selfishly perverted thought that had ever gone through her head was painted irreversibly on that canvas.

In a second, with nostrils flaring, blood in her eyes, and a screaming curse on her lips, she grabbed a heavy impasto knife, and started first towards the artist, and then, when he ducked away, turned her wrath upon the painting. Again, he was faster, having foreseen her reaction, since he had, of course, "painted it in." He deftly grabbed the painting and retired to the closed and locked bathroom. She banged around the room, knocking over paintings, spilling the small amount of paint he had supplied for her rage, and destroying a few drawings he had decided could be sacrificed. She screamed, "I'm sure as hell not paying for this ... this ... abortion!"

He hollered back, "I didn't think you would, madam. It's all right, I'm really proud of it!"

When I asked him about what he had just told me, he laughed, hugged his rotund wife and said, simply, " I think an artist is naturally well designed to explain the word "no" to people who otherwise would seldom hear it."

Chapter 4

OPI: The Emerging Inventor

The vitality of thought is in adventure.
Ideas won't keep! Something must be done
about them. When the idea is new, its custodians
have fervor, live for it, and if need be, die for it.
—*Alfred North Whitehead*

The academic year of 1975/1976 became the most seminal time for the development of the Vallian Coordinate Geometry. Larry was hired as the golden-haired-boy teacher of engineering art and design at the Oregon Polytechnic Institute (CETA II program) in downtown Portland, just across from the main Portland library. In addition to teaching students and being involved in engineering projects with Bill Mosby, a mathematician and the school's curriculum coordinator, Larry spent many hours in the library researching patent law in the Manual of Patent Examiners Policies (MPEPs) and Official Gazettes (OGs). As you can probably tell by now, having only a high school diploma, Larry went on to acquire a variety of self-taught "degrees" in art, engineering, teaching, patent writing, and mathematics/geometry. A partial bibliography is listed at the end of his article, *The Elephant in the Room*; this lists just a few of the books he has devoured over the years. His OPI boss, Robert Bensen, offered to get him a number of "paper degrees." Larry declined. It was here at OPI that Larry did the major work on the development of the both the Ellipse-ease and the "Cubisphere" that, later, would evolve into the Vallian Geometric Hexagon Opting Symbolic Tesseract!

But Larry tells the story much better in his own words.

BENSEN

Something strange and unexpected happened in the fall of 1975: I got a job that, in my wildest imagination, I never expected to get. Like most important things in my life, the mechanics of the beginning were seemingly haphazard and illogical. A friend of my wife told her about a patient the friend had cared for who owned a small engineering school and was looking for teachers. Sherry's friend knew me and told the owner, Dr. Robert Bensen, about me. The word got back to Sherry that he would like to meet with me after he (Mr. Bensen) was released from the hospital. We set up a date to meet with him in his home a week after his discharge. I was happy to have the opportunity to talk about teaching in an engineering school; I had just closed my art studio at 4010 N.E. Hancock and wanted to get back into teaching.

We met at his architecturally-dated, but upscale apartment building, in which he had a suite of eight rooms on the top floor. It seemed obvious that he was doing well; however, as I later learned, this was not quite an accurate appraisal, but I was not looking gift-camels in the mouth at that time. The first thing Bensen said that I really connected with was that he was offering me 2000 square feet for my personal office, shop, and model room, as well as another 800 square feet of classroom space. The entire school occupied a 10,000 square foot area—the entire top floor of a full quarter block at 10th and Alder in Portland.

I had, of course, realized that Bob Bensen was a first-rate con man. He was only a little taller than Sherry, but he talked a good fight. Walking through the penthouse apartment, I noticed that Bensen had not missed many of the good things life had to offer. After the necessary small talk, he took me on a tour. Trophies, cups for engineering achievement, prestigious awards, celebrity-signed photographs, and "sheepskins" from a half dozen universities adorned the walls.

We leafed through photos of a Los Angeles Home Show, where a younger, leaner Bob Bensen was involved as sales executive for a building product called Comp-crete. The demonstration layout took a large portion of the main floor and consisted of a five-room house, made of the material. Comp-crete was composed of wood pulp and shavings, along with a special binder.

The Comp-crete could either be poured in forms like concrete or shaped into blocks with raceways for wiring and plumbing. The material was one-tenth of the weight of concrete, had the same R factor for insulation value, and could be milled, drilled, nailed, or tiled. Its natural color was a pleasant coffee and cream, with a heavily textured surface. It could be painted and/or covered with any kind of traditional wall covering or panels. The special binder that held the material together was some sort of proprietary secret, and after a few of my pointed and incisive questions, it became apparent that Benson was not, nor had he ever been a chemistry major, and he hadn't a clue as to the formula. I believe it was because he knew that I had been working with such a material (for statues) that he was so hot to hire me. It became increasingly clear through our conversations that Bensen was a man unafraid to stretch his own qualifications and abilities while concomitantly diminishing the contributions of others. When we were alone after the meeting, Sherry and I agreed that Mr. Bensen would have to be looked at carefully.

Oregon Polytechnic Institute (OPI) was a small engineering school in Portland, Oregon. It was located in a two-story building across from the Portland Public Library. Bensen's engineering school was financed, in large part, through the government CETA II (Concentrated Employment Training Act), and had not been in business very long. Bensen was president and, I had thought, was the only one I would need to deal with. Then, he explained to me that my contract would have to be signed by the executive vice-president, George Scroge on Monday. I had nothing to lose and had already figured out that Mr. Scroge would undoubtedly try to subdue and renegotiate all that Bensen was giving away.

On the appointed day, Bensen met me at the familiar Portland Public Library, where I had been doing a patent search for my Ellipse-ease.

I looked across the street at the buildings on a block I had passed a hundred times but never really observed. The buildings consisted of lower floors with shops, restaurants, and boutiques, with the entrances to the upper floors of the two large, adjoining buildings that occupied the entire block.

I had dickered for a decent salary, but Bensen had explained that their teaching staffs' base salary was not negotiable, so I accepted it, subject to complete control of my classes and a clear clause recusing the school, its "directors and staff from claims on anything patentable I developed while working there." It became clear that Bensen could and would give away many of the rooms as part of our contract. When I went through the school, I could see why this was easy for him. OPI had offices, drafting rooms, restroom facilities, and an assembly hall; plumbing and wiring were all up to code. The staff consisted of three full-time and five part-time retired engineers. There was plenty of room!

As we toured, I saw that Bensen had given me a shop—narrow but long (~10 by 20 feet)—and an adjoining office and shop of the same size. An additional room was available for my classes and still another room would be made available for any work I was able to do on the Comp-crete project.

Robert Q. Bensen was listed in the schools' staff description as:

Robert Q. Bensen
President and Director, B.S Engineering,
B.A. Geology, A.E. Aeronautical Engineering,
B.A. Business Administration, B.A. Economics,
Instructor in Engineering Technology, including
Alternate Energy Sources.

This was all very impressive, but when looking at Bensen, I always found myself thinking of actor Frank Morgan who played in the movie *The Wizard of Oz* as a character who terrifies Dorothy, her friends, and even Dorothy's dog Toto. The Wizard of Oz is the fat little man spotted at a console behind accidentally parted curtains, manipulating the sound and fury that was projecting the fearful features and voice of the "Great and Mighty Oz."

Scroge

Bensen went home to rest after he introduced me to George E. Scroge, listed as Executive Vice-President, A.B. Business Administration, Business Manager. As I expected, Scroge was an entirely different cup of tea. Before Scroge made any move to offer me a chair, and while I was still standing, I explained everything that Bensen had offered. I allowed as how this was to be formally written into a contract and I would sign it. It was clear by my demeanor I did not expect and would not agree to a dialogue at this point; then, without asking, I did sit down.

He was a good-looking man of 45 or 50 and in very good shape. But he was a type I had seen before: professionally pleasing, but capable of cutting your throat before he finished shaking your hand. I had run off the list of my requirements, including the agreement that only I would have the key to my special areas, which would be locked and off limits to anyone else. I had refreshed his mind on the school's abdicating any rights to any designs or patents I might be working on. I waited for his agreement.

George looked at me, somewhat amused, got up, and walked around the desk to face me. "You don't want much, do you?" he said, in an unctuous voice accompanied by an undertone of warning.

I noted he was now standing so as to block the view of a group of papers he had been perusing when I entered, but I had made a point of looking at them even before I looked at him.

"Mr. Scroge," I said in a firm, flat tone, "just put it all in writing, as described, and I will sign it. This may all be academic in any case. The CIA taught me to read upside down, and I noticed that you were looking at a third and final disconnect notice from the telephone company."

There followed a moment of pregnant silence as the smile drained from his face. He turned and handed me a sheaf of papers. I took them silently, nodded to him, and as I left, said, "I'll have these signed and on your desk before I leave."

George E. Scroge and Larry E. Wahl were not destined to ever grow into close friends!

My Space

At this point, I was still having a hard time believing any of this was really coming to pass. I prepared myself for the real employment decision that I knew would involve Scroge. Most of my space would be in lieu of a decent salary, but I had little trouble with this. In one stroke of an acceptance contract, I would be able accommodate my lathes, a drill press, model shop area, painting studio, and office. It turned out that I would be teaching Engineering Axonometric Art, Shipbuilding, Engineering Layout, and Basic Drafting as well as an Engineering Communication course. I was to have easy access to at least five hours a day, five days a week to use the facilities, especially the "search" facilities of the Portland Central Library by simply walking across the street. My class schedule was such that I would teach two classes in the mornings (nine to one), would have time off until evening classes from seven to nine at night. This meant that the whole middle of my day was open for study and research. While I did both, as well as searching the entire 160 years of OGs for my patent, I found that I had plenty of time to become acquainted with the many retired engineers who were my colleagues and some of whom became friends. And what miniscule salary I was finally offered took care of lunch and dinner downtown.

Bill Mosby

The dean and curriculum coordinator of OPI was William H. Mosby. He had a B.A. in education and was an "Instructor in Engineering Technology." This title was included in the blanket description given everyone who had a breath of some sort of expertise in Alternate Energy Sources; this was the local Sacred Cow of government investments at this period of time.

Bill Mosby was sitting in his roomy, orderly office with Tanya. Tanya had enrolled with her husband Demetri. Tanya and Demetri Korinskova were Jewish Russian émigrés, enrolled in a special U.S. State Department program for recent, highly educated émigrés to the United States. The program was designed to help them make the transfer in their selected fields through the CETA II program, learning American methods and standards in their disciplines. We had about sixteen Russians in our school, though many others were distributed in various schools and training situations across the U.S.

Tanya had been a licensed senior engineer in Russia and had worked on many major projects there. Demetri was an accomplished architect, but because of their Jewish heritage, both had difficulty getting top jobs. When Russian Jews were allowed a quota to leave for either Israel or the United States, they had chosen to come the States. Tanya was beautiful, very interactive with the staff, and about 15 years younger than her straight-laced husband. Behind his back, he was termed Ivan the Terrible by some of the ex-GIs with whom he studied.

There was not much of a dress code at the school, though most of the teachers wore business suits, and I generally wore a dress shirt with slacks, but Demetri was always a fashion plate. His major school project was an elaborate model of the home that he intended to build in Portland. He had been a professor in Moscow and was well known for his skill in teaching, as well as a no-nonsense approach to his students. Impeccably dressed and coldly formal, he appeared to think himself very handsome and very proud indeed [one had the feeling]. He stood out in a school boasting jeans, tee shirts, and combat boots. Tanya just dressed well but, as was said, she would have looked good in a gunnysack.

Tanya stood up as I entered, but Bill motioned us both to sit and continued his talk with her. Tanya had a spread of her design work laid out on Bill's desk and was trying to demonstrate, with charts, original drawings, and pages of math, the work on the lesson that Bill had given her.

Bill looked bored and finally just pushed a parts' source book at her, giving her collection of support material back. "I'm sorry," Bill said, "This is just not acceptable in American standards."

Face reddened and dark eyes blazing, she quickly piled all of her materials into a large backpack and strode wordlessly out of the office, leaving behind the parts' book Bill had given her. She had been rejected and she rejected this stupid book he kept shoving her way. She had been given the simple (for an engineer of her experience) task of selecting and drawing the connections of an electric motor to a set of gears that would then lead to a shaft with a given output in rotational speed and output power.

Tanya had designed dozens of much more complex and extensive machinery for industrial plants in her native land. Yet here was this crazy American, rejecting the designs she had taken particular pride in and pains with, and he did it every time she submitted her work—work she knew was right. Being both young and slimly attractive, she was sure that Mosby liked her, but he seemed obstinate in sending back her term project. She could not graduate without it and she had done everything she could think of to make it more elaborate, simple, understandable… and English! All of the Russians were in America to learn American methods, regulations, and codes, and she was sure that she and "Ivan" were fitting in well with the system. Her English was a little better than her husband's, but both were acceptable. Who really understood the Americans, though, she thought. Professor Mosby should be happy with the quality of the work she had done from the beginning. On most of her work, he had been satisfied, but on this last, most important project, he seemed to be, as the Americans say, "digging in his heels." What in the world did he want from her?

In the office, after watching the interaction between them, I wondered aloud, "Lord knows I'm no machine expert, much less much of a mathematician, but all that stuff looked pretty good to me."

"It was beautiful and beautifully done," agreed Bill, grinning broadly, "but not what is called for."

"What does she have to do—build the damn thing in your office?"

Bill laughed and retorted, "She did look a little like she was going to call in a Cossack hit squad and have me done in, at that."

Bill then informed me this scene had already been played exactly the same way three times before and was about to explain further, when there was a knock at the door, and Tanya burst in. She had a copy of the source book that she had steadily ignored among her resources, having opted for a "from the ground up" Russian approach to the problem. She had detailed studies on the problem, where the various components would be constructed, how they would be machined to tolerances, and even a time scale for their distribution and assembly. All of this is what Bill had been routinely handing back to her.

But now, in a verbal explosion of words, with eyes shining, she explained. "Motor, she is General Electric type d-6, Catalog #41-75 E, vich is conneceted to baze plate type C Catalog, number 47 BPE, vich ess mounted wit bearing of dentrafugal type, bearing and yoke. Catalog number Z 167, vich ess connected to sheeve assembly, Catalog number 457-31 B, all of vich connecets to output shaft!

"Da?"

Bill rose from his desk, clicked his heels together, and shouted, "Da! ... In America we do not reinvent the wheel every day; there are applications engineers who will pull all of this stuff right off the shelves for you." He surprised me by taking her by the shoulders and kissing her lightly on both cheeks, and then bowed silently.

Tanya stood quivering in front of him, breathing deeply, and then slowly said, "Mistaire Mosby, Sir, you are very, very, very bad man." But she was smiling.

Bill answered her in the same marked tones, "No ... I am very, very, very good teacher!"

OPI No More

Unfortunately, while Larry had a wonderful teaching experience at OPI and time to pursue his work on the geometry, it was not destined to continue. Contract negotiations with George Scroge failed, and when Mr. Bensen died in 1976, OPI closed down. It is notable that we recently discovered Oregon Polytechnic Institute located in N.E. Portland, far from its original home, but no information was available on the program or its faculty. We had planned to visit the site on a later trip up north.

Larry had a continuing relationship with Bill Mosby, even after OPI closed. Together they designed and patent-researched special equipment for several businesses. We even had dinner with Bill and his wife several times. The relationship ended when two unusual events occurred. First, Bill insisted that a design was correct that Larry, a much better engineer, knew wouldn't work. They lost the job, fortunately before they killed the disabled patrons: Larry had been correct. And then, at the last of their dinners, Bill and his wife (forgot her name) indicated that they would not mind doing a partner swap. We stipulated that that was not our thing! Larry had really enjoyed Bill and was sad to see the relationship deteriorate, but he did finally figure out that Bill might be a good teacher, but he knew "squat" about engineering design, or marriage, for that matter.

Musing 104 by Larry

On the Road

The buck stops here
—Harry S. Truman

Sometimes I get up at 5:00 or 6:00 AM and start writing. There has to be enough material for you to get the feeling of what you are doing. Sometimes it just flows, but other times it is like pulling teeth. "Maybe you can do it, but why would you want to?"

This morning we are fasting so we can get our blood tested, part of a routine health visit. I am sitting here and thinking of teeth and bones in general, which brings me to growth and development. Both sort-of friend Miles Levine and I were raised, in our early years, on the streets of the Portland, Oregon Ghetto. I capitalize Ghetto because it was memorable and produced a state of mind. That particular Ghetto is long gone and memories fade, but the states of mind persist, probably forever.

As Scientology, or more accurately, Ron L Hubbard, teaches, "A Thetan (soul) has no garbage dump." I translate this in my own words, "The crap you throw over your shoulder and behind you, will not allow for any distance. As you move along, so does it."

This "rule of life" is very real for me. I know that it is true: Sister proved that beyond any doubt. Mark Twain wrote that the bad things one did in life were easily forgotten, but the good deeds—the ones that really cost you—live on forever. It follows the snide rule that "… no good deed goes unpunished." The general gist of the parable of the Thetan (or soul?) is that it must produce an effect. In Scientology, this is taught as the Thetan's one and only edict. We become screwed up when we do something we (the Thetan) really did not want to do. The only other way a Thetan is able to acquire bad karma—or lasting somatics (trouble right here in River City)—is to *not* do something it should have done.

Doing something is never a problem, and this does not have anything to do with physical or legal consequences. The Thetan apparently does not have a back-up co-pilot. The Thetan creates an effect it desires, or it does not; success, therefore, is limited to the individual doing pretty much what he or she wants. The catch is, that if you believe or subscribe to this theory, you are required to do everything you decide is a desirable outcome. Since you cannot choose *not to choose*, the consequences for others of what you have decided trail behind you like an unrelenting and non-erasable wake. Whatever mess—if only in your mind—you have created, you will eventually have to face at some point in this or future lifetimes.

As some rabid Scientologists have discovered, this rule includes those same individual Scientologists, and as an organization, they have accrued some pretty goofy and horrendous karma for themselves. Being able to understand a set of rules, no matter how logical, has ab-soul-utely nothing to do with being able or willing to follow those rules. As has been often pointed out, no rule is simpler than the Golden One, "Love thy neighbor as thyself." But what happens to the hapless neighbor if you happen to loathe yourself?

I spent a decade using the military to get even for what happened to me in the Ghetto, and in Chicago, because it SHOULDN'T HAVE HAPPENED!

Given the Scientologists' rules of engagement, this meant that I must have planned on something else happening to me that had edges, but did not include being beaten nearly to death or starved. All of this occurred before the so-called "age of reason." Apparently the "age of responsibility" is arrived at prior to the "age of reason."

When I worked as a deputy sheriff at North American Aviation, I was caught in a speed trap in Inglewood California, along with a whole raft of other speeders. When I went to court, remembering (of course) to wear my uniform, I chose to be the fool representing myself. Looking sternly at the officer reading the citation, I drew myself up to my full height and said, in a loud, clear voice, "Your Honor, first of all I would like to categorically deny everything the officer has said ..."

At this point, "hizoner" raised his voice to a mocking falsetto and almost leaped off his high pulpit. "OOOOOoooo," he bellowed ... "cat-a-gore-ically!" Then, in a more normal voice, still dripping with sarcasm, he retorted, " ... you were not even on the highway?"

The court roared with laughter. What I had failed to realize was that I had drawn the court jester of judges, but though humorous, he was no fool. I reserved that honor for myself.

Even though the charges were dismissed, I never forgot the point: You are, at the very least, in case of any accident, responsible for ... "being on the road!"

Chapter 5

Of Gardens, Cats, and Corporations

Penetrating so many secrets, we cease to believe in the unknowable.
But there it sits nevertheless, calmly licking its chops.
—*H.L. Mencken*

8020 SW Thorn: the site of the new, official Wahl businesses. Larry had named his last studio in Portland Rose City Art Center Bau Haus. Portland is the Rose City and has an annual Rose Festival, complete with parade and queen and court to authenticate this nom de plume. Larry used this title to authenticate his location as well. But when we got to Tigard and started our corporations, it became RCAC Bau Haus, Inc and was joined by Unit One, Inc a year or so later. I don't know why we needed the second corporation, but I'm sure it served a purpose then. We gathered up interested friends and acquaintances who wanted to be part of Larry's new enterprise: produce and market the Ellipse-ease. As I mentioned, Larry always insisted that I be president (though I had little idea about how to do the job; I don't think Larry did either), and he was director. We induced various shareholders to be secretary and treasurer, and several of us were the board of directors. We were funded by selling stock to our shareholders, but Larry and I put in a lot of our own money, also for stock.

Now, in 2013 and having worked with an accountant and lawyer, I cringe at the amateurish manner in which we conducted our corporate business. Larry had read several how-to books, and one shareholder, a lawyer, helped with the paperwork; we did our best and wasted a lot of our money in the process. But Larry was a natural leader—some would say con man. However, in the Meyers Briggs Psychological Type (MBTI) literature, one of the characteristics of Larry's type, INTP, is " ... able to get others enthusiastic about his projects" (Meyers, 1998), and he was enthusiastic about his product, the Ellipse-ease. Thus, he was able to keep things going for about five years. But he also taught himself patent law by reading all of the materials he found in the Patent Research Room in the Portland Public Library.

But while Larry was in the process of setting up the corporations and beginning to acquire shareholders, several factors temporarily put us below the poverty line: Larry's loss of his studio and classes, his ending up experience-rich but money-poor when OPI dissolved, and my starting a new job at a lower salary, not to mention the expenses of another move. So as I finished my thesis and learned to be a nursing educator, Larry moonlighted as a security guard for Lawrence Security. This period would have been exceedingly grim, except for the, shall I say occult, experience he had in this new job: The Building. Larry describes it in his own words.

The Building

I took a job as a security guard at a literal hole-in-the-ground that was to eventually sprout a twenty-story office building on half a block. The rest of the block was taken up by a landscaped area that was to be an underground parking area, extending to the next block, south. In the beginning there was a tremendous amount of excavation, but from rumors and a strange aura about it, it was opined that this was going to be a very interesting building. I considered this to be a set of several different people's pipe dreams. All I knew was that I was back in a familiar uniform, carrying a weapon, and trying to figure out what and who I was.

The building did not look like a studio, nor did it look like a building. On first sight, it looked like a hole in the ground, three levels deep and twice as long as it ultimately would be.

Multiple trades are involved in any commercial structure, and I had seen many. A hobby of mine was spending hours watching (and photographing) buildings being torn down or being built up. This particular building was strange right from the start. One of the first concrete pours was for a three-story deep electrical vault. In itself, there is nothing strange about this, but the conduit weighs (paths, for the non-contractor) led from the vault, both north and south. South made sense because the nearest main power grid was located in that direction, but to the north, across the street and backed up to the Willamette River, was only an ancient wooden building about three stories high, with no windows on the street. I assumed the building was abandoned. On the several blocks north was the new PGE building; certainly power could be tapped from there. So the south power source made much more efficient and cost-wise sense, rather than extending north to PGE. What was in the designers' minds? I love mysteries!

As construction of the structure proceeded, guards were given new sets of keys. There was one key on the ring of ten keys that intrigued me: it looked like a very old key for a very old lock. The abandoned-looking building had a huge barn-like door facing our block, and I remembered seeing an unusually large lock on its "sally door." A sally door is one meant to allow someone to pass through a much larger door without having to open the latter. I had the key? So ...

About 4:30 AM on my watch, the 2nd guard went off duty, and I was left to patrol the crates, debris, supplies, lumbar, and cables by myself on this rainy, deserted section of the Portland waterfront. I walked across the street to the old building, stood for a long time looking up and down the street, and then tried the key in the massive lock. I was not surprised when I heard it click and was able to open the sally entrance.

Stepping quickly inside out of the rain, I quietly closed the door behind me. A series of heavy bays, all wooden, stretched out on the left, accompanied by pumps and motors. The piece de résistance, however, stood almost in the center of the building: a mill wheel with a thyroid problem. The wheel was all of 20 feet high—that was only half of it because the axel and main bearing were a couple of feet below street level. We're talking 40 feet in diameter and 12 or so feet across. It was now stationary, but was simply, clearly, and obviously a waterwheel—or maybe a carnival ride?! It was unquestionably, sure as hell, one of the largest I had ever imagined, much less seen.

There was a single, 100-watt janitor's bulb sending out hopeful rays of light, which were almost immediately consumed by the dark. The behemoth wheel cast weird shadows in and out of the tracery of the ancient and mighty wooden beams, supports, and infrastructure that held this moose together. The hidden half of the wheel was completely lost in a void of shadows.

As I peered down into the wheel's well, trying to calculate what kind of a water flow would be necessary to move a thing that size, my heightened senses detected a movement near a small internal shack to the right of the wheel. A door had creaked open, and a figure was moving toward me. I turned off the flashlight and walked over to the man, sporting a confidence I did not have.

"Hello there," I said, much too loudly and heard the echoes mock me.

"Eh, hello yourself … Sir."

The "Sir" was added half a beat after he saw the flash of my badge. His voice sounded as though it would take as much horsepower to move the sound past his lips as it would take to move the giant wheel. He was a small-statured man, dressed in dark blue overhauls, wearing an engineer's cap. His face was deeply lined and dark, as though working in the shadows had let the shadows take over his face. My uniform and the fact that I was rattling keys seemed to assure him that I belonged. I pressed my apparent advantage.

"This is on my prioritizing 400 patrol list," I lied, "they said to check with the engineer in charge."

The last ad lib was to offer this old man, who was probably dying of boredom, a chance to talk to another human being; I was acknowledging his position as caretaker of all we surveyed. For the next fifteen minutes, he explained that the waterwheel and the entire operation were much older than he was. He showed me the generators that would operate off the massive set of gears powered by the wheel. Taking me into the shack, he showed me the plans for the Willamette River diversion channel that would feed the beast and the immense gears that would allow the water to flow through a diversion canal and then out again to the river.

An obvious question came to mind. I thought about it for a while, and then carefully phrased my comment so it would not sound like a question. "So, of course, if there is any problem with the city grid, our building across the street will draw power from this source, and all you have to do is open a couple of valves."

He nodded in agreement and proceeded to take me down the heavy walkways to the main bearings. I didn't see the metal bearings that I knew would be needed to support something that weighed more than my three-bedroom house. I allowed, with disbelief in my voice, that they looked like black wood.

"Yah, you betcha," he said in an interesting accent. "Der made from laminated blocks of lignis, harder than iron and der da originals. Gar, dey last forever." He practically bounced with excitement. "And wat do you tink dey lubricate dem wit?"

He didn't wait for an answer but shouted with glee, "youst vater, by Gar, and ve got plenty of dot. Dey vouldn't vare out, ever ... but dey shor as hell vould catch fire."

I spent a few more minutes with him, checked my watch, thanked him, and said, in passing, that I would report that everything was fine, and nobody else would come around again to bother him. He allowed, sadly I thought, that it was no bother.

I let myself out the small door—back into the rain—clicked the heavy lock shut, and went back across the street to the shelter of my small guard shack. I sat looking across First Street at the silent Willamette flowing by and wondered what kind of a strange and weird structure I was watching being born. What was so important that it needed its own power supply?

The Rest of the Story?

Larry guarded that building literally from the ground up, and when occupancy arrived at the highly secure 17th to 20th floors and said occupancy consisted of tall, muscled, marine-type young men, he deduced that this building housed some kind of spy agency. He tried reporting this to a newspaper reporter—he thought the people of Portland should know what was growing in their midst. The reporter abruptly lost interest the next time they met; Larry noted the reporter had been "properly" beaten up.

When Larry was threatened by one of the building "owners" and then fired by Lawrence Security, he decided to protect his family and let go of pursuing the truth of it. The mystery of that building would always intrigue him, but he had corporations to manage, a patent to write, and a life to live.

Zucchini and Corn

Larry decided he wanted to try his hand at gardening—for relaxation, he proposed. I certainly could go along with that, but I wasn't sure about the relaxation ... unless he meant a glass of wine on the patio while directing *me* to pull the weeds. But, he was serious about it. We had a large back yard that supported only straggly grass and slugs, to which we fed beer, the slugs, that is. So, to help us prepare the ground, a neighbor offered to share his Rota-tiller and some fertilized compost he was getting. Larry went ahead and put up a fence that served to define our space and restrain our dog, Muffin, who had already brought home a stolen rotisserie chicken from a neighbor's grill on the 4th of July.

The day arrived, and much to our amazement, our neighbor backed in a truck and dumped a stupendous amount of steaming horse manure all over the bare yard. After things cooled down (literally), Larry went to work with the Rota-tiller, creating a nice fertile bed for our newly to-be-founded garden. It took him a few days and the gentle ridicule of the neighbor to find out he was using the Rota-tiller incorrectly. It had been bouncing all over the yard, not getting much purchase on the ground. The owner of the machine finally showed him its correct use—there is a little "foot" in the back that is locked down to stabilize and "ground" the machine. With this little bit of correction, the whole process went more smoothly and effectively.

Did we plant! Carrots, potatoes, onions, radishes at the far left end; tomatoes, zucchini, cucumbers across the front from the middle on to the right; and one long row of corn from left to right by the back fence (yes, I can hear the farmers and gardeners groaning). We watered our garden every day when it wasn't raining and waited.

Not too many weeks into the season (remember, that was *very* rich soil), we observed the nascency of life and began to anticipate harvest. But Larry wanted to make sure the root vegetables were coming along well (what about root didn't he understand?), so he pulled up some carrots to see if they were growing (Oh, hush, you experienced gardeners). When I explained to him that carrots (and potatoes, etc.) did the majority of their growing underground, and it was best to let them mature there, he sheepishly got it. That was the only thing I was knowledgeable about in gardening. But, from then on, whenever either of us became impatient about the outcome of some project, we would remind the other, often in unison, "don't pull it up to see if it's growing!"

The tomatoes flourished. The cucumbers flourished. The zucchini flourished and flourished and flourished. Our gardener friends didn't tell us that you need only one—I repeat, one—plant to get your summer's worth of that vegetable; we had planted ten! You know what the neighbors found on their front porches. We had a friend who owned a service station and also planted too many zucchini; whenever a customer got out of the car to go inside, Frank would open the trunk and place a box of zucchini therein.

Since I worked full time teaching, I don't know when I found the time, but I canned tomatoes, and made cucumber pickles, and tried every possible recipe I could find to use the zucchini— no *just zucchini bread* for my family. And finally, "the corn was as high as an elephant's eye"—thank you, *Oklahoma*, I think—and, at last, was ready for harvest. We had been drooling for wonderful, fresh corn-on-the-cob for what seemed like ages. But … it was not to be. Larry pulled off one husk and pulled down the silk and there was the cob, but no kernels. Again and again, he looked for kernels—and there were none. What had we done wrong?

The answer came from the smart aleck, manure-sharing neighbor: you must always plant corn in at least 2 rows, even better in a 4 by 4 block—they self-fertilize, dummies! Well, we crawled away from that year's corn, but did note our success with the rest of the crop. We may never get the "4-F Future Farmers of America Award," but, as with many other phenomena in our lives, we learned and changed and, therefore, enjoyed our bounty in subsequent years. In fact, the year of the Mt. St. Helen's volcano eruption, we got a double dose of fertilizer from the ash, but it delayed plant growth to the extent that I had to leave our wonderful tomatoes and my canning equipment to a neighbor when we left for California in September. But gardening was an experience of living close to the ground, and we had thoroughly enjoyed it.

For the Love of Cats

We always had one or more cats sharing our spaces during our married life—in 1980 we named a corporation after our much-loved orange tabby, Tobi. I think I was the one that attracted the cats: I loved them and they seemed to love me. But after they became part of our family, Larry adored and protected them as well. We used to joke that there was a sign on Pfaffle, the main street two blocks up from Thorn, saying, "All felines needing a home—pregnant ones especially welcome—go to 8020 S.W. Thorn; good food and warm house." And we would adopt them, though their first trip was to the Vet! At one time, we had five: a classic tabby (Paddywach), two Siamese (Nick-Knack & Tigger-Too), a beautiful Black Mum (Pywacket), and a shorthaired gray with a bad temperament (Grey Ghost). They all had interesting stories surrounding their arrivals, but Grey Ghost and Pywacket had the most unique beginnings with the Wahl family.

Grey Ghost

Larry had been moderately ill off and on during this period of time, but when he started pacing the floor because of the pain in the right side of his abdomen (a classic sign of gallbladder disease, called "pacing pain"), a trip to the ER was indicated. Bess Kaiser Hospital was in North Portland, about 20 miles from our Southwest Tigard home. I drove and got there in record time, parking in the breezeway by the emergency room door. I leapt out of the car and ran in to get a wheelchair. Leaving the car where it was parked, passenger door open, I took Larry in to the registration desk. After the insurance info was provided and Larry was being taken care of, I went back out to park the car properly in the lot.

After several hours of questions, probing and palpating, pain medicine, and long periods in-between, Larry was pronounced ready to go home, pain pills in hand. I brought the car back to the breezeway and picked him up. He was plenty groggy with pain med, but feeling infinitely better, because of the pain med. He slept much of the way home, but just as we came into the outskirts of Tigard, Larry woke up with a somewhat puzzled expression on his face and in his voice. "Am I having a hallucination or is there something furry under my feet?"

And thus we met Grey Ghost, and a new family member joined the feline cadre. The only way we could deduce how she got in the car was when the door was left open as I transported Larry into the ER. It was a cold night; she knew a good thing when she found it.

Pywacket

It was Christmas time in Crescent City, California (no inclement weather this time), and we were packing the Buick, getting ready to leave for our home, with a planned stopover in our favorite holiday town, Long Beach Washington. We were loaded down with Xmas presents: I could hardly locate Jill and Eric in the backseat, they were so covered with new blankets and comforters, thanks to Mom. Dad came up to the passenger-side window, holding what looked like a black pillow. He indicated he had something for me. Opening the door, I saw that the black pillow had morphed into a small, squirmy black kitten.

"This black cat has been camping on our front porch, and Mommy doesn't want to keep it. I drove it up King's Mountain Road for about a mile and let it out in a safe place. I'll be damned if it didn't beat me back home! Why don't you take it with you and drop it off somewhere up the coast." Of course he knew we wouldn't, drop it off, that is.

The kids were holding their respective breaths—what kid doesn't like a kitten. I looked over at Larry, and he nodded. Larry is a sucker for stray cats; perhaps because he always felt he was one? Kitten was dropped into the back seat with Jill and Eric, and it immediately settled into the new blankets, purring contentedly.

The drive up the coast was relatively uneventful. At a rest stop on Humbug Mountain, kitty was getting restless, and we thought she might need a potty break. I got out with her, and she wandered around on the grass for a few minutes but didn't seem to do anything. Then she walked back to the car, and I scooped her up and held her in my lap as Larry resumed driving. While I was holding her, I could feel that she was just skin and bones, and not much of that. Insight flashed: the poor thing was probably starved. We could get her some food at our dinner stop in Reedsport, where we knew a much-visited buffet restaurant.

We brought her back some small portions of chicken and water in a small, purloined bowl. She devoured the repast hungrily. And we continued on our way.

I had been snoozing when I heard Jill squealing, "Mommy, Mommy, help!"

I noticed an unusual odor, actually a familiar, unusual odor. One would think I would have remembered what happened when we fed solid food to another starving kitten, one who had followed us from our 74th street house to our 13th street house, a trip she made over many months. One would have thought I would have learned the lesson: you don't give a starving animal, human included, solid food for its first meal after a long period of deprivation. But one didn't learn, at least I didn't. The poor kitty, no fault of her own, had shat all over the blankets in the back seat, *the new blankets* in the back seat, and shared a little with both Eric and Jill. We contained what we could while reassuring the poor distressed kitten that she was OK; we were not mad at her. She curled up in the mess and purred, and Larry drove to Long Beach, as fast as the road permitted.

When we got to our motel, while I registered, Larry ushered the smelly group into the room and had the kids get into their nightclothes; the bedraggled cat went into the bathroom! Then he gathered up their clothes, picked me up at the office, and we headed to a nearby Laundromat; it was now about midnight. We sat there for the next two hours while the clothes, blankets, and comforters sloshed and whirled. Fortunately, an airing-out took care of the car.

We had our two, now enjoyable, days in Long Beach (we fed kitty baby food and milk), and then headed back to Portland via a narrow, winding 100+ miles road. As we cruised along, happy and relaxed, enjoying the scenery, our new family member (was there ever any doubt about that? She had initiated us) began to get restless again. Having now learned our lesson, we stopped at the first grassy wide spot we could find. We had been driving for about an hour, and it was getting dark. Kitty got out, and the rest of us joined her to stretch our legs. I kept an eye on her so she wouldn't get lost. I had already buttered her feet so she wouldn't run away (I just read that that is a myth— it seemed to work with our other kitties). As she did before, she wandered around, stopping here and there, pouncing on an invisible insect, nibbling on the grass. She seemed to be taking her time; we were getting a little impatient, but gave her the time she wanted. When she was ready, she went back to the car and leapt in, settling down for the rest of the ride.

We had been driving for about 15 minutes when we came around a long curve, and there were the flashing lights of emergency vehicles and a crumpled car, resting on a second equally crumpled car. Larry gasped when he saw the first car: it had passed us on a blind curve, going much too fast for that road, just a short time before we had stopped for our kitty break.

We named her Pywacket, after the witches' familiar. We were convinced the precise timing of her rendezvous with the grass had saved us from being involved in that horrible fatal crash.

While Paddywach was the boss of our feline household—she was the oldest and the smartest—Pywacket always was special to us. When we moved to California, we made sure all of our cats (Paddywach went with us) had good homes. We found a lovely place for Pywacket out in the country, where she had acres of grass to explore and a family who fell in love with her on first sight.

The Ellipse-ease

Because of all of the time Larry spent researching patents in the OGs (Official Gazettes) at the Portland Main Branch Library—it had the largest collection of information about patents (abstracts) and the governing principles of the Patent Office on the West Coast—he truly believed that he could write his own patent. He had tried hiring a patent attorney with money we didn't have, but that proved fruitless. The attorney kept having him come back, each time adding to the bill. On day while he was waiting for his appointment, Larry saw a patent lying on the secretary's desk marked "abandoned" and heard the attorney, over the intercom, request " ... that abandoned one. I think

I've got a buyer for it." And at that point, Larry thought he now understood the "game": the attorney would keep stringing him along until he ran out of money and would abandon the patent. From the patent rules he had absorbed at the library, Larry knew that once abandoned, *any one but the inventor* could file the patent and claim the idea. Larry requested his materials and walked out of that office, never to return.

Corporations and Investors

At its most active phase, we had, including Larry and me, 15 shareholders holding various numbers of shares, though Larry maintained controlling interest. I didn't have many shares, but I did have a lot of responsibilities, mainly calling meetings as requested by Larry, presiding over the meetings, and especially making sure that reports were written. Larry hated finishing reports. I often had to literally take his notes away from him, type them up, and send them to the shareholders by the agreed-upon dates. But often I felt my position was a sham: the guys in the corporation treated me like I was a second-class secretary. The most annoying behavior they persisted in was when I set up my materials and coffee by a certain chair (the meetings were in our home), they would take turns sitting in my chair, forcing me to move my stuff and myself somewhere else. Talk about power plays! Larry was totally oblivious to this corporate behavior; remember, I was the one who worked in large organizations (hospitals and universities) and understood how power was manifested. Unfortunately, I wasn't able to exert the power of my position, at first. I learned to do so later, but it wasn't much help with this board of directors.

I talked with Larry about how it made me feel, and he promised to talk to the guys (with humor, of course), but somehow it never happened: Larry was too involved in his projects. So I did what I could to support him and tried to put my ego behind me, but the resentment was there and certainly colored how I felt about our corporations and that period of time.

There were some good times though. Larry took me along when we went to various companies in the process of trying to get the Ellipse-ease produced, always proudly introducing me as the president of the corporation; he called himself inventor. Interestingly enough, one of the businesses we went to was called "Floating Point," a term that was to represent anathema in regard to the Vallian Coordinates. We also went to a computer conference in Portland where we first encountered Steve Jobs as he revered his new Apple product and demeaned the Radio Shack personal computer, which he called "Trash 80." Larry began forming an opinion of Jobs at that point, an evaluation that would harden over the years.

Larry spent the majority of his time preparing materials for patenting the Ellipse-ease. He read about a new patenting process called the Disclosure Document Act, which he renamed the DDA. By completing a form and enclosing supporting materials, the inventor could fix the date of his idea or process, proving he was the original inventor if impinged upon at a later time. Larry took this seriously and, post haste, filled out the document and enclosed fifty pages of supportive materials and drawings, including the one signed by Julie and him in 1970. I believe this DDA marked when I officially became his editor (not counting all the reports I had edited). The only patent nomenclature I knew was what Larry had taught me—for years we had a standing joke about whether you used comprise or compose when describing a process; it really mattered in patent parlance. Maybe I didn't know "patentese," but I knew grammar and punctuation—I had published my first article in a nursing journal in 1975. But it was here on Thorn Street and with the DDA that I began my career as Larry's life-long editor, and it was a career that I loved and finally felt useful doing for our corporation.

After he sent off the DDA, with cheers from our shareholders, Larry went to work on the patent in earnest. He spent many more hours in the Patent Room in the downtown library, gathering more general patent strategy (hence, the compose-comprise argument) but also looking for possible infringement from prior art. Larry searched back to the first similar type of patent (draftsmen had been looking for some easy way to draw ellipses for over a hundred years) that was filed in 1847 by (I forgot her name even though Larry referred to her for years!), but even this patent was not a problem. When you write up an application for a patent, it is required that you look for, identify, and argue why it is not like yours every possible patent that is in any way similar to what you are proposing. In big companies, there are banks of lawyers doing this, but Larry, on his own, spent hours and days and weeks thoroughly searching the abstracts in the OGs. I'm amazed he didn't go blind! One day he asked me to stop by the library after I got off work; he wanted to show me something. What he showed me was a drawing that looked appallingly like the Ellipse-ease; I gasped. Then he revealed that he was holding the book upside down. When he turned it right side up, it was not a close match. Larry's comment: "The poor bugger. If he had just turned his drawing upside down, I would be out of luck. It's our good fortune that he didn't!"

Finding nothing like his drawing or his model (in his spare time he built a very good model using his lathe and mini-mat, now housed in the garage), he proceeded to finish writing the patent. It wasn't too hard because much of the material he developed for the DDA translated easily into the completed patent—just change a few words here and there. He didn't file the patent then because he was waiting for acceptance of his DDA by the patent office.

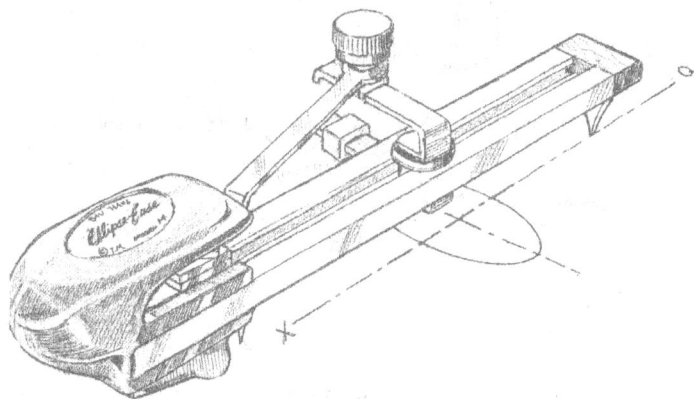

Meanwhile, he hit the road again, trying to find a manufacturer, which he felt was a requirement if we were to get more shareholders and financing. I went with him on a number of those trips, including one when, with four of our shareholders, we drove in a tiny Honda (remember those early ones that we called baby buggies?), with me sitting on his lap, several hundred miles to Yakima Washington where one of our group knew of a sheltered workshop that took on these kinds of jobs for pennies. It was a beautiful trip up the north side of the Columbia River Gorge, but unfortunately they turned us down; producing the machine would be too difficult for their mostly Down's Syndrome workers.

Many days and many dollars were spent in false leads or no shows. The shareholders were getting restless—"where's the money; where's the manufacturer!" Even though their contributions were pennies on the dollar compared to Larry's and mine, they *were* the shareholders. The board of directors was, in effect, giving Larry a vote of no confidence. Becoming discouraged, Larry wrote the following letter to the shareholders.

Director's Message to Shareholders of Bau Haus, Inc and Unit One, Inc.

A corporation, large or small, is very like a family. You may not always approve of what individual members do, and they may not always approve of what you do as the parents, but you are always family.

After many years, some successes and, frankly, many disappointments involving my management skills, I have decided to stick to inventing and leave the directing to someone else. It is never a pleasure quitting any project before it is completed, and I do feel I have developed some special and useful skills. Yet, I have a variety of apparent deficits in the "real world," and it is into that "real world" that the Ellipse-ease must be born.

With this in mind, I am actively seeking equity financing that will put major control of the Ellipse-ease in a third corporation. The Wahl family will have no participation in this third corporation, aside from a personal services contract for engineering, and the extent and quality of even this will be determined by this third corporation.

The final attempt by Bau Haus/Unit One to directly line up a manufacturing facility was a failure, in a business sense, only because the manufacturing company that had had excellent facilities, reputation, and financing, ran afoul of an internal problem of such potential magnitude that it was forced to eliminate most normal out-of-state activities, including our project. For this project, we invested over three thousand dollars, contracted a dealer arrangement, and were truly ready to produce. Except for our potential manufacturer's near bankruptcy, the Ellipse-ease would be now on the market. I just do not have another "cavalry charge" in me. The security and support of large scale, equity financing, costing inevitable loss of control and high return, still will provide the normal and reasonable process by which these tasks are responsibly pursued.

The annual meeting that was postponed because we were in the middle of these proposed arrangements for manufacture will be held on October 10, at which time such details available to me of the corporations' future will be shared with you.

The major complaints against my management efforts have been sincere, consistent, and unquestionably accurate: I am not a team player. Apologizing for this fact would mean denying the reality and benefits of the education and growth that has taken place, not only in myself but, I believe, in each of you. Without apology for "doing it my way," I am prepared, by experience and the benefit of your various inputs, to bring in whatever form of management team that is necessary.

The goal is what is important; the method, within fair and judicious limits, is not. It has taken some maturing time for me personally and, I believe, the same maturing time is necessary for the company to grow and develop, this growth and development resulting in character and strength. Excellent financial achievements are not mutually exclusive, but for me, much time has been necessary to develop adequate flexibility. Strength comes through adversity. Our two corporations have had their share. Difficulty learning cooperation and best utilization of investors' skills is doubtless a serious flaw in our management profile, but it may be important to recognize that Bau Haus and Unit One are essentially "inventive" organizations, and the invention process is uniquely singular. No invention of which I am aware has ever been filed by a committee *(Not true. Several years later he learned that multinational corporations do just that! SW)*.

Among the many obvious disadvantages in the operation of small, closely-held corporations is a major advantage: the necessary and invigorating personal give-and-take among differing and powerful human beings. I would not change any of the past, but I would seek not to necessarily repeat it. We will all remember our experiences and each other.

We hope that you are happy and prosperous and that events in the next few months at Bau Haus and Unit One will improve the standing of both of these qualities in your lives.

Thank you sincerely,

Larry E. Wahl, Director

The Aftermath

How terribly painful must it have been for Larry to acknowledge his deficits and write such a gracious letter. To maintain his sanity, let alone his self-esteem, he vigorously worked on the cubic geometry he first encountered with his "cube" in 1970 and that he now called the Vallian Coordinates. And he also began writing a novel, "It's a Matter of Time," that was to be a science fiction story involving the main character, Count Raveni, a giant mouse living on the planet of Maug. Those of you who have read the 2nd book in this trilogy will recognize the friend who provided the model for this character.

Count Raveni of Maug

When Mount Saint Helens blew its top on May 18, 1980, Larry incorporated that into the novel, and when he interviewed the retired engineer, Winston Bogy, who designed Arecibo (large telescope) in Puerto Rico, Bogy became Wizzer and was also part of the story. I have several notebooks of copy of that unfinished novel: one of these days I'll take a look at it and see what it needs to be finished. More than likely, it really is two novels.

While Larry was looking for "that third corporation" to take over the Ellipse-ease, he was referred to an agent for a business group from a Middle-Eastern country that was looking for a good investment. He met with the agent and one of the businessmen; they were duly impressed with his information and enthusiasm. They had the business framework and about one million dollars to invest. Their one stipulation was assurance that the patent would be filed. Since we were still waiting for the acceptance of the DDA by the patent office, Larry decided to call the patent office and ask for a rapid acceptance because he had a buyer in hand. I will never forget that conversation: the three of us from Unit One who were still friends were on extension phones, listening for the answer.

"Well, Mr. Wahl," a soft voice with a foreign accent began, "this is not what we really meant by a disclosure document. It was supposed to be two pages and a drawing. You sent 40 pages and 10 drawings."

"I just wanted to make sure you understood what I was asking for, and I did include all of the prior art that was relevant," Larry replied.

"Well, Mr. Wahl, I'm not sure we should accept this. It is so unconventional, it might set a precedent."

"Please, could you make an exception in this case," Larry pleaded. "We have an investor standing by, waiting to know if you approve this so I can file the patent. I'm doing all of this pro se."

"Well, yes, I can see you did this yourself, and you did very well. So, I guess we can make an exception this time. Just don't do it again."

While we were all whooping and hollering, Larry managed to get the man's name spelled correctly and a promise from the patent agent to send back the form with "today as the acceptance date." I told you Larry could be very convincing! And he was not shy about announcing how he had changed patent law!

But this episode doesn't end there. We immediately set up a meeting with the foreign investors. At that meeting, Larry described the patent phone conference, that the DDA was approved, and he would be filing the patent forthwith. A discussion ensued of how they would give us some up-front money when we signed the contract in a few days.

Then, Larry did something that I never understood, until I entered his letter to the Shareholders of Bau Haus/Unit One into this chapter. Larry leaned back, relaxed in his chair, and said, "By the way, we haven't had a vacation for all the years we have been working on this. I'm taking my wife on a much deserved, month cruise with the first installment of the money. We can start working on the engineering when I get back."

Both the investors and I were stunned into a lengthy silence. This was not how you do business, this was not how you treat investors, what was Larry thinking?!

Larry said he would wait to hear from them about signing the contract. Needless to say, we never heard. I asked Larry why he did that because it didn't seem like a good plan to go away for a month at the beginning of a new contract. His vague reply was that we deserved a vacation before we started a new round of work. It was never discussed again, but I know now that Larry could not give up the control of his "baby." We never looked for another "third corporation," mainly because in the next year, Larry became aware of graphics being done on computers and decided that the Ellipse-ease would be passé before it could be built and marketed. So the Ellipse-ease patent was written, but never filed, and Larry went to work in earnest on his Vallian Coordinates, while also trying to find design work. I have a copy of an extensive résumé I helped him write. He did do some design work for the Drake-Willis Company that made hemodialysis equipment and machines.

Leaving the Marriage or Leaving Oregon

While Larry was in Oakland California doing an interview of Winston Bogy, the engineer of the Puerto Rican telescope and "dish," Mt. St. Helens did its thing. Actually, Larry was on the train coming home and, without phone access, was very worried about his family. Fortunately, all we got in Tigard was a couple coverings of ash, but were never in any danger. After he got home, he talked about how interesting Northern California was and how much he missed it. I wasn't having any of it. I was just finishing my semester at the University of Oregon Health Sciences Center and was preparing to continue being on the road over the summer to teach our nursing outreach program in Eugene and Corvallis. For working the summer, I was being given the fall quarter off so I could start school again; I had been accepted into Portland State University's Urban Studies doctorate program and had been awarded a full scholarship. I wasn't going anywhere!

Upset by my resistance, Larry went back down to the San Francisco Bay area to visit friend Gordon French. Gordon was a member of the famous Home Brew Computer group that launched, among others, Steve Jobs and Steve Wosniack and Apple computer. Larry had some idea that he might be able to convince someone to look at his Vallian Coordinates for use in graphics and design. While he was there, he took up residence with a woman named Nola, having a vigorous sexual adventure. When he wanted to stay down there and live with her, "How would you like to support me?" she not so gently encouraged him to go back home. Larry has an interesting way of asking for things he doesn't really want!

Over that summer as I traveled 100 miles three days a week to teach in Eugene and Larry kept insisting he was going to move to Menlo Park to be with Gordon, I was in despair from being torn in two directions: Larry or my job, my education, and the home of 20 years I didn't want to leave. I remember staying nights in a motel in Eugene, trying to figure out what to do and having late night conversations with a friend over tea. I even tried going to a bar by myself, but no one paid any attention to me—I was too obviously married. I lost 20 pounds and much sleep. At some level, I knew I was being selfish, not wanting to give up a tenured university position and graduate school. But I also loved my crazy husband. Though, with the number of trips he took to Northern California on the train, I wasn't sure he even still loved me. I also knew he had been having chest pain, but refused to see doctors—some days I didn't even care. This was the most serious crisis we had encountered in our marriage: I considered it could end in divorce. It might have helped if I had been able to see how miserable he was—he covered it up cavalierly—and how the loss of his corporations and abandoning his Ellipse-ease had created so much despair that he needed to began a new life somewhere else. But no, I couldn't see that because I was too wrapped up in my own pain.

My mom and dad lived in a small cottage on Hood's Canal in Northwestern Washington. Dad wanted Eric, Jill, and me to come up and see them since Mom hadn't been too well. Larry was on one of his trips south and had taken the car since he knew I had a State car at my disposal. Talk about larcenous: over several days off, I drove us up to Hood's Canal in the State car (I did pay for the gas). On the way up, we stayed the night in a little costal town in Washington. I was so miserable. I left the kids sleeping on the floor of the motel and tried the bar scene again. I sat at a table for a few minutes, and in those few minutes, I became so disgusted with myself: this was not the way I handled crises. I went back to the motel and, as I was getting undressed, I heard Jill crying quietly. This was my "always happy" Jill. And so I added shame to my self-disgust; my children were in pain too, and I had abandoned them. I went over and held her until she went back to sleep. I resolved that whatever happened, I would never abandon them again.

We got to Mom and Dad's and camped out in the Winnebago parked on their lot. That night at dinner, my folks knew we were unhappy. Mom asked where Larry was. Even though she pretended not to approve of him, I knew she really was fond of him; I told her he was on a trip. About then, the phone rang. Dad answered it and handed it to me.

Larry asked how the folks were and how we were, and then, in a gentle voice he said, "I am going to move to Menlo Park, California; will you come with me?"

Mom and Dad were pretending not to be watching me; the kids didn't pretend. With a smile in my voice, I said, "Of course I will." We talked a few more minutes, and I told him we would leave for home the next day.

After we exchanged "I love you's," I hung up the phone and announced to all that we were moving to California in a couple of months. Mom got it, and she hugged me for a long time. We never did talk about the events preceding this new situation, but Mom said, "Be sure that all of you come to see me before you leave."

Larry brought Eric up to the University of Washington in early September to start his math degree; he had been awarded a full ROTC scholarship based on his SAT scores. Jill and I went to Hood's Canal. Mom was disappointed that Larry wasn't with us, but I promised we would all come up as soon as we were settled in Menlo Park. As Mom and I sat out on their patio silently enjoying a scrumptious sunset, I felt that Mom knew I was going to be all right; it seemed to give her peace. I never saw Mom again: she died on Jan 21st 1981 as Ronald Reagan, her favorite governor, was inaugurated as president.

After we were back home, I had the job of telling the dean of the school of nursing and my friends that we were leaving. One friend, Naomi, said, "You're giving up all of this, your tenured position, your graduate school, *for him*?"

How does one explain love?

I had lived my whole married life in Oregon, so still feeling some indecision, I decided to do a tarot spread to see what might be ahead. The cards were all I needed to fully convince me. They informed me that the move would be the best thing for me: I would have a better career, our marriage would improve, and I would get my doctorate. The cards don't lie!

So, on September 26th, 1980, the three remaining Wahls and one cat, Paddywach, were on their way to California!

Musing 105 by Larry

What Came First: The Child or the Parent?

Your children are not your children.
They are the sons and daughters of Life's longing for Itself.
—*Kahlil Gibran*

April 22, 1980

I lost my temper with the boy and the girl today and really chewed their tails. It seems to be a constant and ongoing process of trying to explain to them that things keep going the same way, day after day and week after week. It seems as if both of my children have a difficult time learning from either their own experience or that of anyone else. They have a problem believing that life is, at best, a grim business. It is not something that just happens to you in a nice way but something that must be lived and worked at if there is any possibility of making life reasonable and continuous. It is not an automatic process, and I am seeing some of the same things that happened to me happening to my children.

I guess what keeps me working on them is that it is obvious to me that there was a lot the Wahls did that was not particularly useful for me, but I will make an honest attempt to change behavior in my own children. If, after I have worked as hard as I could and the children appear to be the same no matter what I have done, I will then, and only then, know that it does not really make any difference what you do with your kids. All the possibilities for their success or failure are actually within them and nowhere else.

The problem is, of course, that this is exactly what I want to believe and what I do believe about myself. It is precisely because I do believe, that I do not give myself the easy way out, and I treat my children as though it is true. I have bent over backwards to make sure that I have done everything I can to help my children become equipped for the world in which they are going to find themselves.

It is hard for me to understand why there is no way to pass on information in a time frame when it can do the recipient any good. What is the good of giving it? And yet, it would seem to be the reason for there being parents, in the first place. The human being produces one of the most helpless young in the animal kingdom, as well as one that needs the most years until it can take care of itself. Perhaps the reason for this extended period of time in which parent and child are together is to make some kind of imprint on the child by the parent. However, from my own experience, I have found that the children in a family often look and behave as if they came from a family entirely foreign to the one they are supposed to be a part of.

A new thought enters my mind: suppose that instead of the children learning from the parents, the idea is that the parents are supposed to learn from the children. Now, that is something I can begin to relate to. There are few parents that I have talked with that have not learned of the futility and individuality of experience. They have learned, from their children, how difficult it is to pass on, in any meaningful way, the results of their experiences, both good and less good.

So let us suppose that we are not to lead the children, but rather be led by them. It seems to me that I read something like that some-place, sometime …. It went like this, "Unless you be born again as little children, you cannot enter the Kingdom of Heaven."

I am able to see my children try to bend facts to fit their desires; I am able to see my children try to find the truth while knowingly lying about everything in sight; I am able to see my children expect to be treated fairly, all the while cheating at many things they are doing; I am able to see the real innocence of the ignorant, falling and hurting themselves as they attempt to take advantage of someone else. Yet, the more I think about it, the more I think that our experiences with our children are for our parenting benefit. We just don't seem to be able to influence them in any meaningful way.

I remember a neighbor, Rosemary, who considered that her little baby was a blank book upon which she was going to write all his early chapters. When said baby was six months old, he crushed the canary; at two years old, he bit and scratched like a wildcat; and when he was three, he had the nasty habit of trying to burn down the house... and like that. What did Rosemary write??? I can't swear to the following, but I thought one time when I was looking at the little stinker, he put a chubby little finger alongside his nose and winked at me ... Rosemary's baby—without capitals so that you won't think he had all the problems of the one in the movie—seemed to be saying, about his mother's blank book theory, "Like hell I am!"

They moved from our neighborhood before there was a chance for us to know if he convinced her of his individuality before or after he became a practicing pyromaniac, or maybe just a hoodlum. I rest my case.

On another note—but I'm never very far away from the original concept—I am hoping my schedule will be a little easier now that Sherry has more time to take an active part in their training (but she seems more willing than I am to learn from them). Since we seem to be unable to pass on our experience, at least we can make sure they have some life skills. We decided to set up a schedule with the division of most of the home chores to give us a break and hopefully prepare them somewhat for the task of making and caring for homes for themselves some day. Sherry, being the teacher she is, set up a "syllabus" with goals and objectives and the activities to meet them, all arranged in a chart, rotating the jobs weekly with performance evaluations and "consequences."

There is so much discipline necessary in the activities I have chosen to do this year, it is as though I had decided to make up for all the things I had not learned in a lifetime. I do know that tomorrow I am going to try and get a painting knocked out before I lose the talent altogether. The painting is what has been absolutely held in abeyance. It is going to be interesting to see what I will do now that several years have gone by. I do know that it will be more naturally disciplined because everything I have touched in these last few years has worked. I have less need to know the facts and more need to decipher how I feel about them. I'm not sure I'm happy with this approach, but a lot of what I'm doing does not have a logical explanation; it seems there is much that needs to be taken on faith.

I'm trying to take a page from my children and learn to take life a little less seriously. And, at the same time, I should learn from my past and play to win instead of just playing to play. If I have to play because it is the only game in town, I might as well play to win. This life is just that: a game. If I've learned nothing else, don't live life, play it! Is this what my kids have taught me??

Chapter 6

Hello California!

There are many truths of which the full
meaning cannot be realized until personal
experience has brought it home.
— *John Stuart Mills*

My introduction to California was less than spectacular. We made our appearance in the middle of a heat wave; the air conditioning in our little "scrubbing bubble"—an AMC Pacer —quit somewhere north of Redding, California. It's a wonder we didn't lose Paddywach: she was so doped up with tranquilizers, she could have fallen out of one of the many open windows, if she didn't first die of heat stroke. Sure, the sun was shining and the sky a brilliant blue, but when I viewed the brown, bare hills along U.S. Highway 680, I was beginning to think my tarot cards had lied.

After the kids and I got home from Hood's Canal, Larry and I had a chance to talk about this upcoming move. He told me that he had put a deposit on a two-bedroom rental in Menlo Park. He liked the idea of living in Menlo Park because it was (1) close to the famous Stanford University where he predicted he would one day teach, and (2) Menlo Park, New Jersey where the revered Edison had done all his inventing. I reminded him that I had just two requirements: plenty of windows and plenty of trees. But all he would tell me about our next home was, "I got us a little shack on the railroad tracks."

As I looked at the brown hills we were passing, all I could think of was Steinbeck's (1939) *The Grapes of Wrath.*

We passed many small towns (was this the ticky-tack of the song?) that were easily seen from the freeway, and the traffic in late September was horrible; somehow I hadn't expected so much. We took another freeway—also too much traffic—and ended up on a bridge: the San Mateo. I was carefully noting how we came, in case I needed to make a fast get-away. But at least here was water, lots of it: the famous San Francisco Bay. From the bridge, another freeway (CA 92) that took us to US Highway 101. At least here was a highway I had heard of. This highway seemed to be running near the water, between two sets of hills—seen distantly through the smog—with lots of fairly low commercial buildings and junkyards. Not a very auspicious beginning.

Finally we got off the freeways and were cruising along side streets: Palo Alto, Larry informed me. My hopes were rising. There were trees, lots of them, and didn't Palo Alto mean something like "high" or "tall tree?"

"Are we there yet?" Jill woke up and asked what was on my mind, as well.

"Soon," Larry promised.

I hoped he wasn't lost, but he turned onto a very commercial street—El Camino Real. Just continuous rows of business after business. He pulled into the parking lot of a fast food restaurant; ah, they had McDonalds here too. "You and Jill stay here while I check and see if our place is ready."

Jill and I practically jumped out of our skins when we heard the loud horn of a train, a train that sounded like it was coming through the restaurant. We were trying to be patient, but our excitement—and anxiety—was growing. Then, I sort of remembered this place: we had stayed with Larry's friend Jordan when we came down here for a quick vacation in August the previous year. I remember we had slept on the floor of his tiny apartment with only light blankets.

The Shack on the Railroad Tracks

I looked up to see Larry and Jordan walking through the door; they had the proverbial "shit-eating" grins on their faces. Jordan gave Jill and me a hug and then said, "Let's go."

Larry drove around the corner and over the railroad tracks, hence the train noise, and then a left turn onto Mills Street. It was looking better and better; there were trees, lots of trees, even a huge Sequoia Sempervirins (giant, old coast Redwood). Larry pulled into the driveway of 1301 just as a loud commuter train went visibly by, and at that precise moment, I wanted to kill him! "A little shack on the railroad tracks?" Our new home was in a nice-looking, two story apartment building, one of five in the complex, with windows—the whole back wall of the living room was floor to ceiling windows with a sliding door onto a small cement patio. There were trees everywhere I looked out of those back windows. We were nestled in between a series of small apartment buildings—Jordan lived on the other side of the fence that afforded us privacy. Inside was wall-to-wall carpeting, up stairs and down, except for the bathroom and kitchen. The walls were off-white—great for showing Larry's paintings. Everything looked pristine. "Little shack on the railroad tracks," huh?! Larry was enjoying watching Jill and I enthuse over this lovely new home. I still wanted to kill him. I don't know how he kept the secret so long and so well; his CIA training, I guess!

Jordan took Paddywach to his apartment—yes, it was the same one we had stayed in a year earlier—so we could unpack the car and wait for the rest of our belongings ... the rest of our belongings: now that was a story all in itself.

The Move and The Gypsies

We had arranged with U-Haul in Tigard to have our belongings brought down in a truck driven by two fellows who did this for a living. They would get several people who were going to a similar area, get a very big truck, collect fees from all of us—half at the hiring and half upon delivery—and load and unload our stuff. It would have been difficult for us, as well as more costly, to rent our own truck, load everything ourselves, and have Larry drive the truck with me bringing our car with Jill and cat the ~ 600 miles from Tigard to Menlo Park. So, it was a great deal for us. Larry had bought us a pair of walkie-talkies and got a CB license so we could stay in contact when he and I thought we were going to drive in two different vehicles—Larry got lost easily—but they would work just as well with our "gypsy drivers."

On the day of departure, friends and neighbors helped us pack. The U-Haul drivers loaded the truck—they were carrying two other people's loads, including a motorcycle that had to go in after ours. Amid hugs and tears, we took off for the first leg of the trip.

Making several rest stops along the way, we drove as far as Redding and stopped for the night. We had heard from our gypsies somewhere over Mt.

Shasta, while still in Oregon. That was the last we were to hear from them, so we crossed our fingers that all was well.

We waited in our empty apartment until about 7 PM when we got hungry: no word yet from our belongings! There was a nice restaurant a couple of blocks away on El Camino, so we left a note on the door as to where we were and directed them to come get us when they got in. It was 9, or thereabouts, and pitch dark, when a scraggly-looking Jake (one of the drivers) came to the restaurant with a sad story: they had run out of gas on the Dumbarton Bridge and didn't have any money left to buy gas. I'm not sure why, but it was decided that I would take him to the truck after stopping to get a filled gas can, and Larry would stay at the apartment with Jill. I would have taken the walkie-talkie, but Jake indicated he had lost it along the way—what had they done on the trip down? His fellow driver was with the truck.

Fortunately he was better at knowing where the truck was located than at keeping gas in the tank, so we found it stranded in the middle of the bridge, about five miles from our new home. Gassed up, we drove back to MP and parked on the street in front of the apartment. We told the guys they could sleep in the empty apartment, and we went to a nearby motel.

The next morning, we had them unload most of the kitchen stuff, linens, clothes, and other necessities in the apartment and then the rest of the truck contents was unloaded directly into a U-Haul storage locker we had rented. We gave Jake the certified check for the balance we owed them and sent them on their way, while we went to a furniture rental store to get a bed, couch, et al delivered ASAP; we had sold everything in Tigard.

When we got back, we found the guys sitting on our porch steps. The bank wouldn't cash the certified check without us verifying that they were the intended recipients. So off to the bank we went (we had set up an account with the California Bank that had a branch in Tigard so we would have access to our money without delay) and once again bailed out our movers! They finally left with money in hand.

Our initiation to Menlo Park was interesting, if weird! We were glad we had planned the move so well, and most of the planning was Larry's, my supposedly un-organized husband. Furniture arrived the next day. Now I could concentrate on making a new nest!

The Beginning of the New Life

The first few months were not easy. Larry immediately took Jordan up on his offer to share his small office on Crane Street, a few blocks from home. Jordan had invited Larry to come to California, promising to teach him how to use Jordan's very large PDP 8008 computer. Since Jordan had been part of the famed "Home Brew Club" that launched the personal desktop computer, he had a lot of knowledge about computers, which Larry lapped up! They had arranged their work schedules so they wouldn't be in each other's way; Larry spent most of that Fall of 1980 writing his novel (begun in the 70s in Tigard) and picking Jordan's brain. Larry also had the hope that Jordan would be able to hook him up with his contracts from Apple and "the Club." But Jordan kept putting him off, so Larry wrote but also worked on refining the Vallian Coordinates—his geometry featuring the tesseract. We even had some dinners out with Jordan and his new girlfriend, Sally, but they drank a lot more than we were comfortable with, so that activity petered out.

Disappointed with Jordan for not following up on the introductions to Silicon Valley folks, Larry tried to maintain a low profile and just keep to his time schedule, primarily writing on that cumbersome computer. But Jordan became irritable with Larry because he thought Larry was using too much paper to print out his writing. Larry paid Jordan for any supplies he used, but the relationship began to deteriorate when Jordan started showing up during Larry's allocated time to work, saying he needed to use the office. That tiny office (another closet!) could not support two strong-willed geniuses, so in early January 1981, Larry moved out and began working at home. By then Jordan had moved out of his apartment and in with Sally in Mountain View; he exited the Menlo Park office shortly after Larry moved out.

A few years later, Larry chanced upon Jordan in Palo Alto, and they arranged a dinner with spouses for the next night. When we arrived at the restaurant, both Jordan and Sally were quite a bit "in their cups," as it were. We endured the dinner, but never saw either of them again.

Larry never did receive that invitation to meet Jordan's computer colleagues; we found out later that Jordan had been requested to leave the club, even before we got to California, so he actually was a persona non grata.

We had a miserable Christmas that first year because Larry was so discouraged by Jordan's "dark" behavior. But on the bright side, Jordan did get us to California, and Larry did learn a lot about computers from Jordan. Larry transferred what he had learned to a small hand-held Texas Instruments (TRS) scientific calculator/minicomputer where he worked on math and did some programming. I was so sorry that Larry had lost his friend, one who dated back to high school; Larry didn't have a surplus of friends.

While Larry's drama with Jordan was developing, I was enjoying the excitement of learning about our new town and the surrounding area, but the Oregon pension fund that we had cannibalized to finance the move wouldn't last much longer, so I had to go about finding a new job. I hadn't wanted to go into teaching again right away, but that remained a possibility: there were two major state universities equidistant from home. I had it in my mind that I wanted to get a job at a hospital doing staff in-service; there were many hospitals in the area as well. Unfortunately, when the personal directors looked at my résumé and saw my background in management and intensive care, that's what they wanted to hire me for. That I really didn't want!

So, on one very hot (90s+) day in early October, I drove the Pacer to an appointment in San Mateo, sans air conditioning; the first thing the personal director did when she saw me was get me a bottle of *cold* water. I met with the director of nursing Lee, for whom I still have great admiration. She had a notion of a position for me—they already had two nursing staff educators. She had looked at a different aspect of my résumé and noted that I had done a special project for the Portland Veteran's Hospital that involved evaluation of record keeping and follow up on accident reports. From that, she offered me the unique position of "Department Developer," whatever that was.

I was intrigued by the prospect, but over the next year and a half, I was up to my watermark in projects in which I had no idea what I was doing. It was an interesting concept, but my qualifications and skills did not match Lee's need. The only thing I did that made me feel at all competent was setting up the new Statewide Nursing Program on site for the hospital's nurses who wanted to get a bachelor's degree. It was during that project that I met

Virgil, faculty at San Jose State University, who was to be my mentor for many years. When Lee and I mutually decided to part, I called him and said I was out of a job. "No, you aren't. Call me tomorrow and I'll get you on our faculty." That was a propitious day for me and our family.

The Search for Apple

For the first six months of 1981, Larry continued to work on his geometry, using the TRS scientific calculator. He even got me a little one and showed me how to program; my first and only accomplishment was a program to determine your mental, physical, and emotional biorhythm cycles. I discovered Larry and I were at cross-purposes, biorhythm-wise, most of the time!

Starting in June of 81, Larry began trying to make contact with Apple; he hoped to be able to get an Apple Foundation Grant to adapt his geometry to computer graphics, an upcoming endeavor in which Apple was at the forefront. Larry just had to convince someone at Apple that his Vallian Coordinates were so much better than the Cartesian system that was currently in use. Unfortunately, he kept being told that an amorphous someone would "get back to him." Not getting any call backs, he wrote to Apple Computer Vice President, M. Williams offering Apple the rights to the Vallian System in exchange for equipment and help in programming the graphics application. No response!

Then, at the end of July, he wrote to Mr. Steven Jops (misspelling his name—an accident?) outlining his attempted contacts with Apple to date. His letter went like this:

Dear Mr. Jops,

I am writing to you at the recommendation of your office staff. Attached is a copy of the letter I sent to Mr. Williams after a series of unsuccessful attempts to arrange an appointment or even a telephone conversation. The letter met with the same fate as my previous interactions with Mr. Williams' office: no response has been forthcoming. If the company were not interested in talking with me, an assertive "No" would be most acceptable. It is impossible to do a good job of any sort, certainly nothing requiring "cutting edge" research, without acquiring a tough shell. Any innovator should understand this need, as I believe I do. Having participated in many of my own and others' business affairs, I have, up until now, usually received "normal" courtesy and communication from the companies with whom I have dealt.

René Descartes developed a system of mathematical manipulation that solved some local problems for him; however, since it was so basic in nature and fundamental in operation, it slowly revolutionized the theory and practice of mathematics of his time. From it, developed large sections of the Calculus.

My system, The Vallian Coordinates, is a natural extension of the Cartesian Rectangular Coordinate System. The Cartesian system understood the existence of eight natural divisions in space—octants as Descartes described them. He decided to use only one of the eight sectors, referring to the other seven as "unchartered territory." He wished to stay only in the positive sector to avoid negative values since there were no mechanics for handling the square root of negative numbers.

The Vallian Coordinate System uses all eight sectors, including the minus (-) divisions. Since the matrix system derived from this process does not use negative roots, as such, there are no system limitations mathematically. Cartesian Coordinates are the graphical realities derived from the state of algebra in Descartes' time. The Vallian coordinate system is the child of descriptive geometry, a system in which one can solve hundreds of graphical problems without ever entering a number. Numbers are inferential to this system, but when induced, are absolute and compatible.

A few typewritten pages cannot encompass eleven years of developmental work; therefore, I am most desirous of meeting with the person who understands math and engineering and who is in a position to make some recommendations and/or decisions regarding our future relationship, if any. Unfortunately, my only meeting with your staff was a very uncomfortable five minutes in the lobby with a young woman engineer who informed me immediately, "I know nothing about math, but ... ."

It is somewhat difficult to explain an innovative mathematical system under such circumstances!

My reasons for selecting your company initially are outlined in the attached letter [to Mr. Williams]. I will be most appreciative if you or your selected representative will arrange a time for us to discuss my proposal at your earliest convenience.

Thank you for your time.

Sincerely,

Larry E. Wahl

Two weeks later, Larry was contacted by phone by Mr. X of Apple Corporation and Stanford University (Professor of Mathematics). Mr. X told Larry that Apple assigned him the people who "fall in the cracks." Was that an apology of sorts? In the 2013 movie, *Jobs*, X is portrayed as a long-haired hippy professor from Stanford, whose only purpose seemed to be to hang out with Jobs and colleagues.

Mr. X listened to Larry for about 20 minutes as Larry described his invention and its superior use in computer graphics. Larry thought he would get just a few minutes of X's time, but 20 minutes, that was miraculous … until X said, "How would you feel about my name being on it?"

Larry was speechless, but not for long as he came back with, "Let me get this straight. I've worked on this for 11 years, and you have known about it for 20 minutes, and you want your name on it? I think not!" There were probably some expletives as well.

So, exit Apple, for now. Years later, after I was thoroughly entrenched in Academia, I wondered if Larry missed out because he did not know that maybe X wasn't suggesting taking it away from Larry, but rather doing what professors often do with students they are mentoring: having both of their names on it! We'll never know. But from that time on, and especially after the VP of Tandy Corporation called the Vallian Coordinates pure hoax, Larry lost any awe or respect he might have had for big corporations. For the next many years, Larry continued working to refine the coordinates and writing his novel.

Look Ma, We're Modern!

In May of 1982, we bought our first computer, the Osborn. It was a tiny thing with a built-in disk drive and a screen the size of a camera; you could only get about 20 pages of writing per disk. But it was exciting for us—the first of many computers to come. That nascent computer was developed by Adam Osborn, also of the Homebrew Club. There was even a user group you could join called FOG (First Osborn Group), but since it was too far away in the East Bay, we didn't join. Later, after Larry got a larger computer with more space and graphics capability, I used the little Osborn to write several learning modules for the Statewide Nursing Program, the same one I had helped set up at my previous employment. At 20 pages per disk, you know I accumulated many disks in the process!

In the fall of 1982, a new studio was born—I no longer remember what number this one would be, but I do know it was the last one he had outside of our home. This new "closet" resided in Palo Alto at 415 Cambridge Ave, on the 2nd floor at #19, and the business to be located there was christened Lewis X. Vallian, Associates. In case I haven't explained, Descartes' coordinates were called "Cartesian," so Wahl's coordinates were called Vallian, not "Wahlian," which would have been awkward at best. Larry found the location of his new studio auspicious since it was only a few blocks from Printer's Ink Bookstore and Café, a hangout for Silicon Valley types. With a TRS 80-12 business computer, he began this new venture in earnest. At this time he was not only writing his novel, he was working on his autobiography, writing short stories, and using a TRS Handheld Scientific calculator/mini-computer to began writing code for the Vallian Coordinates. But … there would be "rocks in the road" over the next few months.

Preface to Theory 201

Descartes' Dismay

Transition to theory

When I conceived of writing book III, I thought that I would concentrate on our lives as related to Larry's work: art, writing, and geometry. The plan was that I would read his theory materials and translate the content into something more digestible for the average reader. When I shared this idea with friend Michael, who had known Larry quite well and had been on the other end of Larry's theory dissertations, he suggested that I "let Larry speak for Larry." I was somewhat taken aback, until I more fully explored that idea. And I knew then that Michael knew of what he spoke: I was not qualified to "translate" for Larry. Larry couldn't translate for Larry! He spent years trying to explain his Vallian Coordinates, to get someone to program them as he conceived of them; all I had done was take dictation and correct grammar and punctuation. If I didn't understand something he was saying, I questioned him until I felt I had a maybe, sort-of understanding. That is how we wrote *The Elephant in the Room*, which we did publish locally (it has an ISBN number), but understand his geometry … I don't think so!

So the plan that evolved from that insight (thank you, Michael) is that I will write my perception of our life with art and geometry, but I will include a selected few of his actual writings as theory chapters, leaving it to the reader as to whether he/she wants to further investigate Larry's very complex data. But later, in a special book focused on Vallian theory, I will publish many of the sometimes tortured, always intense, written discourses by which he tried to seduce others to assist him in the development of a useable product. My hope is that this information will reach the eyes of someone who can do the programming that Larry was unable to accomplish. Or … perhaps someday Larry will reappear on this earth—presumably in a different time and as a different person, hopefully a mathematician—and have another go at it himself.

So, you have been forewarned, but I hope you will at least take a crack at his theory—it is fascinating stuff. I loved looking at his drawings and sincerely wished I could have helped him more … but I have a very different brain.

The following theory exposition is one of Larry's first attempts to formally document his new geometry; the last paragraph of the introduction was added much later, written sometime in early 2000, after his patent had been granted.

Theory 201

Descartes' Dismay

Part I: Introduction

Where the territories of early maps ended—although what was drawn was more fiction than reality—and just uncharted space was left, the legend read "Here Be Monsters." Uncharted territory has always been full of monsters until someone with more foolishness than good sense discovers there is just ... more territory.

Picture a seaman who, by thinking as well as looking, concludes that the distant horizon falls down away from him on both sides. Considering this for some period of days, months, and years, he comes to the extremely dangerous conclusion that the earth must be round. He does have wit enough and a deep sense of self-preservation to keep this conclusion to himself because he lives in a world determined by "wise men" to be flat. It will take Copernicus' research to prove the seaman's guess, but only after Copernicus had properly recanted and, after his death, the Church's position had softened.

Several hundred years go by, and René Descartes appears. He is a philosopher, mathematician, scientist, and logician. He thought, therefore he was, but as a geometrist, he was as far out of his time as was the lowly seaman. Descartes breathed life, in the form of breadth and depth, into Euclid's observations on Plato. With the x and y of the new algebra, Descartes made depth and width an infinite set of variables. In a Euclidean universe, this was more than sufficient—sufficient to register plots, plats, and territories on, to all intents and purposes, a still flat earth.

Descartes had the perfect system, but when he tried to codify the 3rd dimension, his system crashed. It was like one of those terrible monsters and it had a name: it was zed, or z. That z literally tore up his perfect 2-dimensional system. It defeated him geometrically, mathematically, and philosophically. He recognized that there was a GUT (Grand Unified Theory) that should collapse the 2nd, 3rd, and n-dimensions into one exquisite, simple, elegant mathematical/geometric order. What was needed was a set of useful, generalizable concepts and constructs that would lock 2-, 3-, and n-coordinate systems together. He did find such a system: the Cartesian Hexagonal Octet. The system itself was not new; it had been used unwittingly by artists and draftsmen for decades, unwittingly because the draftsman in that time—and many draftsmen of today— remain blissfully unaware their system is the cubic octet. But Descartes knew.

In Descartes' theory, to physically arrive at an octet, it was only necessary to take a cubed piece of wood, cheese, or any other semi-solid substance and make three cuts, parallel to the edges and crossing the center of each face. With one horizontal and two vertical cuts, the single cube resolved into eight cloned cubes. Interestingly this eight is the very foundation of themathematics of the modern computer: octal. Of course, Descartes could simply use his computer, right? Wrong! Because of his mathematical approach and an attempt to introduce square roots, he fell into the grievous mathematical, geometric, and even religious problem of negative square roots.

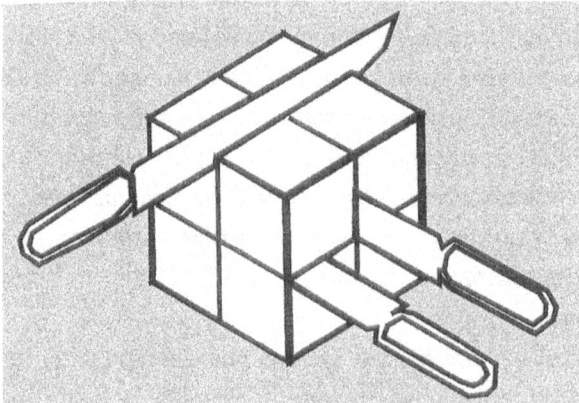

Cube cut into 8 cloned cubes

Picture, if you will, Descartes sitting in his local Starbucks looking at his octet. He knows it is perfect. He knows it is simple. He knows it is elegant. He knows it is impossible! Now picture him 350 years later, sitting in our local Starbucks with his laptop, in total dismay because "they" haven't learned a thing. The moderns have imaginary numbers so no problem with negative square roots; they have relatively instantaneous speed and infinite memory, but they still have not managed to conquer the octet.

If he had had our tools, unified with his logic, he would have long since created a workable octet and, more importantly, designed and developed a useable geometric system. It would bear the title of "Cartesian" Geometric Hexagon Opting Symbolic Tesseract and would be listed as U.S. Patent # 5,982,374, but ... he left that job for me.

Theory 202

The Birth of the Cube

Drawings by Larry

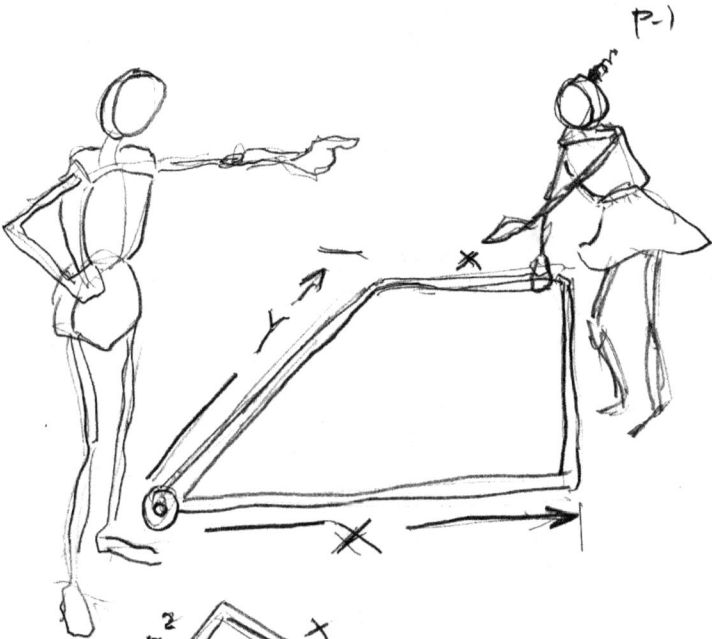

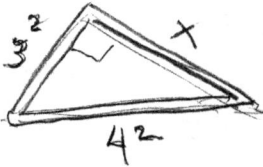

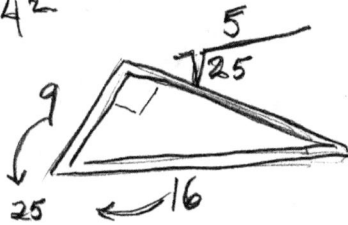

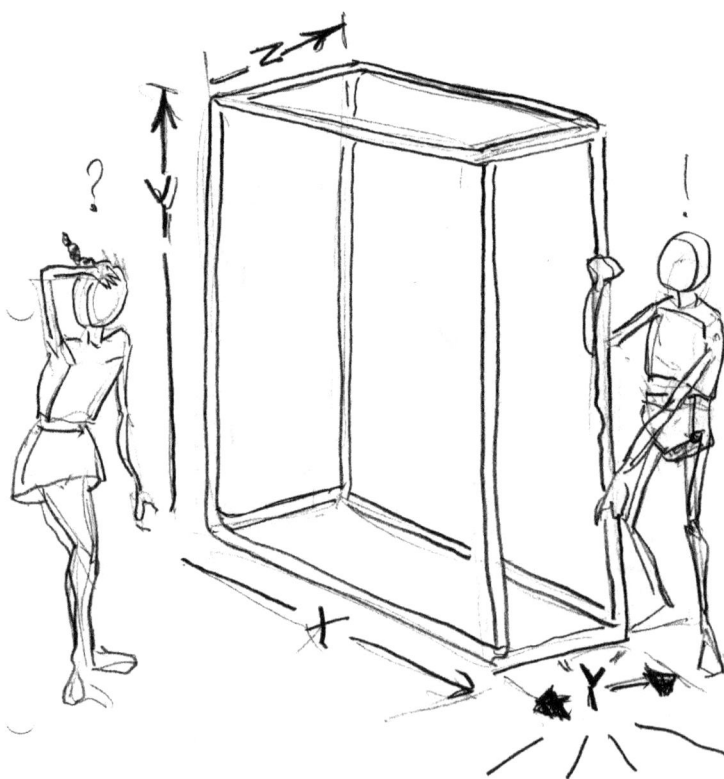

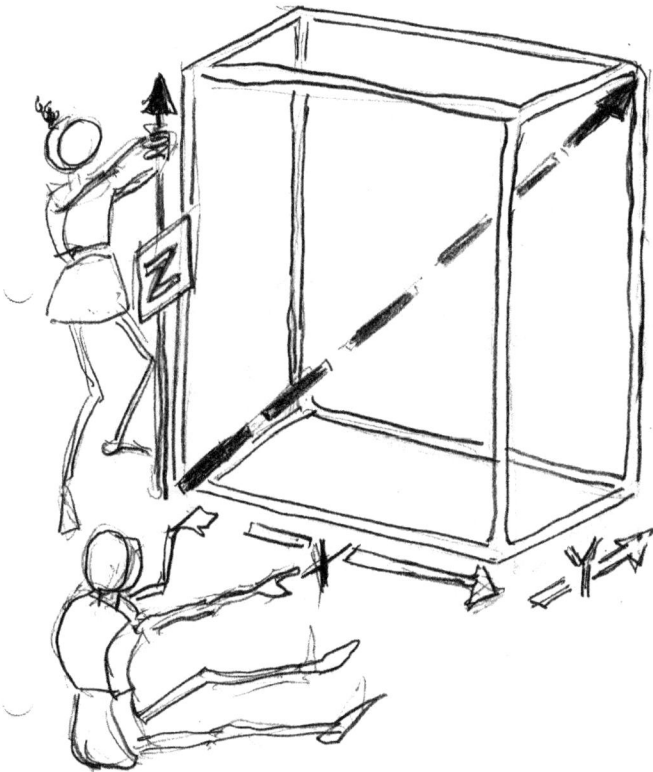

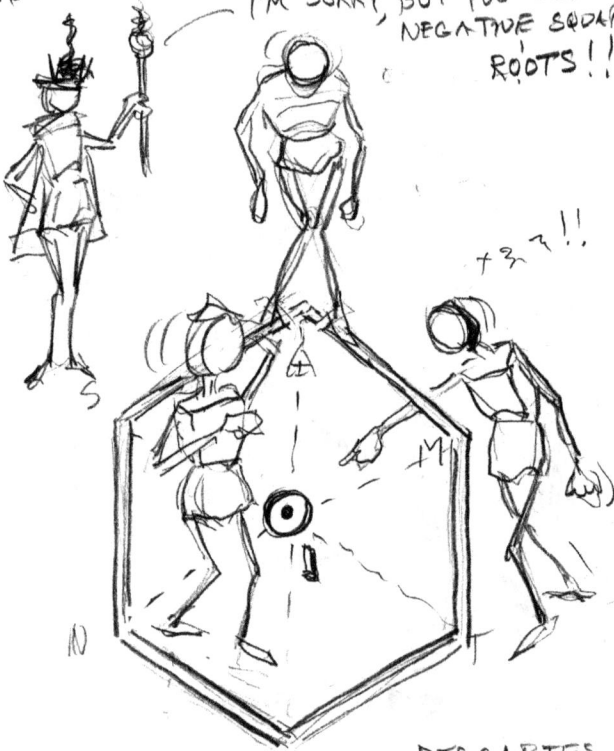

Cube = 6 FACES
= 8 Vertices
= 12 edges

TO THE BANK!

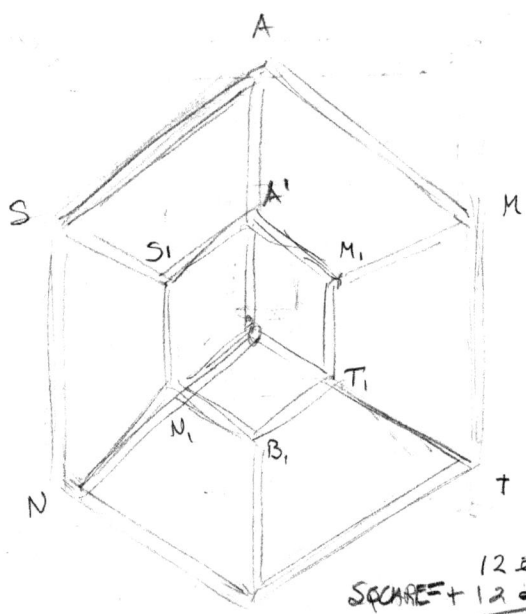

A

S   A'   M

   S₁   M₁

N₁   B₁   T₁

N   t

B

POINTS = 16 (VERTICES)
    + 12
= 28 VERTICES

                12 edges
SQUARE + 12 edges
         ─────────
          24 edges
        + 12 edges
         ─────────
          36 edges

FACES = 12 (NORMAL)
      + 12 (TRAP.)
    ─────────────
    = 24 FACES

A CUBO-OCTAHEDRON ON THE OUTSIDE — WHICH FOLDS INTO A DOUBLED OCTAHEDRON ON THE INSIDE...

A

S

M

ICE

N

T

B

SEEN AS A Valban VIRTUAL

Articulated Super Tesseract

'THE TUVAST.

Musing 106 by Larry

The Beginning of the Rest of My Life

In each venture is a new beginning,
a raid on the inarticulate
—*T.S. Eliot*

August 1, 1981

Today is the beginning of the rest of my life, as the old saw goes. It is, at the very least, the beginning of the rest of this month. This may be the month that makes up for the somewhat catastrophic nature of the summer, up to this time.

There are several things that I have wanted to see done before this day arrived. I have accomplished those over which I have the most control, but there was a large proportion that I had little, if any, control over. It was a little surprising to me, for I had the feeling that "The Old Man" and I had gotten to the point where I finally had some kind of an idea of His sense of humor; it does seem to be a sense of humor that is occasionally strange. Finding myself spending much of the previous month scratching from head to foot, the result of some kind of weird virus that made me feel like Job (the biblical one!), even if I didn't look so bad. All and all, it is fair to say that July was not my best month.

Now, on this first day of the new month, I have seated myself at the easel and have roughed out the beginning of a gallery of subjects, human or otherwise, that will go into the book. And I have started this journal again, seriously, two of the three "666s" I want to get done in this period of my life. The last of the three tasks is the publication of the Vallian Coordinates. I have put together the listing of the program that is the backbone of the system, and there is little else to be done

125

now except to sell it. I have been surprised by the difficulty of even getting to see or talk to someone at Apple Computer, though this has not really discouraged me since it did not come as a surprise.

Mostly the book has been sitting on the back burner, just simmering. Before this night is through, I am going to review the beginning revision so that I can, in fact, state that I have been working on all threads of my major projects on this one day. For me, beginnings are among the most important part of events. It has taken a long time for me to see the various patterns of my life and how they are arranged.

This has been a time in which the full meaning of mortality and infirmity has dawned on me. I know I have a great deal of strength, but also that there is a good deal that is faulted in me. I have tried to make 1981 a year in which I catalogued some of the most pernicious habits that have plagued me and a year to see all the things that I had held important that thinking has proved they are not important at all. I have found there is much that I thought I could not live without that I have been able to live without very well. More importantly, there are numerous things I have never been interested in, which I thought silly and banal, have gradually taken on more significance, if only because they are valued by some of the people who are important to me.

My course in life has changed so many times that it is hard to see the work of any helmsman—even a drunken one—in the wake I have left behind me. There are so many shifts in my activities that the only pattern I can see is that there is no pattern at all. What I do see is that I am going to be interested and involved in computers for the last half of my life.

The main error with the foregoing is that I have described my life as being involved with "my course." It should be obvious to someone, anyone, even someone with as much ego as I can command, that people are not in charge of "their course." There really is a Master of the Course, but it is not always easy to understand Its commands or to see that there should be Someone to whom we have to answer. It is true that there are long periods of my life in which I insisted on being the one who would call the shots. Strange that these are of the times in which I have done the most devastating damage to the people whom I claimed to live for and love. The only time I was on any kind of a course was when I set out to try to do the necessary things to become part of the world for which I have so little love.

For me, it is usually enough to know what is going on and enough to find out what this universe is packed with. It has always been enough for me to be the smartest kid on the block, with only myself as the judge of what things fit those criteria.

If the beginning of faith is to put oneself firmly and fully in someone else's hands, I am sure I am now doing that; I am doing the things that The Master seems to think that I am supposed to do. I have found there is nothing I have decided to do that is not full of hundreds of activities I would rather not do or consider myself ill equipped for. It seems that I am not allowed to do any of what I am good at; I am going to run a railroad, but someone else is going to set the rails. Day-by-day, I may not even know where I am going, much less what passengers or freight I will be taking with me. Actually, I have not minded the chaos of my life, although I have occasionally wondered why it seemed that I was destined to involve so many other people.

I am part of a good many different people's karma. I have always known this. I supposed that it was because I felt that in some way, through writing or painting, I would be the instrument of leaving a record of these historical heroes and heroines. I am, of course, stuck with the heroes and heroines; I have had them with me from the beginning. I have always been on the cutting edge of the individuals I have been around.

My first larger-than-life characters were introduced to me at Providence Academy by all of the books I read there. It was clear that they weren't necessarily real people, yet I thought they were the blueprints for the kinds of people that I would later recognize. I have not been disappointed. I have met many of them; I have met many more than were in the books I read, and perhaps, on occasion, I have been able to be one myself. But were I not a hero, then at least, I will have learned that there are such people and I will know when not to be a coward. I'm sure that when I die, as I must, I will not die the many deaths of the coward.

There is, of course, no school that you can go to that will teach you to recognize heroes. I know this is true because I have seen many people who did not know that they were leading heroic lives, even though they lived around people who knew they were.

I can see this first journal entry is not going to be full of any great writing, and yet, that is the greatest writing of all: it is the writing that you do when you have nothing to say, and all that you can hope to do is sit at the machine and create copy. It is writing in the sense that you are making marks on a piece of paper, but it is not writing when merely pedestrian words are going down on that piece of paper. Yet, this is often the time that you are doing the most important work, for it is the day by day drudge effort that is the process of getting your can out of bed and out of the doldrums. And it is getting into it—the writing—when it is the last thing on earth you want to do. It is the courage to do the things that you must if you can't do the things that you wish.

I had promised myself tonight that I would sit down and type five pages. It is a beginning. For the most part, it really is only typing practice, but that is something too. It will take a lot of these little steps to round out the journey that I am planning for this family, but all the little steps count.

I have a good deal of work to do on the computer. I am going to get a letter written to Eric sometime, either tonight or tomorrow, and see if there is some way that I can explain to him what this family is all about. Torrents of words have passed between us. The blessed thing is that now I have the opportunity to take time to think about what I'm going to say and to try to be sure that the words are what I really think and will be of some use to hear. It is hard to realize that there is so little I can do or say that will make a difference, but

(the copy ends here as Larry ran out the bottom of the paper of his 5th page!)

Chapter 7

Forty Days and Forty Nights

At times it is strangely sedative
to know the extent of your own powerlessness
—Erica Jong

Since we were new to this San Francisco Bay Area, we had no established health care providers. Thus, now working at a local hospital, I began to ask my fellow nurses whom they would recommend as a family doctor. The vote was unanimous: Dr. Craig Miller. I hope he is still alive so he can read my singing his praises. He was a terrific family doctor and, as fortune would have it, the only doctor from whom Larry would have taken medical advise at that time. Not only was Dr. Miller a general practitioner, his frequent attendance at a variety of medical conferences assured that he usually had an answer to our questions and usually the correct diagnosis. He was also holistic in his thinking and practice, willing to try the unusual with the patient's consent. He even did chiropractic. When Larry had severe pain in his heels, which apparently was caused by cysts of some kind, Dr. Miller injected the area with a concentrated sugar solution. Voilá! End of heel pain. He was also an expert in nutrition, which had more influence on Larry's eating habits than I did; Dr. Miller and I often exchanged recipes for healthy meals. But, the main reason that I adored Dr. Miller was that he saved Larry's life—three times.

In June of 1982, Larry began the "pacing pain" again, the same kind that he had been treated for at Kaiser in Portland several years previously. But, he seemed a lot sicker this time. I called Dr. Miller; he said he would meet us in the emergency room at the hospital. They wasted no time whisking Larry off to the operating room with Dr. Miller on their heels. After Larry was recovering in the ICU, Dr. M. told me that Larry's gallbladder was so gangrenous (rotten) that the surgeon accidentally shoved his finger through it when trying to remove it. Because of this, I had my first opportunity to actually contribute to saving Larry's life, the first but not the last.

I stayed with him in the ICU (the advantage of being a nurse employed on site) and identified the beginning of septic shock: a peripheral mottling (a blotchy, purple/blue discoloration of the skin) that crept up from his feet and ankles to his knees, an early sign of the vascular disruption common in gram negative septic shock. The doctors in the OR had flooded his peritoneum with a strong antibiotic solution, but apparently the infection was so massive that some of the bacterial critters escaped. I notified the nurse of my suspicions, and Dr. Miller was called immediately. Larry was started on a cocktail of intravenous antibiotics, and the crisis was averted. After nine days in the hospital, Larry went home to finish recovering. Once again, we were in debt to Dr. Miller, but also to the hospital doctors and nurses. Larry's experience was memorialized in an article on septic shock that I wrote for a nursing journal (Wahl, 1989). In fact, Larry provided me with a lot of case studies for my writing and classes!

The rest of 1982 was uneventful. In August, I started my new job, teaching at San Jose State University. Since I was a newbie and was being hired semester by semester, my position consisted of supervising nursing students four days a week at two different South Bay hospitals. I particularly remember this for two different reasons.

Larry often liked to take me to work and pick me up afterwards, but on this one day—it was my birthday—I had gotten a ride to the hospital with a colleague, so Jill and Larry were to pick me up at that small hospital in Los Gatos, after which they were taking me to dinner. Finishing my shift and having sent my students on their way, I sat in the beautifully decorated lobby and waited for my ride. And I waited, and I waited, and I waited! It was 5:30 PM, and they supposedly knew that I finished about 4. I was beginning to feel rejected; after all, it *was* my birthday. And then I was angry, and then I was sorrowful, and then I was … and then they came wheeling up to the door about 6 PM. I composed myself the best I could. They were abject in their apologies: they had gotten lost in the *Los Altos Hills*. I couldn't contain myself, "For Gods sake, don't you guys know the difference between cats and trees?!"

A sense of humor saved the day, and we had a lovely dinner. I never let them forget it. But, they never let *me* forget that, in Spanish, "Altos" means "high," not "trees"!

The next experience was not so harmless. It was February 2, 1983, and this time I was at Kaiser Hospital when I got a call from the nursing school: it was a call from Larry that they were transferring to me. He tried to be very calm, but I could tell that he was very anxious.

Often Larry and I walked around in our neighborhood and to downtown Menlo Park. I had noticed that he would stop for a minute, in a pretense to examine a flower. Looking closely at him while we were stopped, I saw that his nose was very pale, almost white in comparison with the rest of his face— I had seen this before in people who were having an adrenalized reaction to pain. I asked him if he was all right; his response was always that he was fine, he just got tired. While we were still in Oregon, he had admitted to some bouts of chest pain, but it didn't last, and he had registered no complaints since we had moved. Now I was concerned, but he would not admit to any pain. Dr. Miller, having his own suspicions, had scheduled Larry for an angiogram, but it had been cancelled; I'm not sure why.

On the phone, Larry was quite direct as he told me he had had some pretty severe left chest pain and had called Dr. Miller, who told him to go immediately to Peninsula Hospital where they would do the angiogram to check for blockage of the arteries to his heart. Larry said he was now at the hospital and would be going for the test shortly. I told him I would be there as soon as I could—it was a 20 mile drive; the school had already sent another faculty person to take over my students.

When I arrived, Dr. Miller was there to meet me. He explained that the angiogram showed that although Larry had not had any damage to his heart muscle, four major coronary arteries that fed blood to the heart were almost completely blocked. Since there was no time to waste and the cardiac surgeon Dr. Ulloyt was available, they were going to take Larry directly to the operating room for open-heart surgery; Dr. Miller said that he would watch from the observation area. So I wasn't able to even hug Larry before he went for a potentially life-threatening procedure. Our phone call was to be our last contact until the surgery was over.

I need to explain: When I was in Portland, I was the charge nurse who took care of the open-heart surgery patients immediately after surgery. There were no ICUs in those days, so my staff and I were it. I worked with Drs. Al Starr and James Wood, Dr. Starr being the co-inventor of the Starr-Edwards mechanical heart valve. I had seen a lot of patients get well and had seen a lot die. And I had had the opportunity to observe in the operating room when the surgeries were being performed. When they were finished operating, I was a witness as they "shocked" the heart back into functioning. Thus, I was very well informed about open-heart surgery, now called a CABG or coronary artery by-pass graft.

So, I sat in the hospital waiting room, where the doctors could find me, watching TV but not seeing it. I was trying very hard not to visualize the surgery being performed on my beloved husband. It was a very long afternoon. And as I'm writing this, I don't remember where Jill was. I'm sure some friends were taking care of her, but I don't remember. My energy was focused on blocking out what *my mind* wanted to see.

At about 7:30 PM, Dr. Ulloyt came bouncing into the waiting room—he really was bouncing. "We did it, we replaced four vessels and gave him a mammary artery transplant for good measure. We 'cheated' your husband out of a heart attack. He's going to be just fine!"

I think I may have hugged him, or maybe he hugged me, but I was so grateful. He went on to explain that I could see Larry in about an hour in the ICU, but he probably wouldn't be very responsive until the next day. Dr. Ulloyt did admit that there had been some excessive bleeding through the chest tubes (inserted to assist the lungs to re-inflate by draining fluid from the chest cavity), but it had been controlled with medication. Dr. Miller showed up about then—more celebratory hugs. They didn't even look tired, and they had been at this for over four hours.

I kept extensive notes of Larry's post-operative experience, which I'm grateful for having while writing now. I must have known I would need them some day. I have lots of emotion available about the next six weeks, but would not have been able to tell this story as thoroughly without my notes.

All the tubes were out by the 2nd post-op day and ambulation was started even though Larry complained of severe pain. His weight had increased by 20 pounds from before surgery; he was given medication to help his body eliminate the fluid—20 pounds is the equivalent of 10 liters (quarts) of water. To me, that indicated how seriously ill he had been for some time—the body retains water as part of the inflammatory reaction to illness and injury. Some retention is expected after surgery, but Larry's was excessive. The doctors had no ready explanation. He also had a heart arrhythmia that had to be converted back to a normal rhythm. Through all of this, he had periods of confusion, memory loss, and depression, possibly related to the disruption of body chemicals during surgery and the fluid overload.

Over the next few days, Larry began to get some strength back, but he didn't seem interested in walking, which was an important part of his rehabilitation. Even though I knew I shouldn't make comparisons, I noted that man who had had surgery in the morning before Larry was trotting up and down the hall, while Larry seemed only able to walk a few yards. But I needed to remember that this was the 2nd major surgery he had undergone in the last 9 months, and he had incisions on both legs, from ankle to groin, where they harvested the veins that replaced the clotted arteries in his heart: how painful that must make walking.

I continued to stay with him as much as I could; the nursing school told me to take as much time off as we needed. Jill was still in high school, so I wanted to go home and be with her in the evenings. I brought her in to see him one time, but it was too difficult for her to see her dad like that. One thing that concerned me was that Larry seldom displayed the spark of humor that we were so used to; in fact, at times he seemed apathetic. But finally, on the evening of the 8th postop day, the doctors pronounced him ready to go home, accompanied by pain medications and a follow-up appointment in a week. He was happy to be going home, finally, but was very tired.

At 5:00 AM the next morning, he woke me, complaining of severe chest pain and difficulty breathing. His blood pressure registered at 50/20. I called 911, and the ambulance took him, this time, to Stanford Hospital—it is only one mile away while Peninsula is 18 miles. In the emergency room, they started intravenous lines to give him fluids and measure the pressures in his vessels. The doctors reported that he was "3 liters down" in his fluid volume, thus the shock (very low blood pressure), but also a CT Scan demonstrated that he had a cardiac tamponade—fluid in the pericardial sac that was compressing his heart and impairing function. They removed that unnecessary fluid. By 9:00 PM, Larry looked better than he had since before his surgery! He stayed at Stanford for five days and then went home again, still tired but feeling better.

Not very long into this second recovery period, Larry again began to have less energy and wasn't eating well. He was short of breath with very little exertion, but would go out for short neighborhood walks with me; he didn't initiate activity on his own, except for going to the bathroom and upstairs to bed. He complained of frequent burning pain in his leg incisions. While I felt he should be getting more activity, I tried not to be a nagging nurse/wife. He was gradually experiencing more difficulty catching his breath, even without exercise, and while his calf incisions were healing well, the inner thigh incisions were inflamed and painful.

On the fourth day after his discharge from Stanford, I noticed that his breath sounds were diminished (*was he retaining fluid in his lungs?*) and his entire left leg was somewhat swollen. He was cheerful and said he felt better, especially after a shower, but his exercise level still seemed to be limited by shortness of breath. I was concerned, but trying not to be panicky. Larry thought his lungs needed more expansion, that he wasn't breathing deeply enough. He had always prided himself on having such great lung capacity, so the breathing problems were emotionally distressing to him. He felt he could do much better, so we worked on a plan of deep-breathing exercises. This went on, including the swollen legs, for three more days, and finally, with some protest from Larry, I called Dr. Miller at about 10 PM. I told him of Larry's symptoms and then had Larry talk to Dr. Miller on the phone: Larry's trouble breathing was very obvious, as he frequently paused speaking to catch his breath. Dr. Miller had me come back on the line, and he said, "Bring Larry to Mills Hospital right away!"

I drove instead of calling an ambulance because they would take him to Stanford, and we wanted him to be where our regular doctors were. Larry insisted on getting dressed so, by the time we were ready to go, it was almost midnight. As we drove, I noticed that Larry seemed excessively drowsy and was breathing very rapidly. Months later, Larry and I had a good laugh over what I did next. Fearing he would become unconscious before I could get to the hospital, I told him to tell me jokes. He perked up, looked questioningly in my direction, but complied and kept telling me jokes, mostly the same ones, until we arrived at the ER. I had kept him from "falling asleep"!

In the ER, it took a while for anyone to see him (priorities?), and by the time the cardiac doctor-on-call arrived, Larry was hyperventilating and moaning with pain, not only in his legs but now his chest. The doctor decided that he was hysterical, that the hyperventilation was causing his pain. He never looked at his legs. He instructed the nurses to have Larry breathe into a paper bag—a supposed method to alter the oxygen-carbon dioxide balance and stop the hyperventilation. Both the nurses and I were very skeptical, but we followed the doctor's orders (nurses did that in those days!). After a few minutes of bag-breathing with no noticeable results, I said, "This is enough. He is in terrible pain and can't get enough oxygen. That's why he's hyperventilating!"

The nurse called the doctor back. Dr. K was the senior partner in a group of very respected cardiologists—was he too old and tired to deal with Larry's distress? I was being generous! Finally he agreed to send Larry to x-ray (*now* the doc looked at the swollen, red legs) and had the nurse start oxygen. The x-ray showed that his lungs were not aerating (moving air) in the upper lobe of his right lung, and most of his left lung was not functioning. He was admitted to the Coronary Care Unit.

It was now the middle of the day, and still in extreme pain—Dr. K had only ordered Tylenol—Larry was sent to x-ray again for a venogram to check the blood flow in his legs. We were later told that they could hear him moaning and coughing three floors away, so extreme was his pain. The venogram results? Larry had bilateral venous thrombosis (blood clots in the veins) that had migrated to his lungs, becoming pulmonary emboli (PE) and blocking the circulation of blood through large areas in his lung tissue. Larry's hyperventilation and extreme pain are classic symptoms of PE, which often results in the death of its victim. He was immediately started on an IV Heparin drip (anticoagulant) to start dissolving the clots before they could do any more damage.

Later in the day, Larry was still in a great deal of pain. I asked the nurse if she couldn't get him something stronger for his pain. This big, beautiful nurse wrapped her arms around Larry and said, "I can't now. I tried but Doctor K (who shall remain unnamed) won't order anything else. If you can just hang on until 7 PM, Dr. Cohen will be here on-call, and I know he will medicate him properly."

Right at 7, Dr. Cohen came into the room, sat on the bed, and held Larry's hand while he administered intravenous morphine. Larry became pain free for the first time in almost 24 hours. Dr. Cohen was to be Larry's cardiologist for the next 30 years, until Larry died, and was the only reason we didn't sue his "esteemed" colleague for malpractice.

After Larry seemed to be resting, and I felt he was now in good hands, I drove home to update Jill and pick up a razor and toiletries for Larry. Jill had a number of good friends in the Unitarian Church youth group she had joined, so she asked me if it was all right for her to stay with one of them for a few days while I was at the hospital. Of course I said yes; from her friends she would have the support I was not able to give her. Also I needed to let Eric and our friends in Seattle know what was happening; they were under the impression he was still recovering from the initial heart surgery.

As I drove back to the hospital, it started raining, so the windshield wipers were sloshing, back and forth. I decided to audiotape a letter to our friends; the windshield wipers were quite audible in the tape and set a mournful tone. I still have that tape, now 30 + years later, and it is still as poignant as it was when I did it. I did not know, while I was taping, whether Larry was going to live or die. When I played it for him after he was home, Larry told me that he really wasn't sure I loved him until he heard that tape. What does that say about me?

I am still consumed with guilt that I did not "blow the whistle" on Larry and get him medical treatment when I first noticed his increasing difficulty breathing and his swollen legs. I knew all the signs and symptoms of venous thrombosis and pulmonary embolism, they were right there in front of my face: red, warm, swollen legs; difficulty breathing; chest pain; even his altered mentation. Talk about denial ... I have no excuse. The only reason I can think of is that, after the difficult time he had recovering from the heart surgery and sequelae, I just couldn't accept that he was having *more* serious problems. No wonder he didn't think I loved him—a good wife, let alone an expert nurse, would have taken action far sooner than I did. I know Larry didn't blame me, he said *he* thought he was faking, but I don't know when I will fully forgive myself for all the pain I let him go through.

For the next two weeks, Larry stayed in the CCU with Heparin running into his intravenous line. He also received IV morphine as he needed it, but it seemed to affect him mentally. He had periods of irritation and lashing out, confusion and hallucinations—he looked out his windows at downtown San Mateo and thought the Long Beach, California airport was just behind one of the tall buildings. After he was changed to oral pain medication, he was more alert and oriented, but he continued to be short of breath and needing oxygen—not surprising since half of his lung tissue had been destroyed.

During his time in the hospital, I stayed with him as much as I could— even bathed him when he asked me to, but I made an effort to make life as "normal" as possible for me. One incident occurred that helped me realize I was not making "normal." I was teaching a class at Mills in leadership to a lovely group of nurses that were part of the program I had set up there when I still was working at Mills. I had my back turned to the class and was writing on the board when one of the students came up and put her hand on my arm. "Sharon, go be with your husband. What you are writing on the board is nonsense."

I looked, and of course she was right—it was gibberish! One of the nurses from this group had brought me a casserole and settled me in the family room so I could stay the night, when Larry was first admitted. Other nurses brought me coffee many mornings. These kindnesses were special to me.

We had only been in California for a couple of years, and I had been working at San Jose State University only for two semesters, so I didn't have many friends and didn't even know our neighbors; I wasn't very good at making friends under any circumstances. I had not told anybody about what was happening to us; my students knew by virtue of Larry being in their hospital, and they were empathetic enough to sense my pain. I remember feeling deserted by my work colleagues and the people in the choir where I was singing: I felt no one cared. I was so desperately alone.

Sometime into that final two-week recovery period, the doctors discovered Larry had another complication. He had coughed so violently—the body was trying to get rid of the necrotic lung tissue—his mid-sternal sutures from the heart surgery had broken and the incision was starting to open up. He was not happy when he had to go back to Peninsula and have the heart surgeons rewire him.

Finally, he was allowed to get out of bed and walk a little. With that, he began to look and sound like the Larry I knew; we believed that Larry was on the mend. He still hurt in the chest and legs, but was now sociable, kidding around with the nurses and doctors, as was his usual mode. He had periods of introspection, telling me he was reflecting on the meaning of this illness. He told me that a few days after his heart surgery, he had a dream—or a hallucination, he wasn't sure. In this dream, Yosemite Sam—a cartoon character that carried two large guns in holsters at his sides and whipped them out at the slightest provocation—came up to Larry and hit him in the chest with a large axe. A plethora of green, gooey stuff streamed out. "Thanks. I needed that," Larry said he told Yosemite Sam. Was all of this pain and consternation his karmic payback for earlier sins? Was he metaphorically getting rid of a lot of accumulated "pus"? He hoped so.

On March 11th, Larry went home and planned to stay there a good long while. On my calendar for March 22nd, there was noted, "Larry helped Sherry out of her guilt and depression." During his at-home convalescence, Larry celebrated his new health by walking the three miles to his studio. By April 5th, he was back to work at said studio.

We both recovered from this adventure, but it had a profound effect on both our lives. I wouldn't take having Larry for granted ever again. For Larry, he began the long road to changing his habits and behavior. When he was having chest pain while we were still in Oregon, I had bought him a book titled, *Type A Behavior and Your Heart* (Friedman, 1974), which talked about the noxious effect of anger on the body in general and the heart in particular, the hallmark of Type A Behavior. As Larry said, after this present siege, "I walked around that book for years. Now I'm going to read it!" And he did.

About a year later, early1984, Larry said he wanted to give something back for all he had received from the nurses, doctors, and hospital staff. At that time, I was writing learning modules and developing supplementary learning materials in pathophysiology for the Statewide Nursing Program—yes, the same one I started at Mills Hospital. I was now the regional director and an instructional designer. I don't know who initially suggested it, but when I told Larry that I was working on the module for heart disease, he said maybe he could thank all the hospital folk by telling his story. From there, we decided that we should make an instructional video, complete with breaks in the content for student discussion. Obviously Larry and I aren't movie-makers, but when I proposed the idea to Jerry, the leader of the instructional design team, he was very excited. Larry and I wrote the script and taped his story so they could find an actor that looked and sounded similar to him. They even let Larry do the introduction so he could thank people; inadvertent humor was provided by a noisy bird that chirped all through Larry's speech.

The video was a great success; it won some kind of award for educational videos. And my students were delighted to meet the author on film and in person. I shared the video with my fellow faculty at the school of nursing, but I was feeling disappointment when the showing was finished and there was only dead silence. I thought, "They didn't like it. I've embarrassed them," until I saw tears in many eyes. I hadn't intuited the impact the story would have on people who knew us. They said they had no idea what we had gone through; I hadn't been one to share our troubles. That had been, as Larry observed, our "forty days and forty nights."

As I was sorting through Larry's papers in the fall of 2013, I found a letter that he wrote sometime after his ordeal, probably to our friends in Seattle. I feel it really needs to be included here—"Let Larry speak for Larry!"

Hello There,

I am now ensconced at my model 80-12 TRS, prepared to write a humongous letter. I am not in the slightest sure what in the devil was happening three years ago when I last wrote, but I will try to keep you aware of what is happening now, at least to the best of my ability. This has been a wild and crazy year, and the last six months have been the busiest of my life. Shortly after I returned from the hospital, I got down to the business of business as usual. I realized I was going to have get the ol' bod back in shape in a hurry and was going to have to make some changes in the way that I lived that would ensure I would continue to live.

In the early days of our marriage, Sherry worked with several doctors who were into heart surgery, and so I knew most of the things that happen to heart surgery patients as a result of the surgery but mostly by the kinds of things that they did to their minds themselves. The doctors suppressed most of this kind of information because, in most cases, it indicated that a person having heart trouble of a protracted nature would be at risk for ever going back to work. Sherry had done a study, following up many of Doctor Starr's patients, that showed, among other things, if they were off work for a year, ninety percent never went back to work again, even though all of the physical problems had been corrected. *[I didn't do that study; it was actually from a citation in my master's thesis. Ed]*

Since I had helped Sherry with the construction of the statistical analysis and display format, I had that information in the back of my mind when I finally realized I was dying of heart trouble. It was not a sudden realization: I do believe that I tested fully my beliefs and understandings of life as I navigated this period of time.

I had set a very high standard of exercise performance for myself at the health spa and was working out, on the average, three days a week, two to three hours a day. This schedule continued apace, even though my heart was in the process of shutting down. But I found that I was subtly changing the type of exercise I was doing; I was doing less and less on the bicycle and more just upper bodywork. As the weeks went by, I found that effortless walking became diminished, so long before I went into the hospital, I knew my heart was going to hell in a hand-basket!

Now it happens that I have some very peculiar attitudes toward life in general—my own death in particular. I really did think about dying and weighed all of the consequences. I finally decided not to give in because I figured that Sherry needed me. I also liked to think that my son and daughter did too. And when I fully realized that I was dying and it would take a certain combination of events of great power and expense to keep me alive, I did an additional survey of my life and reasons for continuing it.

I really do believe I have been here before, that I was Leonardo da Vinci, and that I have been able to span across life-times with a good deal of memory persisting. It is the conclusion of these beliefs, and the life in which I now find myself living, that there is a damn good reason not to span lifetimes. I am glad that I have done it, but it is not something that everyone needs to do, or that everyone is constitutionally quipped for. I do not find it any big deal, and I have a couple of books full of information why it is not routinely done. What comes through as the most important prohibition against remembering past lives is that from the vantage point of the now, you see all of the stupid decisions that you have made ... without the ability to change them. You may find yourself in a new life with an almost certain assertion that you will screw up this one just as you did the last. It is a concept that fills one with a depth of despair hard to put into words.

Anyway, the hospital saw to it that I lost over 30 pounds in a couple of weeks, and after the first few days, I knew that I had made the transition, that I had decided to live. I also knew that I was going to have complications that were unusual and bizarre, that would leave me dangling on the end of the string we call life, for some time. I knew that I had to come as close to the edge as it was possible to come.

With that behind me and with the family finally aware that I am, in fact, mortal—an idea that I have always discouraged in them and one I still refuse to accept even in death. It is the body that is mortal and not the soul—even by Christian figuring and is true in spades for the Spiritualists.

There are several books in me. I do not know if the world needs to read them, but I do know that I need to write them, so the first thing is to get my house in order. I do not know about other people, but I do know that a good deal of the difference between Sherry and me is in the kind of "housekeeping" we do. Sherry lives in a house that has a hundred thousand rooms. There are various doors between these rooms. Some are simple swinging doors without locks or hooks, which will swing open anytime you merely lean on them; others take special keys that only certain people possess and some have trick processes for opening them. Most of the latter Sherry herself does not have keys for.

My house is larger than Sherry's, I think, but it is one huge, disordered, world-sized room, expanding in all directions with no doors at all. There is nothing that is hidden by doors, but there is much that is hidden by disorder. In all of my life, I have found that the simplest way to confuse my enemies is to tell them that the evidence to hang me is in a certain place and then let them look at this huge mess that is my life. Few enemies feel like taking the time to try and figure out what is valuable to steal or ruin in that junkyard.

I rearranged my life before the operation—the important part that consisted of trying to get a little order into the chaos. I did this quite successfully, I think. When the physical operation was over, I was able to set up my life so that it finally looks to me as though it will now make some kind of sense. For all of the things that I always had other people do for me, I was operating on the basis that they liked to do it and it would take me a long time to even be mediocre at it. When I finally realized that I could make no more sense out of that giant room than could a stranger stumbling into it, I took it upon myself to make changes that I had never taken the time (read: never had the courage) to pull my own strings.

Almost immediately, I had to get a new computer with the capacity to do all of the tasks that I was going to get into and one large enough to remember all of the material I was going to pore through to write the space novel and, more importantly, to finish the autobiography. What I settled on after weeks of examination was the TRS 80-12. Immediately, I ran into a problem of compatibility with the software. I have just finally, after almost all the entire summer, resolved the problems. I am now ready to sit down and really start hammering things out.

My office is really terrific. It is just perfect for what I am now doing. It is full of the various things in my life that I consider important and full of things that I still have to get rid of. It is relatively small, but is located in an area I have fallen completely in love with. It is in Palo Alto, in an area called the California Avenue District. My office is only a block off California, on a street called Cambridge, but it is California Avenue that is the "gas." The street runs at right angles to El Camino Real and is a couple of miles south of the University Avenue, that being adjacent to Stanford University. University Avenue is considered by some to be the real Palo Alto. It is curious and quaint in its own way and is affected by every nuance of its being by the prestigious college.

California Avenue was once a small city called Mayfield, but then Palo Alto annexed it, making it a second-class suburb of the "real" Palo Alto. This little district consists of old homes and even older money. The main street, which had always been called California Avenue, ran about six blocks from El Camino to the railroad tracks, but what a six blocks! There is an EST center, a massage/Rolfing business, numerous bookstores, exotic restaurants pushing health foods, and a nearby banking center that deals in much of the high tech money made in the Valley. At the end of the street is a new condominium, located only two blocks from one of the raunchiest "good ol' boys" bars that I have ever seen, as well as a huge rock concert center.

PhD's and characters too weird to be described occupy the street in about equal numbers. One morning, at about 10, I was walking over to my office and saw this group of what, at first, looked like circus clowns making erratic rounds through the neighborhood. Since they were an evil-looking lot, I watched them for some time. They did not seem to be interested in my attention, and so I was finally able to figure out what it was they were doing. It was a tour, a ragged tour, consisting of a head bum showing the touring bums the best garbage cans and refuse containers in the area. The deference and rapt attention the group gave their leader reminded me, uncomfortably, of the sheep-like quality of me and others at the last Computer Symposium I attended in San Francisco.

Anyway, there are many semi-famous writers on that street, loads of college profs, and more characters per square foot than you can shake a nightstick at. It is a perfect environment for me. I would be finished with the book by now except for one glitch. After getting access to all of my first floppies, I discovered that I had 33 chapters with more than 30 characters and that the book had expanded, in spite of me, to at least a third longer than the million words I had already written. As time went on, it became clear that I had never had "a" book, but had, in fact, written a trilogy from the beginning. It has taken me a month to recover from that shock. It means, in simplest terms, that instead of one socko opening and one socko close, with stuff in the middle, what I now have to write is three socko openings, three socko finishes, and three middles, and I have to make all of them hang together as books in their own right as well as hang together as a trilogy! This realization almost broke my heart since I had known at the beginning I had enough stuff for one book. But crafting a trilogy is a very different project and not for the faint-hearted.

You may have noticed that in this letter, I have been talking about myself almost exclusively and have not asked much about you and yours. The thing is that I have been out of contact for such a long time that anything you want to tell me about your life will be greatly appreciated. I am very happy to be alive. A great part of that joy is knowing that people like you are the best part of that life and the main reason I did not let it slip away. I feel that there was enough pain and suffering in this hospitalization for me to have paid off what karma I have accrued through my lifetimes. I am starting off even and hope that by making myself more accessible and useable to you and my family, I will leave this world a little better than I found it. I know you do not share many of my beliefs, and you consider many of the things I do foolish and prideful. You are probably right on all counts, but you have never restricted your love on the basis of our differences. That is probably why I love you so much and will continue to call you my friends throughout this life ... and as I see it, many, many, more to come.

Love, Larry and Lewis (X. Vallian, that is)

Little Toy Soldiers and Grapes

by Larry Wahl

At best we play second fiddle
In the Creator's orchestra on high
And scramble the tune with disjointed rhyme
For the lyrics of Who, How, and Why.

Burning shrubs, parting seas on stand-by,
Special miracles, two for a dime,
Insistently bizarre and spectral
Pointing blindly to space out of time.

Whom does it profit to cling to the Truth
Of the trusty oak beckoning there?
Though the branches be strong and protecting,
Deep-rooted and safe, yet anchored in air.

You can find every message extended,
Tune in radio, tape, or TV
Up full bore, then open the good book,
"Garbage in, Garbage out," don't you see?

The senses are five most will argue
Or six, seven, eight as some think,
But trying to follow on their tortured paths,
Only dulls all those senses like drink.

We can't tell how high we are going
Without donning our fast running shoes.
Acres of silver or rivers of gold
Buy only more rehashed bad news.

Going up isn't good if you're diving
And down's not too good if you're flying.
A lie isn't good when your goal is the Truth,
But pure truth's a disaster when lying

"Give me Liberty or death," cried Pat Henry,
But I'm not sure that always is true.
Liberty for some leads you straight to the grave
But death gives a choice: Door One or Door Two.

Is maniacal laugh of a killer at large
Just the grown laugh of children at play?
Does sunlight annihilate blackness of night,
Or does waning night just slip away?

If we would, could we all get together?
Will it ever make sense or be right?
Should we all be as loose as the ashes,
Or hermetically sealed, pure and tight?

Will we learn what we need if we open
Every door or each window we find?
Or is carefully screening each errant idea
The way to get clearer of mind?

Does He want us to think less and feel more,
Demanding one more than the other?
Does He want us reflecting our demanding Dad,
Or our loveable "chicken soup" Mother?

The fast tracing finger has scratched its behind
Near the terminal end of the gland,
And a translated message appears in the mist
Reading, "Welcome to My Disneyland."

I have been on some ships going nowhere
And a jet that has no place to land,
But I got there before I had left home,
These were messages all writ in sand.

If thinking "won't make thought your master,"
It is sure as Death or High taxes.
You'll find you've made great wooden handles
For cutting through steel-headed axes.

If you arrived with pole, line, and bait,
And others with ball, mitt, and bat.
If you make yourself safe, so quiet and mousy,
You find out your roomies a cat

If you dry out, the gang has gone swimming;
If you're soaked, then you're meeting with queens;
If you're Sherlock, they'll all cheer the villains;
If you've found all the ends, they want means.

Is there ever some point or some answer
To these questions, enigmas, and 'plaint?
Must man always be so wicked and vile
While just traveling the rough road to saint?

If God wanted us funny and witty
You would think He'd have made us that way.
If He wanted just workers or serious drones,
He would have left out our needing to play.

Is He a designer bedeviled with quirks
With no real heart nor brain in his head?
He makes sure we all want success,
Then issues the proclamation, "You're Dead"!

What we want we can't have till we've lost it,
Just to have it appear "elsewhere."
He adds extra pounds to our mid-life gut,
Then decimates most of our hair

He squeezes our tubes till we're empty
Used up, spindled, and spent.
Waiting all of our lifetimes for journeys,
Over-trained and prepared—never sent.

But then, I remember my soldiers of tin
Along with their guns and their tanks.
I would bivouac, force-march, and waste them
By battalions, long files, and wide ranks.

After hours and hours of playing my games,
I would put them back in large drawers.
I would gather them up by the squad, by the gross
Where they'd wait for my next scheduled wars.

So maybe Life's real fighting soldiers,
Who wait in an unmoving line,
Testing honor and purpose and intrinsic truth,
Should remember we're only grapes on the vine.

Be it one tin soldier or sweet little grape,
Does it matter who's won, what's the score?
For I knew not the name of my hero tin men
But I loved them not less – no, much more.

For they moved or they stood as I ordered them to,
Even wounded or wickedly bent.
But each responded to me—their God—
The reason they came, stayed, or went.

I never gave thought when I played with those toys,
Wasting time stumbling deep, deep in wine,
With no thought of remorse for a one of my men
Nor of grapes growing ripe on the vine.

If I was their god, then thoughtless was I,
And knowing this left me no pride.
I did understand that the men in each squad,
When ordered to, laid down and died.

Ripe grapes would die sooner or later
Either crushed to fine wine or left fallow.
Like all of the soldiers, the grapes have no plan;
At the end of each life stands a gallows.

And so, just as grape or tin soldier,
I must do what the day seems to order.
And when I am called to that far distant land,
Walk hopefully towards that far border.

If the "One God" meets me, smiling with pride,
And rewards me for battles well fought,
I will try to remember all sunsets and risings:
Those memories I've ordered and bought.

But if no such wonder will happen this time,
And life shifts from bright to dim gray,
I'll strive to remember, like soldier or grape,
The days that we lived not forgetting to play.

When all working stagehands or actors try
To believe every truth that they say,
What enters upon this, then magical stage.
Is as real as the sweet month of May

But, if no such wondrous God meets me there,
I will still know I've done all that I can.
So if He won't tell me, I'll handle that truth:
I may have been acting, but I am a MAN!

Chapter 8

The Interlude

Write a non-fiction book, and be prepared
for the legions of readers who are going to doubt your facts.
But write a novel, and get ready
for the world to assume every word is true.
—*Barbara Kingsolver*

After the intensity of Larry's illness and recovery, 1984/85 was a relatively calm time in our lives. Once the script for the teaching video was completed, Larry resumed working on his novel, *It's a Matter of Time*, and I began actively recruiting students for the Statewide Nursing Program (SNP) and teaching its classes. Dr. Parsons, who had helped me set up the program and got me the San Jose State (SJSU) job, had me take over his position as regional director for SNP so that I was halftime SJSU and halftime SNP. That meant that I was traveling all over Northern California, setting up new sites and recruiting students for those sites. Larry would usually go with me, especially since some were far enough away that an overnight was necessary. When weekends were involved, as they often were, Jill would come along too, so we made them mini-family vacations. Since I was allowed to use a state car, I would avail myself of one for the longer trips, like Clear Lake and San Luis Obispo.

It was on the way back from Clear Lake that Jill's first experience with "deer-on-the-windshield" happened. It was raining hard when we came up over a slight hill, and there it was, staring at us, illuminated by the car headlights as it careened off the middle of the windshield. Jill screamed, but there was nothing we could do—it was gone as fast as it had come. The front of the car was another story; I was going to have some explaining to do when I returned the car. Jill said she never would forget the look in its eyes.

But in general, our trips were uneventful. That job also involved my going to Long Beach, California for 3-day meetings of all of the Statewide Regional Directors. Larry also went along on those; we became well known at the quaint Long Beach Airport. An interesting event occurred on one of the trips when I went alone. The meeting had gone overtime on the last day, and I had to make a dash for the airport so as not to miss the last plane to San Jose. Again it was raining (yes, it does rain in California), but this was a deluge. When I got to the airport, they had already loaded so the clerk called out to the pilot to hold it for me. I ran the distance to the airplane (no inside ramps), getting soaked in the process. When I got there, the stewardess asked for my boarding pass; I told her I didn't have one. She said, "You have to have a boarding pass. Go back to the airport and get one."

I didn't know what to think, so I did what I was told: back to the airport through the drenching rain. When I told the desk clerk of my dilemma, while dripping rain all over the floor, she said, "Oh, for God's sake, what was she thinking?! I'll call the plane. You go on back and get on so they can take off."

Back I went, through the blowing rain. The stewardess let me on, without a word and not looking at me. Some nice passengers made room for me, and one woman gave me a towel. I'm sure I dripped all over them as well.

Larry had a good laugh when I shared this anecdote, but how could I *not* tell him: I looked like the proverbial drowned rat when he picked me up.

The Crystal Skull

During this time, and continuing for about the next two years, Larry joined a metaphysical group headed by Mick Martino, who was the leader of the group by virtue of being the owner of a crystal skull that was deemed to have mystical powers. According to one of the members, Norma Sabine, who became friends with both Larry and me, Mick didn't as much lead the group as he did guide them in areas of the metaphysical realm. She stated that they had workshops where they "could practice their gifts and interests among like-minded people." (Sabini, 2013). Larry enjoyed this group very much and admired Mick. I didn't have much involvement with the group because of my heavy work schedule, and I was preparing to go back to school.

Larry, Sharon, and Friends at Mick's Christmas Party

Norma did send me some pictures from a Christmas party, and said she will try to send me more of her memories, which I'll include.

Unfortunately, Norma, a beautiful soul, died in late 2014.

There were several of the mystical experiences Larry told me about. One of the members had a friend whose daughter had been kidnapped by an ex-spouse; she didn't know where the girl was and she wanted her back. According to Larry, the group used mental telepathy to visualize the location of the girl. When they shared their information with the member's friend, she recognized the place they described as in Hawaii, and thus the girl was recovered. Since Larry had been involved with telepathy and telekinesis in his younger years, he enjoyed this group very much. At the same time, I was teaching "Holistic Wellness" at the Rosicrucian ("a mystical organization") Summer University, so obviously Larry and I were reading in the same book, just on different pages!

I just found one of Larry's essays that is very pertinent to what was discussed above, so I would like to insert it here.

Man and Magic
By Lewis X. Vallian

Man has worked to understand and control his destiny from time immemorial. Magical thinking has proceeded lockstep with development over countless eons. It is the prehistoric fountainhead of all our history, art, and science. It is everywhere preeminent, though usually unrecognized in our daily conscious thought. If one diligently strives to exorcise this magical thinking from this location, it simply digs itself a firmer stronghold in the alleys and back streets of the psyche. It is not necessary to believe in the Magical; it believes in us!

Mick Martino is the "Magician as Man" and the "Man as Magician": alive, alert, sensitive, and giving. He is also strange, tough, humorous, and irascible. He has helped hundreds of students construct their futures and fortunes on the basis of his teachings. This article will attempt to portray the life of a Living Treasure, for it is fair to say, "One may love him or one may hate him, but few will forget him.

In modern times, we are witness to a resurgence of Spirit not seen since the Renaissance. Experts on every aspect of the Divine, the occult, and the paranormal have arrived, risen, or escaped from every nook and cranny. Most of them are honest, open, and helpful. Some, however, are ill-equipped but earnest; some are simply greedy and rapacious. Still others long to convince themselves and followers of the great, long, and treacherous journey they have been upon "lo, these many years."

It is with a strange combination of tolerance and quiet frustration that Mick has seen some of his students—neophytes a year or two ago—appear in print, convinced or convincing they are a channel for Fra Contuti Contuti, the Magnificent from the planet Gorp, through multiple lifetimes. The problem usually is that the new, just revealed material is more often than not, amazingly similar to what Mick has been teaching for over 50 years.

Perhaps because of faulty translations into terran languages, many brilliant channeled masters do not speak "well" English. However, even if one finds whole, lifted passages, it continues to be difficult to serve papers for plagiarism on Fra Contuti Contuti, the Magnificent, since extradition agreements with the planet Gorp have not yet been finalized. Mick, when viewing such non-attribution of his part and parcel teachings, just looks skyward and, in a soft voice says, "God bless 'em."

Mick Martino is a fountain pouring forth good and powerful magic, mostly free. He has legitimate standards and practices, having started as an apprentice at age seven. He has gone to jail, having been fiscally attacked and pilloried in the McCarthy-like atmosphere surrounding the reactionary attacks during the forties to the late sixties.

Scientists, for over a hundred years the sworn enemy of parapsychology, have finally caught up with the knowledge of their own disciplines, finally getting their theory bases designed to see what the ancients knew was obvious. Suddenly "discovering" psychic wheels rolling along since before Adam and Eve, they now, once again, rush to the head of the line where they assure us they have all the keys to the kingdoms.

One would think they would start out by quantifying such common imponderables as Faith, Hope, and Charity since most people, religious and otherwise, will stipulate to these existing. But no! One scientist, with a faultless engineering and scientific background, is sure his specially designed, cut, polished, and patented improvements will make one "know" the power of the crystal. The price for this "scientific" improvement in natural crystals will only cost the unwary $600.00 to $1000.00 plus, available F.O.B. San Jose.

And ... Mick smiles, "God bless 'em!"

My Very Own Office

In September of 84, we became aware that the tenant in #4 of our five-plex was moving out. We took that opportunity to trade in our two-bedroom apartment for the three bedrooms in #4. While the other four apartments had only two bedrooms, our new home had three, by virtue of an extra, long, thin room that was situated over the utility area—garbage cans, water heater, and laundry. This was perfect for me to use as an office, since I was doing so much writing—learning modules and chapters in nursing textbooks. I had been using a corner of the not very big living-dining room downstairs in #2. We lost no time in fitting out my room (the long, skinny bedroom) with a computer desk for the Osborn (Larry had since abandoned it for his TRS 12-80 that he had at his studio), bookshelves, a futon for guests (I occasionally mentored students at home), and even some selected hanging plants by the windows (full height of the room at each end). I was in heaven. But, I should have known not to count my angels too soon.

Cold Ham and Warm Cold Duck

It had been 4½ years since we had visited our Seattle friends, so we decided this would be a nice year to take the train up for Christmas and New Years, stopping off at Long Beach, Washington for several days on the way. It had been a family tradition to stay in a favorite motel over the holidays, a tradition facilitated by my teaching position that allowed time off at holidays. We were sorry Eric couldn't join us for Christmas, but since he was also in Seattle, he would be with us at our friends' home for our traditional New Years' Eve game of Hearts, which also included their two daughters (who grew up knowing us practically as family); we were always a lively group!

We got off at the Portland, Oregon train station and rented a car for the 100 mile drive west to Long Beach. While Portland is generally colder and wetter in the winter than Menlo Park, we were nevertheless surprised at how cold it was when we got off the train. But, of course we knew that the beach never had to cope with freezing temperatures, so happily we went on our way. The place where we usually had stayed, Chautauqua Lodge, had changed ownership, and we had decided it was now a little too pricy, so we made reservations at a nice, but much cheaper motel—a Day's Inn, I think. It didn't have the full kitchen like we were used to, but I figured we could probably borrow some time of the oven at the manager's residence to cook the ham I decided to get for our Christmas dinner; motels at Long Beach at Christmas were not usually that busy.

We stopped at Ray's Market on the way to the motel and stocked up on groceries for the days we would be there: a nice ham, already sliced, just needing heating; assorted vegetables; and a couple of bottles of a favorite red wine—Cold Duck. Even though Jill was not old enough to be legal yet, we were sure a little celebration wouldn't hurt—she was a senior in high school, after all, and since she kept company with the flaky Unitarian church group, we were sure she had imbibed at some point! So we were set for a nice, enjoyable holiday, with music and TV and walks by the ocean.

Surprise! We noticed, as we drove into the registration area that, other than several PGE (Portland General Electric) trucks, we were the *only* car there. Larry quipped, "Guess we didn't need a reservation."

When I got out of the car, I almost fell on the ice-covered driveway. Oops? Had we inadvertently driven to Mount Hood instead of Long Beach? At the registration desk, I noticed that candles lighted the area. The manager smiled at me sheepishly and said, "I'm sure you were looking forward to a nice holiday at the beach, and it still may be possible, but we had heavy rain a day ago, followed by a hard freeze. The ice weighed down and broke many of the power lines, so as you can see, we don't currently have electricity. The guys are working on it," she pointed to the PGE trucks, "so they hope to have it on by tomorrow. We do have some lanterns and battery-powered heaters, but we'll be glad to refund your deposit if you want to turn around and go back to Portland."

I excused myself, saying I would go talk to my family and let her know. After minimal discussion, we decided to stay the course; we liked adventures, didn't we? So with unanimous consent, I went back in and got our keys. She had given us a room in the middle of the motel on the non-ocean side and had turned on the heater before the power went out, so it was quite cozy. Since we were tired from the train and the car ride, we gratefully sacked out. This was Christmas Eve.

Christmas Day greeted us with brilliant sunshine, but no power. Larry, Jill, and I, wrapped up in many layers, with gloves and knitted caps, tried to go for a walk on the beach. The thermometer on the side of the motel registered 7 degrees F. We lasted about 10 minutes of heading into the freezing wind; I commented that I didn't know sand could freeze! So much for leisurely strolls along the ocean—at least *it* wasn't frozen.

So we opened some of our gifts, the few we brought along—the rest we had shipped to Seattle. Then we thought about dinner. Since the power outage was quite widespread (how had Ray's Market escaped?), there were no restaurants available to rescue our Christmas dinner. So I borrowed some plates, wine glasses, and silverware from the manager, and we had cold ham and Warm Duck for dinner. We might not make Arctic explorers, but we know how to make the lemonade when the Universe gives us lemons. After dinner, we sang some carols and then played Hearts (practicing for the big game on New Year's Eve), while we finished off the warm Cold Duck. It was an animated game!

The power did come on for a few days, so we stocked up on food that didn't need much cooking. But on the morning we were to leave, I heard on the radio that another storm was imminently due to arrive. Not telling Larry about this possible complication—we *had* to catch our train to Seattle that afternoon—we packed up and got on our way, after thanking the manager for making the trip as nice as possible under the bizarre circumstances. While Larry was packing the car, what I had also heard on the radio was that the road we needed to take might be closed. The highway between Seaside and Portland was a good highway under usual weather, but there was one mountain—about 1700 feet up—that we had to traverse to get to Portland. This could be problematic.

We were cruising along quite well when I heard a report on the radio: State Highway 26 was closed at a specified area, until further notice, due to snow and ice ahead. Larry was in his own space and not listening. Since we had already passed that specified area (it hadn't been closed when we went by), I didn't bother telling Larry; I knew what a good bad-weather driver he was, so we were sure to get through all right. And if we didn't make that train in Portland, we would have to buy new tickets, which we really couldn't afford.

The snow was getting serious, and Larry was driving well, but he was looking a little concerned. Jill was asleep in the back seat. Larry noticed the men in the yellow/red vests as we went sailing by—they just stared at the little brown car heading for, they thought, disaster. Larry was now much more concerned as the snow pilled up along the side of the road and the previous sanding was not visible. But like an airplane, we were at the point of no return: further to go back than to go forward, so Larry hunkered down and drove. I silenced my inane, nervous chatter.

We pulled into a Denny's in Northwest Portland to get a much-needed cup of coffee, and after we had slip-slid over the solid ice on the walkway into the front entrance, I finally confessed to Larry what I had been guilty of withholding. "What were you thinking?" he questioned.

"I knew you could do it, and we just couldn't miss our train," was my insipid response.

Larry just looked at me and shook his head; Jill had slept through the whole trip.

We had a great tale to tell when we got to Seattle, as we gratefully ushered in 1985. Larry never let me forget that one. It more than made up for him losing Los Gatos!

The Book, The Corporation, The Fire

Larry was on fire with his book! He wrote and wrote and wrote and wrote. I swear you could see smoke coming from his little office, #19. As he noted in a letter in the previous chapter, he had discovered that he had enough material and characters (and, I should add, plot lines!) for two or three books. But, because he wanted to have more time to devote to the further development of his Vallian Coordinates, he made the decision to find an ending point for the first book, which, in case you forgot, he called IAMOT, or *It's a Matter of Time*. Since Larry had tied the novel's plot to the volcanic eruption of Mt. St. Helens on May 18, 1980, sometime in 1982, we took a special trip up to Washington so we could time the trip Larry's main character, Wizzer, would take from US I-5, east along US 12, the White Pass Highway, down WA 25 around the damaged mountain, and back to Portland. It was a fascinating trip since the mountain was coming back to life, but you could still see the trees laid down like toothpicks. I'm not sure where that ended up in his book, but the trip was great fun.

I do have the written material of IAMOT that Larry organized into notebooks and a synopsis of the first book, which I may include as an appendix—

just the synopsis, not the whole book. I suspect my next writing endeavor will be to scan or transcribe all of that writing and see about publishing it. Larry would be pleased.

Our Poetic Son

Sometime in the early 80's when we were visiting Eric and Jill in Seattle, we discovered that Larry wasn't the only accomplished writer in this family. Eric amazed us by reading a series of poems he had written, using multiple rhyme schemes and literary devices. At first, Larry didn't believe Eric had written them; as far as we knew, other than high school classes and English 101 at the U, Eric had no special, let alone advanced, writing or poetry training. But we knew our son: he was incapable of the kind of subterfuge or cheating that would be necessary to have copied them from a book and presented them as his own. But what solidified the poems' provenance was the content of the lyrics that were very personally oriented.

Of the hundreds he has written over the years, I'm including only two. The first, called Thorn Street, correlates with my discussion of our gardening experience in Chapter 5; the second (my favorite), a lyrical love ballad, displays his mastery of linguistic strategies in the fluent use of metaphor, simile, alliteration, and enjambment. I especially enjoyed the following alliteration: "How her shy, serene smile flooded my sullen, shame-burdened soul with sudden sunlight!"

I don't know why we were surprised at Eric's expertise with language and vocabulary: he is his father's son—he came by it genetically! We are very proud of Eric and are honored to share these poems with you, with his permission, of course.

                              thorn st

spring of 1973;

                                        we signed up to rent

one of twenty-eight

                                        routine jerrybuilds

lined up to fill

                                        a three-fingered cul-de-sac.

one of only two that had

                                        an actual fireplace.

Spray-painted a cheesy brand

                                        of dark olive drab,

                tarpaper hung out over the foundation sill
                        like a social misfit's t-shirt.

an attached garage was designed

                                                to fit two cars

but our staunch buick

                                        remained outside so

                        dad
                could convert the space into a machine shop
                for the manufacture of his patented schemes.
                the upper loft was left for the neighbor cats
                        and dad's unsold paintings.

i couldn't help

                                                boasting

to my friends

                                        that *we* had

a sunken livingroom and

                                        shag carpet.

dead center

                        in the postage stamp

front yard

                                        sat a lone stump,

ghost of a tree long gone

                                        that neither owner nor we

could uproot

                                        if our sorry lives

depended on it.

                        the backyard;
                a huge squashed polygon
                which did double duty

as our right neighbor's front
lot, consisted entirely of
constructer's clay
mixed with misbegotten moss and
weed spores.

nevertheless

        mom wanted

to grow veggies so

        our cross-street neighbor

came over with

        a truckload of

horse crap and a

        cranky rototiller.

and dad and I,

        armed with

shovel, hoe, and rake,

        sculpted a

prizewinning

        garden that

served us

        seven full

seasons with

        a cornucopia of

let me see

        if i can remember...

corn, tomatoes
zucchini, snap beans, zucchini, watermelon,
zucchini, beets, swiss chard, zucchini, carrots
zucchini, spinach, zucchini, zucchini, zucchini
bread
        which we delivered like a smalltown bakery
to all twenty-seven neighbors free of charge.
        mom purchased hordes of ball jars so we
canned
        tomatoes for sauce,
cukes for bread-and-butter pickles,
        watermelon rind for pickles and relish.
what a glorious time in our lives!

ROMANCE ON ROUTE TWENTY-EIGHT
OCT 30 1985

After one of those dirty drab days,
when three hours hard labor
felt more like thirty,
I slogged down Nickerson Way
towards Bleitz Funeral Parlor,
and crossed Fremont's bridge
to stand weary, wobbly watch
for Number Twenty-Eight.

—

I sported a pair
of shiny-kneed corduroy breeches
and a terry-cloth shirt,
equipped with matching holes in each underarm.
My tennis-clad feet;
sorrily soaked with dishroom-floor floodwater.
My hair;
an unkempt, mopsy-flopped banner
of frighteningly low self-esteem.

—

There I stood;
catty-corner
from the plaster-faced Interurban throng,
facing the faded skeleton
of a tormented tavern,
under the umbrella
of a Greek dinner house
where Feta and Pita made nightly appearances.

A moist gray sky, wanting to make rain,
kept changing its mind
like an indecisive Christmas shopper.
Fall,
doing the forty-yard dash through Boeing's land,
was just getting ready to hand off her baton
to an early winter.
I was headed homeward,
Metro's routine path etched permanently
upon the wetware of my world-warped mind;
only Martin Luther's bio in paperback
was to stand between me and seated sleep.
Maybe walking a mile or three would revive me;
yet I could not-- or would not-- recant my tired feet,
and so, like Brother Martin,
there I stood!...
waiting...
—

Somewhere near where Leary Way
mates with Eighth Northwest,
she got on!
Angel...faerie sprite...soul of my dreams...she!!!
The onboard atmosphere
now rocked and reeled with dangerous delight;
I no longer needed Wittenberg's dog-eared testimony
to guard me from slumber!
—

She took a seat, straight across from me,
next to some talkative lady with angry red hair.
With store-bought bags between their feet,
they conversed in tones of relaxed confidentiality;

they might have been next-door neighbors, or perhaps
they'd had an old boyfriend in common.

—

There she sat;
a fashion study in tea-rose and eggshell.
A full overcoat
draped itself demurely around small sweet shoulders,
offering only the briefest glimpse
of her subtly slender waist.
I took kindly to her gently creased nylon slacks
and wondered at her wistful white sneakers.
Her dim-blonde hair was so strikingly lovely
for all its shoulder-length uncertainty.
Her eyes spoke volumes of timeless treasure;
complex layers of Celtic mystery lay deep within.

—

How her shyly serene smile
flooded my sullen, shame-soaked soul
with gracious sunlight!
How her posture told a tale
of complacently nervous joy,
just waiting to be boldly broadcast as gospel
to a cynical world.
She looked an under-fed waif,
but carried herself like an uplanded princess.
I could taste the winsome religion hidden within
her childlike aura.
And yet,
never a word between us,
no looks exchanged.

There was no need;
double-headed vectors of love
were doing all the talking for us!

—

Ballard gave way to Broadmore,
as Eighth turned to Third
then back to Eighth again.
A setting sun peeked out shyly once or twice.
Clouds pregnant with rain
held their wet breaths to see
whether two awkward half-souls
would become one that Wednesday afternoon.

—

The final leg of route Twenty-Eight
drew us up a grassy, green mini-canyon
spoilt by a multitude of decrepit houses,
presenting an uneasy contrast
with the golfed meadows of The Highlands,
gated villa for the moneyed benefactors of Seattle.

—

145th caught up with Greenwood;
my stop...her's too!

—

I followed her off the bus
at an ecstatically reverent distance.
At a bus shelter cross-street,
she sat down next to her shopping burdens
patiently awaiting the next carrier.
My steps became deliberate molasses
as I drew near her royal bench.
Suddenly, as I passed before her kiosked shrine,

she called out a free and friendly greeting to me
in a voice like innocent honey.
I reflected her hello back to her gentle ears
as my hopeful heart boarded
a one-way shuttle to purple-sky heaven.

—

Oh, how I desperately desired
to stop and chat about the weather...
and whether or not
we could be more than anonymous ships
passing upon the cold seas of society.
But my arrogant legs had other plans;
I was carried rapidly past her to keep
a pressing engagement with an empty house!

—

I spent the bored remainder of that lonely evening
burning stale cardboard in a forlorn fireplace.
Every song on the radio threw kindling embers
upon noble dreams about the glorious maiden
I'd nearly snatched from flames of loneliness.
The sky wept raging tears of frustration
all through that night!

—

Next afternoon at three,
I went forth to seek an audience with her
at yesterday's bus stop.
But my bonny Bitter Lake princess
had abdicated her spritely throne,
returning only to be cast
in matinee daydreams and rarefied night visions.
The autumn-drab sky no longer felt my pain.

Disaster!

On October 15, 1985, we birthed a new corporation, TOBI, Inc. (Transfer Operations by Image), named after a beloved orange tabby cat we adopted and lost to a series of accidents. TOBI was formed to hold the copyrighted material for IAMOT and the Vallian Coordinates. Of note: the only business trappings that Larry liked better than corporations were initials that he then found words to fit; more of these will be apparent as we go along.

Then, on October 16, 1985, a fire destroyed my recently decorated office at 1301 Mills St. # 4. Larry was a stickler for safety and insurance, and I'm certainly glad he was; we had a smoke alarm in the upstairs hall outside my office and excellent renters' insurance.

It was about 9:00 in the morning—we had been up late that night, which was usual for us—when we heard the smoke alarm go off. I ran to look in the direction of the smoke and saw, outside my west window, flames scurrying up the old tree that stood there. Larry called 911 and urged me outside; I grabbed a robe and the cat. Just as we were out the door, a fire engine drove up—Larry said it was like an old Mack Senet comedy routine; we were later told they had been driving by and saw the flames. Paddywach took off, and after Larry had roused the neighbor next to us (we weren't the only late sleepers!), we stood and watched. I was devastated—my beautiful room—what had I done to deserve this?

Due to the fast action of the firemen, the fire was confined to my room, the wall by the stairs, and the roof of our apartment and #5's. The landlady also had good insurance. We were able to get back in to get clothing, personal items, wallets, purses, oh, and yes, the tickets we had purchased for the Hearst Castle Tour, which amazingly had been spared. But the smell of smoke was awful, so we spent the next few days in motels trying to hook up with our insurance adjuster. When we went back to check the damage, we saw that the fire had done most of the damage to the apartment structure. However, all of my books and a large pile of student papers, housed in that west end, were burned, and the water destroyed my electronics, desk, futon, and what the water didn't get, the smoke did. My Osborn computer had a meniscus!

The insurance agent was thorough: Allstate paid almost $7200 for books, equipment, office furniture, and the cleaning of all of our clothing and the apartment, including painting. And they also paid for six weeks of motels and eating out while cleaning and repair were ongoing. However, because of Paddywach and the need to find some normality, we moved back in as soon as the apartment was habitable; we lived with workman as they repaired the structure of my office. In the meantime, since we had the tickets, we went to Cambria and joined our friends Kathy and Bill to tour Hearst Castle. I don't think we were very good company.

Sometime in late November, Larry purchased our first Apple computer—the SE, I think—with some of that insurance money. That was the beginning of our life-long love of Apples and Macs and ... the pattern of Larry getting the new computer and handing down the old one to me, which was OK with me. Because I had begun my doctorate program that spring and had papers to write, I inherited the "big refrigerator" TRS 8008 computer. I was so intimidated by it that I would read my papers to Larry and he would type them in. At some point, though, I got my courage up and conquered the beast! And Larry was able to go back to work on his geometry.

By the way, in September, Apple Computer, Inc sued Steve Jobs, its former chairman, to keep him from using Apple technology in his new company ("Jobs charged with 'nefarious scheme'" *Times Tribune*, 9/24/85). It was to this company, Next, Inc., that Larry later sent a package of material on the Vallian Coordinates.

I summed up the year with the following:

December 12, 1985
  Just a quick Christmas note to our friends: we've had quite a year!
  Larry launched the Vallian Coordinate System (patent pending), and TOBI Corporation has been formed to get it (VCS) to the software market.
  Jill started college and has declared herself a speech pathology major; she wants to work with deaf children.
  Sharon started her doctorate in education and is struggling to balance all the hats. The BOOK (IAMOT) is awaiting her editorial skills, in her spare time!

She is also on "The Road Less Traveled" and "The Way of the Peaceful Warrior."

Eric took a leave from his advanced mathematics at U of W and is working and living and writing poetry in Seattle.

Paddy has had an uneventful year—she's 12 years old now, but Tobi (the new kid on the block, a 2 year old orange tabby) has had several learning experiences during his first year as a Wahl. First, he learned that you don't walk up to a Doberman and say "Hello," and, second, that cars are bigger and faster than cats! His fractured pelvis has healed well, and he never lost his smile.

To put the proverbial icing on the Wahl Family cake, we moved to a larger apartment in September and one month later were purified by a fire that wiped out Sharon's new home office, along with newly-acquired furniture, computer, mucho books, and student papers. Our lives were displaced for over a month—motels are hell! But, here we are, ready for Christmas, healthy, happy, and a whole lot wiser.

Hope you have a great '86.

Love from us all ...

Musing by Sharon: Humor

He is winding up the watch of his wit;
By and by it will strike.
—*William Shakespeare*

A Risible Life

Larry made life beautiful for me with his humor. He helped me see the unusual, the amusing vignettes that are present in everyone's prosaic lives, those vignettes that can pass by unnoticed if there are no available receptor sites, if there is nothing to extract the humor preserved within. Larry shared that talent and, as a result, unearthed my suppressed, hidden appreciation of the absurd. I will always be grateful for that gift.

One example of these unexpected, amusing events happened on an icy Portland morning. As we were slowly inching our car toward downtown, we observed a professionally dressed woman running, unsuccessfully, after her bus. She slipped on the icy sidewalk, threw her briefcase underneath her bottom, and as she was sliding down the street, nonplussed, she consulted a schedule, presumably planning to catch the next bus. No time-waster her! (You had to be there).

Another time, we were driving behind a fire engine going code 3—speeding with sirens squawking. The young fireman on the back was vigorously carrying out his assigned job—managing the wheel. Suddenly, sighting a pretty miss on the sidewalk, he interrupted his energetic mission and tendered a tiny wave toward the girl, then instantly resumed his importantly serious assignment. The brief wave, accompanied by a silly grin, was so incongruous and happened so fast, I might have missed it had Larry not trained me in the art of split-second, absurdity observing. We relived those frequent happenings many times, always enjoying the shared pleasure and humor.

Larry loved to mimic special characters from comic books or from his assessment of the comedy of life. My favorite was his Irish leprechaun —this never failed to elicit a giggle, each time he launched that persona. He had some other disreputable representations that would not qualify as PC, and so will remain unmentioned.

Eric inherited Larry's punster creativity. When they got together, they would bat puns back and forth as if they were playing volleyball; they could go on for indefinite periods of time without either of them dropping that ball! Jill would often chime in, but since my mind doesn't work that way, I would just sit by and listen with wonder—how do they do that?

But a discussion of my family's humorous escapades is not complete without "The Parable of the Elephant." See what you think.

The Elephant

I'm not exactly sure when I told him how best to manage my "snits," but it was to be a foundation upon which we were able to progress in our life together. From the beginning, Larry could make me laugh. So, some time into our marriage, I told him, "If you want to get me out of a bad mood or change the direction of our fights (we had many throughout the years), just use humor—I find that hard to resist."

And so he has. Sometimes they are belly-laugh moments, sometimes they are just plain silly, but they are nearly always effective. I would like to share one such humorous event and the resultant ritual that has maintained us through many arduous times.

In 1986, our life had been especially harsh: a beloved kitty had tragically died; Larry had lost a long time friend and his attempts to get others involved with his new geometry system had stalled; and we had a fire in our home that disrupted our lives. Deciding that a change of scenery might provide some relief, we decided to go visit the San Francisco Zoo.

As we walked the various paths, heard the howler monkeys, and viewed the exotic birds and shy koalas, we suddenly came upon a huge enclave containing one large elephant. And as we stood observing his grandeur, he abruptly decided to entertain us—he began to empty his bladder. As we stood watching in amazement, this act of micturation continued for an inordinate period of time. Did we mention the elephant was standing on a large flat rock? We could not contain ourselves: we began to double over with laughter. Barely able to speak, Larry quipped, "Look at that. He is peeing buckets full, he is peeing barrels full, he is peeing… Volkswagens full!"

And with that, everything came into proper perspective: we had our sense of humor back and a line from a favorite poem came to mind. "And whether or not it is clear to you, no doubt the universe is unfolding as it should." (Ehrmann., 1927, pp 33-4). We were going to be just fine.

When we got home, Larry proffered the following that has become a ritual for invoking our senses of humor whenever we get too gloomy about life:

"Elephants have eyelashes—put your thumbs on your eyebrows and wiggle your fingers; elephants have ears—put your thumbs in your ears and using your whole body, wag your hands back and forth; elephants have trunks—grab your nose with thumb and finger of one hand and reach over and grab the extended hand of your partner, sway your attached arms back and forth."

The preceding can be implemented with one other person or in a group. We used to embarrass our children by doing it in public places like restaurants—but we always got smiles from other patrons, if not from our children!

This exercise is guaranteed to get a smile from everyone. It is especially fun when done in a group and people look around at others looking silly and enjoy the moment.

So, we invite you, the reader, to become a member of the Society of Peeing Elephants (SOPE). Send us an email (scwahl@earthlink.net put "elephant" in the subject line) with your desire to join, and we'll send you an official membership certificate. And be sure to teach it to your friends and family.

The following illustration demonstrates how to "Do The Elephant"!

occasionally

When Things ⋀ get too serious

DO THE ELEPHANT

1st. Stop what you are doing.
2nd. Put your hands to your head and do one of the two following exercises

EX.-1

WITH THE TOP OF YOUR WRISTS PRESSED AGAINST YOUR EYEBROWS, WAGGLE YOUR FINGERS IN A PROVACATIVE WAY, ALL THE WHILE IMAGINING THEM TO BE EYE-LASHES.

EX.-2

STICK YOUR THUMBS IN YOUR EARS AND WAGGLE THE FINGERS WITH GREAT EXPRESSION. REMEMBER THAT THERE IS NO NEED FOR SYMMETRY

Now, don't you feel a whole lot better ?!!!

174

Musing 107 by Larry

All Soul's Eve 10/31/84

Oh God! I could be bounded in a nutshell and count myself
a king of infinite space, were it not that I have bad dreams!
—*Shakespeare, from Hamlet*

My favorite day of the year—ugh, sob, gasp, groan! If after the twelve o'clock witching hour, I still find myself among the living, I will live for at least another twenty years.

We had a lovely dinner before the rush at The Good Earth and are now at the church. Sherry and Jill are in the main auditorium with many other people who are members of the choir. Jill is dressed in her angel costume, and Sherry is wearing a very attractive, bright orange dress. Someone is playing the piano, just kind of softly, easily sliding around on melodic chord sequences. Now there is a change in the background noise indicating that the choir director is getting ready to get the troops going in some particular direction.

Before the evening is over, I should have some idea what the Christmas program is going to sound like. I find myself really looking forward to this Christmas. We are driving up the coast to Oregon, spending a couple of days at Newport where I will be doing some research on the bridge, and from there, on up to Long Beach. We will stay a couple of days, and then go on to Seattle to visit our friends. I have a feeling the girls will have jumped up in growth in the last two years. The passing years have taken on a train-like trance state in which more and more events seem to be packed into smaller and smaller time units. This time contraction is all right with me now that I am almost convinced I will become an old man.

I began to see, dimly but tangibly, a future filled with writing—writing based on remembering the old things that have happened to me, yet leaving wide-open spaces for the present. I find myself guarding time as never before. It is becoming real that as time races by, I will find more and more decisions already made for me, and yet, these decisions come about in me and through me, only as a result of all the millions of decisions that proceeded from the time "before I was" and stretch in an unbroken parade down to this present heartbeat.

People have always existed for me. These people have always been "real and alive," but until a very few years ago, not a single one of these people was as close to me as a distant star. Those who were closest were big giant mechanical dolls: they looked real, they sounded real, but they were marvelously mechanical. They had spells when they pretended to love; they had times when they pretended to hate. They drank, laughed, worked, cried, fell down and were hurt, but somehow I knew that, at some predetermined time, whatever or whoever was operating them would grow tired or busy or bored and would leave.

I would see, as indeed I often have seen, a pretty young thing stop in mid-sentence with all animation leaving her face, while she showed only a blank, manikin stare. Others seemed not to notice these periods of nothingness, or if they did, they let them pass unmentioned. From this I came at last to realize the manikin's point of view: for very long periods of time, they were alive and real, but for certain, momentary, transient periods, they simply CEASED.

From the first moment I saw this behavior, I was drawn to those strange, silent sounds. I worked with my mind imagining these little cracks in reality, much as a crazed prisoner might dig frantically at the tiny chinks in huge, cold stones with a pitifully bent and dull spoon. Beyond the fortress (jail), if only the opening could be widened, there would be different air, different land—someplace free and open. The *reality* of the stones would become more and more bearable because the hole was gradually getting larger. Soon—sooner than I had dared to believe—I was able to pass through the hole into a vast opening, and the prison disappeared.

At first I ran. Then, finally convinced that no one sought to catch or stop me, I slowed, drinking in great drafts of pure, free air. I was free, alone, ecstatic, and complete. Then there would be a sudden clap of thunder, and I would be back in that cell—the once huge hole, just a miniscule chink. My life would again be crowded with fellow prisoners, who alternately laughed, loved, cried, and periodically stopped completely—silent and cold—as if the very life had oozed out of them.

My fellow prisoners did not seem to see the chink in the wall, did not seem serious about escaping. As for me, I had to know "what lay beyond and even beyond, beyond!"

Years passed before I realized that I had never dug a hole in that massive wall; instead, I had become able to instantly shrink small enough to pass through. I learned this with a shock as one day, while passing through, I turned to look at my fellow prisoners and noted with amazement that one of the dull-eyed, transfixed manikins was obviously … me. After that, the hole was always available: I could leave any time I wished.

I flew on the winds, I sang with the birds, I stalked and was stalked, I killed and was killed, I loved and was loved, and all the while the manikin remained in the great, grey prison on the brow of the hill that I had named Life.

And now, as the years hurry by, I can no longer believe it is a prison for indeed it had never held me. I think of it now as a castle. It may be a castle, containing the thoughts of a prisoner, or it may be a prison containing the thoughts of a prince. In any case, since I cannot conceive of it being both simultaneously, I must consider it neither! As I spend most of my time some distance from it, I have come to believe that it is really only a stage for the manikins. There must be a stage and curtains, with scrim and flats to hide the strings and paraphernalia that move the manikins. But more than that. Of late, I have come to believe that in some time or in some place, I created it all: prison, castle, stage, manikins … all. But how can that be? I do not know.

Lately, on my walks far from the "stage," I have found myself passing a large rock with the most wonderful structure and texture. And as I looked at it more closely, it seems I have discovered a kind of time hole in the lower side, not really a hole—you know, something finer that that—a sort of chink …

LXV

Chapter 9

What Do Patent Attorney, China, and Leonardo daVinci Have in Common?

A man with a new idea is a crank until it succeeds.
—*Mark Twain*

Patent Attorney

In a previous chapter, I mentioned Larry's feelings about the patent attorney experience he had in Portland with the Ellipse-Ease, but those did not seem to deter him when he was thinking about patenting the Vallian Coordinates. Thus, in February of 1986, he paid a prominent local attorney a retainer of $250.00; at the end of March, the attorney credited the payment, indicating that he was awaiting further disclosures from Larry. Larry had originally sent the attorney a letter with a description of the coordinates, including many drawings. It seemed to me that Larry expressed his ideas better in drawings than he did in descriptive words, but not all people have Larry's spatial intelligence (Gardner, 1985) and are not able to see abstract objects as clearly as he does. I have not located any copies of the materials he sent to the attorney Mr. Rock, but I expect that they are much of what he included in his 1990 disclosure document (DDA).

Larry didn't immediately follow up with "more disclosures" for Mr. Rock. In fact, it was several years. During that time, we had a family emergency (my dad) that took up a lot of time, my doctoral program, and, best of all, our trip to China.

China

The Statewide Nursing program (SNP) had an arrangement with the Nurses' Association of Mainland China, whereas a selected group of 20 Chinese associate degree nurses would come to California to take the general education and some of the nursing courses required for the baccalaureate degree (BSN), but then would return to the hospital in Nanjing China for their community health, research, statistics, and senior experience. During the Cultural Revolution, because the Red Guard had eliminated most of the university professors—many became farmers and hard laborers—the Chinese universities were rebuilding a cadre of qualified teachers. The nurses were to eventually achieve a master's degree in nursing so that they could educate the next generation of BSN students.

The regional directors of SNP—of which I was one—were offered the opportunity to teach the classes in China. Since I was also half time for San Jose State, I had to select a date that would not disrupt my classes at SJSU. That time was March 30th to May 1st. Unfortunately for me, the content to be taught that corresponded to that time slot was Statistics! I had taken a lot of math classes in Portland when I was preparing for a doctorate program, including statistics (three times), but I still had just a vague, hazy notion of how statistics worked—And I was to teach those unfortunate Chinese students statistics??? Fortunately for me, and certainly for them, one of the media experts had put together three very lucid workbooks to be used in the class. Now all I needed to do was make the content real, i.e., real life examples. Because there has always lurked a storyteller in my being, I had a great time making up scenarios that illustrated the content and that also could be used as testing material; one had something to do with men, beer, and blood pressure. However, I was always only one chapter ahead of my students. But I had my storyteller husband with me to provide more stories and to help me understand what I was teaching.

I am not the adventurous one in this family: Larry is. So the thought of going to a foreign country, especially a Communist one, was extremely unnerving for me, while Larry was drooling at the thought. Fortunately, I was able to make an arrangement with SNP that, instead of "combat pay," they would pay for Larry to go, including accommodations—but not the wet bar! Because Larry was with me, instead of living in the hospital dorm, we were housed in Nanjing's luxury hotel and transported by our "handlers" to and from the hospital classrooms. On Saturdays, they would take us wherever we wanted to visit, but Sundays we were on our own.

One of the trips we took on Saturday was to the Buddhist Monastery in the mountains, to observe the in-training monks at prayer amid the visitor chaos. A sad note: during the cultural revolution of the 1970s, the Red Guard had decapitated all of the Buddhist statues on the campus and had set up the ubiquitous orange soda stands for the curious Chinese visitors.

We also went to Wuxi to see the silk factories and—not an expected part of the trip—experienced the citizens' fear as we were "held captive" by some very large Chinese militia until the reason for our bus trip was established as "innocent." Another time we wanted to see Confucius's temple, but were put off about its availability; finally our guide admitted with embarrassment that it was now a shopping center!

I took a lot of photos. I loved seeing the geese in the back of the bike-carts, even though I was sad that they were headed to market and they joyously didn't know it. On the Wuxi trip, I was asked not to take photos of the passing scenery. What they did not want me to record was the utter poverty of the living conditions for the people in the countryside. What I saw were houses— shacks really—where I could see from the front door through the back door because there *were no doors* and no floors, just dirt. But what I also saw were seemingly happy groups of people brushing their teeth in the "front yard" and sharing food from a common pot cooking on outside fires.

Larry mentions the lack of cars in his "newsletter," but what he didn't expound on was how bad the drivers were. Because the roads were essentially bike lanes, the cars had to negotiate their way around the plethora of bikes, as well as pedestrians. So when in town, the cars crept, but once out of the city, they made up for lost time, barely missing a bike-cart full of geese or a stalled truck. For many years after that trip, whenever we saw a slow, erratic car in the fast lane on the freeway, we would say, in unison and in non-PC, "new Chinese driver!"

On our Sundays, Larry and I explored the area near our hotel, often causing people to fall off their bicycles trying to get a look at us: few Chinese in Nanjing had even seen a blond women and a tall, husky man in a safari jacket. I have pictures of us where you couldn't miss us among the masses of black hair! One young man thought I was as beautiful as Marilyn Monroe—if only!!! Often young men would approach us and ask to speak English with us; some even insisted on buying us a meal, but others thought we were rich Americans and wanted us to sponsor them in the United States. When we went to buy things (we never did find a good bottle of wine, just the "diesel fuel" they drank), we had no idea what their coins represented in money, so we would just hold out a handful, and they would take what was needed; I don't believe we were ever cheated.

The students were wonderful, and I loved every one of them. I spoke no Chinese; they were fluent in English, thank goodness. I learned that many made great sacrifices to come to the program, leaving home and family for the time required to get their degrees—a couple of years, I think. One woman, who lived over a thousand miles to the west, had left a weeks-old baby with her mother; she wouldn't see him again until the program was completed. Because we were there for our 27th wedding anniversary on April 10th, they insisted on giving us a party; they wanted to hear our love story! At their request, I even gave a lecture to the whole hospital staff—through a translator. That was some experience, especially since I'm not comfortable talking to large groups, even when I know what I've said!

The students weren't the only ones who liked parties. Since we were their guests, the president of the hospital—a general in the military—and the director of nursing gave us several dinners. The only problem was they liked to drink and to toast frequently, using their "diesel fuel" liquor. I think now it must have been Sake, but it curled my toes even to smell it! Apparently the purpose of the many toasts was to "drink the guests under the table!" I quietly refused more than a sip, even when challenged by my nursing counterpart, saying that I would let Larry do the drinking for me. And boy, did he! I have a vivid memory of the general, with all his metals blazing, gently sliding under the table as he "sloshingly" said to Larry, "You're incredible!"

Larry and Sharon at our 27th Wedding Anniversary Party
Given by the Chinese Students

On our last day of class, I noted that my usually very attentive students (I was introducing their next class—the research process) were very restless, not really listening to me. Finally I said, "OK, what's going on here?"

One of the leaders stood up and quietly said, "Mrs. Wahl, May 6th is Nurses Day, and we want you to teach us an American song we can sing at the celebration." Here she handed me a songbook—in English.

The discipline I'm least qualified to teach, after statistics, is music, specifically how to sing. But I wouldn't disappoint them, so I gave it my best effort. We had no musical instruments; I would have to sing the song to them, in whatever key I happened to pick out—I don't read music that well! So, first I found "Red River Valley," but after a couple of choruses of that, they decided it was too sad. So then I found "Oh Suzanna," and we had a winner. I still have the tape recording of them singing "Oh Suzzie-anna" in perfect pitch. It was a wonderful finish to our time together.

On our way back home, via Beijing, we had planned to walk the "Great Wall," but because the weather had changed so dramatically—from snow in March to humid heat in May—and because we had ingested a little too much polluted water from teeth brushing, we were not feeling at all well, so we missed that once-in-a-lifetime opportunity.

The Class, Larry, Sharon, and Hosts

Larry loved China—the system analyst and engineer went crazy. He asked questions of everyone who understood English and did hand gestures for those who didn't. He even inquired about their sewer system and which color in the river represented raw sewage! I, on the other hand, was so aware that we were representatives of America in a Communist country that I was afraid to say much. Larry didn't stand on convention, and they absolutely adored him. Later he wrote several different pieces on his thoughts and feelings of China. Since I've been describing my experience, I'll now let you hear directly from him. This first piece was written like a newsletter, which I believe he started while we were still there.

A Special China Adventure

Warm-Wise

China—what a special reality is present in this simple five-letter word. In the five weeks my wife and I spent in China—all but two of the days in Nanjing—I was able to monitor the heartbeat of a typical medium-sized city and get, what I believe, was an accurate portrait of these very special people. The people we met in Nanjing were excellent hosts, and the original concepts I held about the difficulties I would have communicating because of my total lack of Chinese language facility were dispelled upon entering our luxury hotel. The Jin Ling: 36 floors with massage center and small dispensary in the basement, immense meeting rooms on the mezzanine, and crowned with a large restaurant, revolving around a bandstand and discotheque. While Sherry, my nurse educator wife, spent her most of her time in the Jin Ling Military Hospital with her 16 Chinese nurses, I literally lived in the hotel.

We arrived about 8 PM on April 1st, having spent one night in Beijing, and deposited our baggage in room 2405. I took note of the well-stocked bar. Then I went down to the main floor where I spotted the "Why Worry Lounge." It turned out to be a large room with a piano bar and a middle-aged Chinese chanteuse, singing along with six or so Chinese businessmen. They had just finished singing a soft, gentle Chinese melody as I sat down and, to my utter surprise, they broke into a chorus of "Old MacDonald Had a Farm" in fairly reasonable English. I was in the act of formulating some sort of thank you for singing in my native tongue, when they took off on "Red River Valley." As the evening progressed, and they continued to intersperse Chinese and American songs, I realized that this was something they did on a regular basis and had nothing to do with my appearance. At 11PM, they promptly closed the bar; I went up to our room where Sherry had been unpacking and organizing her material for class the next day.

That morning I noticed that our huge room windows looked south into the Dijin, or Purple Mountains, guarding or threatening the city as they had done through the hundreds of years Nanjing had been a city

(it was the capital at one time). And they were there through its peril-
ous past with the Japanese invasion of World War II, the long years of
revolution, and most recently the cultural (Red Guard) revolution that
had closed China to the outside world.

After only a short time living with and learning about these people,
we were naïve enough to believe all their troubles were behind them. It
would indicate some kind of super sensitivity on my part if I could tell
you I had been able to foresee their latest political upheaval, wracking
their land from Tiananmen Square to the fertile South; however, our
experiences only showed us the unity and the sharing, caring spirit of
the people we met and observed first hand.

The staff at the hotel spoke excellent English, and from many of the
informal meetings of foreign businessmen and other visitors, I realized
just how powerful the English language is. There is almost no possibility of a Chinese person advancing in any business without the ability to
speak English. In the hotel, I noted German, French, Dutch, Swedish,
Italian, and English businessmen attending meetings and seminars, but by
far the greatest number of foreign business interests were represented
by the Japanese and Australians; however, the United States, Taiwan,
and Hong Kong were also well represented.

From my window on China, I overlooked a central district with thea-
tres, huge office buildings—built and being built—and a large shopping
center: old and new, nestling and surviving side by side as they always
have. It was not unusual, but it was strange to see a workman with a
modern welder working alongside a traditional carpenter using a bow
saw a hundred years old.

In some parts of the city, I could see old sections giving way to new
ones. By observing carefully from my 24th floor perspective, I could see
some sections where bricks were disappearing from a group of buildings being torn down and, over a period of weeks, could watch them
apparently rearranging themselves into the ongoing construction of a
modern building a few blocks away. At night, mystical flashes of blue
lights would illuminate the locations of a hundred night shifts working.

At no time of the day are the ubiquitous bicycles absent. Several multi-lane roads led into the square that housed the hotel complex, and though tens of thousands of bicycles can be seen during the day, there is a smaller, but regular flow at all hours of the night: special bike-carts carrying produce in from the country, materials moving from one spot to another, people going to and from their night jobs, and even a fairly constant, but very light flow of vehicular traffic. Actually there are few, if any private cars in China; as we were guests of the government we were afforded a car and driver.

Off in the distance, I was able to observe a compound, clearly a jail, and closer in was a building that had saffron robes hung from its many rooftop clotheslines, clearly living quarters for Buddhist monks. I could see them doing Tai Chi shortly after dawn on their roof, mirrored by civilian groups doing the same in the park below. Up on the mountainside twinkled the observatory, white and aloof on the dragon's back. Further to the left, blocked from my vision, was the Buddhist Temple, which we had the good fortune to visit when I was able to convince my hosts that I was indeed a Buddhist.

6/22/87

It is almost midnight, and I feel a very real desire to sit down and write. It has been quite a while since I have just let things rise off the top of my mind. I got news today that the Spa has closed down, and it will take $25 dollars a month to maintain a schedule at the swimming pool. I am not sure that is what I want to do this summer.

There were so many things that happened in China that I could probably write at least six articles on the subject. It is true, strictly speaking, that much of it was very personal, yet at the same time, it is a land that is very interesting to Americans. It is, of course, the country with the largest population, and it is bound to involve the wellbeing of many other peoples in the world. I find that the feelings I have for this strange country are varied and deep. Much of what I saw there has a direct relationship to the many parts of my own history. I have told anyone who cared to listen that I was, in fact, Chinese, although there is certainly nothing in my present gene pool that will support this belief. I think the proof positive is the feeling of being completely at home in Nanjing, even though I was limited to talking to people who were able to converse with me in English. I was able to say "please, thank you, hot water, cold water" in Chinese with a modicum of fluency; past that I was in deep water. It turned out that my inability to speak Chinese was not much of a barrier since the people with whom I would wish to speak spoke English. I was amazed to find, for example, that a group of Chinese reporting on the numbers of students who had been sent overseas by the Chinese government on student visas and the various problems that arose (many defected, including two of the original group of students Sherry was teaching!), these reports were all in English, even though all of the people in the discussion were indigenous Chinese.

There is a desire among the educated Chinese to speak English, not because of any innate love for the language, nor any great affinity for English-speaking people, but because after almost 40 years of self-determined isolation, they are suddenly engaged in accepting trade, education, concepts, and mutually desirable goals with other nations of the world. Because air transportation was essentially invented by Americans, and English is the language of air controllers, no matter what part of the world you may be in, English became the "Rosetta Stone" into which all of the diverse languages of the world would be translated. With this caveat, understood by all who would have transactions with the Chinese, English became a transfer language in which all Chinese made it their business to become fluent. For this reason, I was able to overhear business, social, and even political seminars for every foreign group that passed through the Jingling Hotel, where we were staying.

The Chinese are a race of Type A's—they drive that way too. Education is not something in this country that you can take or leave. It is clearly understood by everyone—down to the last man in the street— that there is no way to move up in any job without a good working education. In order to use this information, you must be able to express yourself in fluent English so that you can communicate with all of the peoples of other lands that are interested in doing business in China.

China is supposed to be the classless society, a perfect Marxist state, but people seem to fall into two classes: the people who know they are poor—poor in education, poor in health, poor in experience, poor in future—and those who know they are not. Life being what it is and people being what they are, it is necessary to understand that a poor student from a farmer's family and an inept student from a powerful family will not be considered on the basis of their scholastic aptitude. This was made very clear when I learned the movers and shakers had more than one child.

As you may well know, in China it is a strictly enforced rule that one should only replace himself (emphasis on the him!). In the poorer classes, this is enforced by giving additional wages, better jobs, and nicer living quarters to those with one child. If they have a second child, these are all taken away and punitive considerations are added, such as parents working different 12-hour shifts or even being sent to different provinces. And because of the one child rule, if the pregnancy is a girl, it is often aborted—parents know they need a boy to care for them in their old age. After years of this noxious law, the result was too many men and not enough women. I'm not sure how the Chinese government remedied that problem, but I can guess!

On a trip to Wuxi (pronounced Woo-shee), we were able to see into the farming heart of China. We witnessed grinding poverty, and yet, in Wuxi we ate at a restaurant that was one of many owned by an individual farmer. There are almost as many exceptions as there are rules. The strange thing is that the people, whom you would think most ill-used by these variations, seem to understand and accept them; using trite phrases like, "honoring the rule of the people," even while they are clearly aware that some Chinese are more equal than others.

There is in Nanjing, as in most medium and large cities, building going on at a frantic rate. However, many of these buildings are not going to be used to directly help the people waiting for better and more efficient housing. Many of these buildings will be factories, luxury foreign hotels, and the like; for each one built, there is a large housing complex that is not built. The explanatory message given to the people is that foreign travelers must be lured to China by the knowledge that there will be adequate, substantial services provided for them. And without buildings to house the foreigners, there would be no money to build homes for Chinese families.

It is within the memory of many older Chinese—and some not so old—that while things are tough, they are not starving and they are not being attacked by foreigners, situations that have gone on for eons in Chinese memory. They know the history of rape and pillage, murder and tyranny, not only from the accursed foreign devils, but also from previous centuries of civil disorder: rampant internal uprisings; takeovers by many separate warlords who heaped riches on themselves; and poverty, terror, and death for hapless and hopeless subjects. In this stead, they can now, and just now, begin to see a totally unified China that will be strong, alert, ambitious, and world-class in every meaning of the word.

Home Sweet Home

While we thoroughly enjoyed our sojourn in China, we were glad to be home. I probably will never get used to what happens as you cross time zones (and the international dateline) when you travel thousands of miles. I have a memory of waking up on the airplane at midnight and seeing a blazing sun through the window; it remained with us for the next six or so hours until we landed in San Francisco.

The first thing I was confronted with after we came back to our seemingly spacious apartment (in Chinese standards) was a request—or was it a demand—from the SNP to give a graduation speech to the group of RN students who were graduating that Spring. I'm sure it was an awful speech my jet-lagged brain put forth, but I had complied—did I have a choice after being given the experience we had just come home from?

My bleary public appearance was tame compared to what Larry went through. The night after we got home, he became so dizzy and nauseated that I finally took him over to Stanford ER. We were there half the night as they gave him all sorts of tests, but found nothing too out of line. With some anti-nausea medicine, we went back home with a promise to see a neurologist the next day. The neurologist did the standard neuro checks as well as a CT scan, but also found no pathology. A few days later, Larry woke up with the same vertigo, nausea, and visual anomalies, so this time we went to see Dr. Miller. As it happened, the good doctor had just been to a conference on headaches. Given Larry's symptoms, plus the information that we had just gotten back from a five-week, intensive excursion, Dr. Miller (we called him Craig by now) diagnosed Larry with "silent migraine." Larry had suffered intermittently from migraine headaches from the time of high school and through several years of our marriage. Apparently, when "migrainers" get older, they no longer have the pain, but continue to get the visual effects as well as nausea and vomiting, especially in the relaxation period after a stressful event. So, this time, Larry went home with special medication (ergotamine or Cafergot), relieved that he didn't have a brain tumor or stroke. Craig to the rescue, once again!

Leonardo Arising

For the next couple of years, Larry worked on multiple projects, ranging from identifying applications of the Vallian Coordinates to drawing figures and faces in various modes, as well as writing the book IAMOT, carving sculptures of his IAMOT characters, and fiddling with all sorts of electrical projects (I don't have any idea!). Throwing in essays and capturing events from his childhood in writing, he qualified as the energizer bunny. He didn't even get back to Sam Rock (the patent attorney) until 1990.

Larry had such a potent, potential product in the Vallian Coordinates, so why did he keep finding different ways of describing it with different names each time, and why was he doing all those other projects? If you had read Larry's previous books, especially the second one called "The Learner," (Wahl, 2012), you would be aware of all the different jobs he was drawn into, but he was always learning something new and expanding his knowledge of whatever came his way; he had many pots boiling on his stove. I found something in a book that makes me think I know why he scattered himself about so.

In *Learning from Leonardo*, Fritjof Capra (2013) notes that Leonardo da Vinci had many ideas to explore and many things to draw and build, and that he wanted his finished products to be perfect. For that reason, Leonardo (and Larry) didn't finish many of his projects. Capra goes on to describe the genius of Leonardo da Vinci based on "a set of mental attributes, that, in addition to exceptional talent in a given field, seem to be distinctive signs of genius" (as listed by Lykken, 1998, p. 2-8): "relentless curiosity, intellectual fearlessness, capacity for intense concentration, attention to detail, holistic memory, commitment to the empirical method, and pervasive systemic thinking."

Capra also observed that Leonardo never published, and there was no evidence of contact with other notables of his time, though he read widely in scholarly manuscripts and books and undoubtedly discussed his ideas with associates. Only his notebooks, which he attempted to hide because the all powerful, 15th century church would consider his findings heretical, had an accumulation of his thinking and discoveries. And they were not appreciated by scientists until the 18th century. Capra notes, "like modern scientists, Leonardo was always ready to revise his models when he felt that new observations or insights required him to do so. In his art as in his science, he always seemed to be more interested in the process of exploration rather than in the completed work or final results." (p. 7). Capra inferred that, because of Leonardo's systemic thinking, he needed to work on many projects simultaneously to see the connectedness.

As Capra has indicated, Leonardo did not publish, a characteristic Larry might have mirrored. Larry was more than content to investigate the mysteries of his tesseract and to tell anyone who would listen about his geometry; the only publication he initiated, and thank god for that, was his patent. The marvelous stories of his bizarre life would never have been written—told, but not written—if I had not taken on the project of corralling his many pieces of paper and computer disks into a coherent whole. Leonardo may have had an excuse for not publishing, but what was Larry's? I pushed him to publish because I sincerely believed his story needed to be told and, most importantly, because he was here to correct that Leonardo failing *this* lifetime. Foolish idea, perhaps, but his work speaks for itself!

Lykken (1998) evaluates the various theories of the origin of genius, essentially the old nature vs. nurture (including extreme environments) argument, but he sums it up by saying, "The answer is [whether or not genius is passed on in the genes], I think, that genius consists of unique configurations of attributes that cannot be transmitted in half-helpings." (p.30)

Larry frequently said that he had been Leonardo in a previously life, although to him that was no big deal because he obviously had to come back to do a lot of things over, correcting his Leonardo mistakes! Recently I found a part of a letter Larry had written, probably in the early 80s and probably to our son, in which he offers comparisons between Leonardo and himself, and not very complimentary ones.

On the face of it, it might be a little hard to see my shotgun-totting, pistol-lugging, assassination cruises as being the persona that da Vinci would have been comfortable with, but that isn't as simple as it sounds. Leonardo was a real hard case; I'm not overjoyed with his character. He was a deeply troubled and unhappy man, and I don't find it difficult to see my transition from CIA to art when, after all, Leonardo built public projects and then devised military canons and other war-going equipment. He lived in a time when existence and death were pretty much in evidence as unequal partners in the game called Life. There were wars, rumors of wars, assassinations, oppression, starvation, disease, poverty, and pointless brutality. This was, of course, the time of the Borga—not the nicest people you might want to meet.

Leonardo was a bastard, literally. That was what marked him at the deepest level, that hurt him, and it is the same characteristic that marks me. I think where I am right now is making peace with all those bastard parts of myself and with all those bastard parts of Leonardo da Vinci.

There has never been a time in my life when I have been impressed with money, power, or position; if I didn't like something, it was not unusual for me to walk into the office of the high muckety-muck and tell them. Of course I got my ears pinned back for my efforts, more than a few times, but that never seemed to "learn" me: I never changed my attitude of being my own man. But that is a joke at a Cosmic level because it is obvious that "no man is an island."

Leonardo made a pretty good attempt at being that kind of an island. He was thoroughly loved by those who saw him at a distance, who experienced his talent and skill; they assumed a character that would match, in attitude and civility, the range of his gifts. What they didn't know, and what, to his sorrow, he did know was that the two do not go hand in hand. You can write soft peaceful material, draw soft peaceful drawings, and paint soft peaceful paintings and yet be utterly tortured and savage. One of the mysteries of life to me is the number of famous, accomplished men who, upon examination, prove to be pretty despicable. They have marvelous talent. In this sense, talent is power: all power corrupts and absolute power corrupts absolutely (to coin a phrase). I think this was probably Leonardo's condition and position in life. If he had met his commitments as they came up—he would have been famous in any case—he also would have been useful. As it was, he buried everything he did in the Codex, which was not interpreted for hundreds of years, and his inventions weren't utilized for centuries. He was a manifestation of the parable of the talents.

Larry undoubtedly continued to pursue these thoughts, but that was the end of the available portion of the letter.

On a more positive note: to support his–and my–thesis, I will take each of Capra's (2013) examples of Leonardo's genius and will compare them to Larry's genius. I strongly encourage the reader to read Capra's wonderful book; I don't do it justice here.

1. Relentless Curiosity and Intellectual Fearlessness.

Capra documents Leonardo's "intense curiosity and enthusiasm for discovery and understanding." (p. 2) He notes that Leonardo found something new to discover and explore everywhere in his life and environment, that he involved himself in many natural occurrences and was not afraid to try out new disciplines. Leonardo would challenge accepted wisdom, especially that which had religious overtones, and would labor until he found evidence to prove his theorem.

Like Leonardo, Larry was interested in everything he saw or heard and always sought out the "why" of phenomena. He seldom accepted opinions without some sort of expert verification, principally from several reliable sources. He talked about his fascination with the ivy that grew on our patio: what fueled its tenacity (which he identified with); how did it know where to grow and how to attach to fences, brick walls, even houses; what did it hide in its density; besides man, what was its natural predator—if it had any; and so on. He attached similar questions and observations to the many things that passed through his daily attention. Larry's intellectual fearlessness was manifested as he went up against the mathematical brains of Silicon Valley, trying to prove to them that $1 = \sqrt{2} = \frac{1}{2} \sqrt{3}$, the basis for his innovative geometry. He continued to promote this even though he was "shot down" by every mathematician he encountered. As Lykken (1998) noted, "[Edison, Feynman, Land, and Newton] ... were able to take seriously hypotheses that others had thought implausible (or had not thought about at all)." (p. 34)

2. Intense Concentration and Attention to Detail.

Capra points out that Leonardo had extreme patience and could wait until an idea or fact would reveal itself. He would work on several projects simultaneously, putting a brush stroke here or a nature sketch there, sometime leaving long periods of time between activity on individual projects. Leonardo demonstrated attention to detail in his human body drawings and scientific discoveries and anomalies.

Larry left behind thousands of drawings of faces, human bodies, geometric figures, machines of many sorts, ships, and even abstract shapes, all done in slavish detail. He drew hundreds of eloquent illustrations of his geometric processes. Many of his paintings and drawings were not signed because "they were not finished." To my consumer mind, they looked very finished, indeed! Weekend after weekend, we would sit in Starbucks in silence, silence because he was so intensely concentrating on his sketches or drawings. (If he thought I did not like his drawings or his projects, it was because when he was working on them, I ceased to exist!) And, while at this stage of the book you don't have the information, by the time you finish it, you will realize that he persisted in his art and his geometry, intent on improving them until the end of his life, over 50 years of work, but for him, pleasure.

Lykken (1998) saw mental energy (and perhaps motivation) as an important factor, with the person so endowed able to work many hours, even days, not being aware of the time going by or the needs of the body. He stated that "... there can be no doubt that some people have more of this resource than others." (p. 35). In Chapter 2, it was discussed how Larry poured a cup of hot coffee and, on the next sip, noted it was ice cold: he had painted all night without knowing it. Also, we almost didn't get together because we had a dinner date that he showed up for ... two days late; he had been painting and forgot the time!

3. Holistic Memory.

Leonardo apparently had the ability to keep in his mind huge amounts of information that he committed to memory, acquired from many sources: direct observation and reading scholarly books and documents. He used this memory to find the interconnectedness of things. He often worked for days on paintings, without eating and drinking.

Larry also acquired and retained everything he read, saw, heard, watched on TV. He was a font of information that he used in his work and, often, in educating me—I know, I have the doctorate degree, but Larry is many times better educated across the board, all self-directed. His library consisted of several hundred books (or as many as we could pack in our offices and home) of philosophy, psychology, science, mysticism, mathematics, geometry, art, drawing, and military topics, to name a few; the only novels Larry read were the detective stories we read together. For his monograph, *The Elephant in the Room* (2011), he listed 21 books in his references and bibliography, including such names as Brian Green, Roger Penrose, Buckminster Fuller, Olive Whicher, Lawrence Susskind.

Like Leonardo, Larry also would work on the geometry and painting over many hours and days, often alternating between several different projects, including his novel and autobiography. He could lay aside projects, sometimes for many months, and then resume them as if he had never "been away." He did that in his storytelling as well, wandering into irrelevant topics, but always eventually got back to his original point. And regarding his memory: as his editor, I would occasionally change a word or phrase because I didn't think it was what he meant. Forget that! He would invariably say, "That word you changed is better," or "No, I meant something else." He knew every word he wrote, even material he had written years before. The only thing he couldn't remember was where to put the commas! I don't know if this is memory or systems thinking, or both, but Larry had this amazing capacity to "mock-up," as he called it, several pictures or geometric models in his mind and manipulate them inside his head to solve problems; he thought everyone could do that!

4. Commitment to the Empirical Method and Pervasive Systemic Thinking.

Capra discusses empiricism and systemic thinking in the context of the time in which Leonardo lived: In the 15th century, scientific method did not exist. Leonardo developed his own by making systematic observations, using logical reasoning, and developing some mathematical formulas. Then he tested his theories, repeated experiments, and recorded his findings, in drawings and writing, in his notebooks. This, centuries before the process was accepted as scientific rigor. Capra also cites the tendency of Leonardo to think in the gestalt (Field Theory of wholes and parts that was not evident in medieval thinking) and see and demonstrate, often in his drawings, the interconnectedness of nature, human physiology, and mechanical processes.

Larry credits the beginning of his geometry with his 1970 cube, but there is evidence that he used the empirical method much earlier in his life. He reports that he developed the police idento-kit, tested it, and recorded it decades before it came onto the commercial market—his idea came from an integration of concepts from comic books, like Dick Tracy. He often was in trouble in his jobs because he could see problems, but his suggestions for solving them went unheeded; the disaster was the proof of his theory! And, alas, the probable end of that job.

As to his geometry, he used systems thinking to connect the cube with what he discovered mathematically by drawing ellipses that then eventually, with years of starts and stops, morphed into the tesseract, the basis for the Vallian Coordinates. He used his drawing and sculpting skills to develop models, which he then described in exquisite detail in his patents. Also, with the patents, he used empiricism and systemic thinking to refute potential infringing prior art that he carefully, systematically, and thoroughly researched by reading patent after patent in the Patent Office Official Gazettes.

One area of observation that Larry conducted, tested, and wrote about extensively was optical illusions that, he contended, comprised the difficulty architects and draftsmen had in illustrating objects in 3 or more dimensions, a event complicated by computer graphics. In *The Elephant in the Room* (2011), Larry wrote, "My skill in illustrative art is displayed in the drawings done for patents, and my interest in mathematics is intimately conjoined with my interest in and occupation with art: illustrative, fine, and engineering. But my key interest, in which I have invested many hours of study, is the field of visual anomalies, generally called optical illusions." (p. 3) He then goes on to describe the many aspects of these anomalies and their effects in everyday life, as well as in many graphic art disciplines.

I cite these examples as illustrative of his empirical and systemic thinking. I believe that Larry always perceived the interconnectedness of events, objects, phenomena, and beings, human or otherwise. I don't know if I have convinced you that, if he had not been Leonardo, at least Larry had very similar genius characteristics. I could have written another book on this topic with many more illustrations.

After living with Larry for 53 years, I am currently plowing through the volumes of paper and projects he left behind—drawings, scientific notes, writings on various topics, multiple evolutions of his new geometry, multiple physical models, and patents written and discarded until finally one was granted. But he wasn't satisfied with even the published patent. He continued to explore and develop his ideas, continued to create new drawing and sketching techniques, continued to write essays and poems, and continued to find new and novel ways to express his innovations and spiritual thoughts, in writings and drawings. I believed that he was Leonardo, but I really didn't appreciate him as I should have; after all, when you live with a genius, he does many things and has many faults that a non-genius does and has, and it is sometimes hard to understand, let alone value, his many talents. What a joy it is to *now* appreciate this special man.

To answer the title question of "What do patent attorney, China, and Leonardo have in common?" the answer is simple: Larry!!

CHRISTMAS SERMON FOR 1988

From Larry

Greetings! May all of those you love be near you, if only in thought. For you who know me and you who think you know me, it is only important that you know I once thought seriously of being a priest or minister. Fortunately for posterity, this was only a transient ambition. The desire to help others has remained, perhaps fueled by the frequent help I have asked for and received from countless folks. If you will bear me out with your usual tolerance, I will explain.

This has been a year of tremendous shifts and changes; some, if not all, of these have been consequences of actions taken—or not taken—years ago. In order to make some sense out of this chaos, I decided that this would be the first year I would write a sermon for Christmas, although actually it is a kind of a summing-up of the old year and an attempt to make some sort of defensive moves before the new year has us by the throat. With this pithy excuse for the following "exercise," I give you:

THE FIRST ANNUAL WAHL CHRISTMAS SERMON

Our daughter Jill seemed to start it with her definitively vague ambitions and the reality that she was not going to be a college graduate without divine intercession. My wife Sharon is well educated and has the letters to prove it while I am educationally deficient and have the scars to prove it. So my attitude toward my daughter was mixed, to say the least. I decided to force her toward training ... any kind of training ... in lieu of a more formal education. She answered this ploy by moving out of the house. She voted with her feet.

Seriously, I have no great affection or disaffection for formal education, and I certainly know there are different channels for some people. For some, they are not only better channels but, given their individual natures, perhaps the only channels. A quote, which is a favorite of mine, allows as how "experience is the greatest teacher, and fools will learn at no other school."

With Jill gone, a whole series of events proceeded. It was clear that it had been time for her to get out on her own, but I loved her company so much: that lilting, tinkling laughter, the non-stop love interests, the activity ... the whole sweep of watching a modern young woman grow up. Jill and I have always had a special bond; I knew the leaving would hurt, as indeed it did. In its place was left a series of decisions about what to do with the room, how to restore the income from her rent (we had an agreement: if she didn't go to college, she had to pay rent), and whether to keep the room as a studio, which I felt I needed. But, probably, underneath these obvious and prosaic mechanistic questions was the greater one of what would happen to us, the mother and father, who now, somehow, had to face again being only husband and wife—husband and wife who had both grown in separate ways and were at different levels.

Fortunately we had always tried to keep the channels of communication open, although with both of us, tortured parents had made us poor marriage possibilities and potential disasters for parenthood. But, some primal force in each of us, some kind of compass, allowed us to give the best we could to our children and assisted us in picking, cultivating, and keeping deep and abiding friendships with some very remarkable people. Because I had been an orphan and believed I always would be, I started out distrustful and aloof from people, as a matter of course. Sherry has always kept her own counsel and would rather break her back doing a job than trust others to do it. And yet, from these inauspicious beginnings, it seems as if we have been able, through the years, to assemble a group of friends so varied, so catholic that it begs the imagination. They are our riches, our bankers or granary, our warehouse. They are the rivers from which we drink and the trees from which we pluck all manner of varied fruit.

I have known the famous and the infamous and have found all of the obvious differences one would expect, and yet, for all those differences, one comes at last to the street-fighter's rock base of reality ...

"Like, ah, he's the kind of a guy who'll back ya up in a jam. If they's a whole army taking ya on, this the guy you'll find protectin' your back!"

There is not one of these, whom I have called "friend," who has not had the opportunity, and met it, of "protectin' my back" at some point in our relationship. As marriages are not made in heaven, neither are friendships. We may find our friends, sadly, making asses of themselves, or worse, of us. We may find our friends diffident and weird. Sometimes we may find them self-destructive, and in a few cases, an enemy will take them down. Though we are willing to be at their backs, often we can find no one to battle because the enemy and minions are hidden inside the friends, and they will quickly sink into this quicksand with nothing we can do to save them.

We have now weathered the squall of Jill's departure, and she is with us on Christmas morning, as she was with us for Thanksgiving. Her tinkling laughter is a joy, and the pleasure of her company is intense. She is still my daughter, but I have given up being her father in the same way that I was before. It is better in some ways and worse in others, but most importantly, it is different. She is truly an adult; it is not my job to approve or disapprove of her.

In the time Jill has been gone, I have had more time to study the face of my spouse and partner, time to reevaluate her. I find myself listening to the sound of her voice as if it were music, somehow not listening to the words but just to the music. As she talks, she will stop suddenly, aware that there is a strange, far-away look in my eyes that she recognizes as departure. "Are you listening to me?"

"Oh yes, I am," I will answer, both telling the truth and lying, for the music is beautiful to hear.

In our earlier days of marriage, there were times neither of us would believe or rely on the other, "standing our backs," and in many cases that belief was more than justified, but now, and for many years, we have accepted who we are, together and separately. Now there is no question in our minds, there is no question in our souls about standing for or behind each other.

Eric, our son, found Jesus and, at first, found the experience unique—as it is and always should be—but then found it separating and self-aggrandizing. The wedge between us was deep and looked, for all the world, as though it were permanent. The years rolled by, and I grieved and was bitter for the loss, not just of his presence but of the hole it appeared he had dug, so deep as to be impossible to bridge.

We wrote, carrying the war to words, hurting and cutting each other with sharp edges. One final letter from Eric, a terse recital of my past failures—some of these only too real—and a final resolve to cut all ties forever. The warrior in me rose up in all its majesty and, with the skill I have as a writer, I employed a scathing return in kind. It was a masterpiece, it was the final word, it made my ego feel wonderful! I did not send it immediately and, upon reading and rereading it, I realized that although the ego felt good, justified, and satiated, nothing else in me felt anything but loss, sorrow, and shame. I did not send the letter.

A few weeks later there came a letter from our son of such honesty, such depth, such reality that it put me in shock. It was assertive, it was loving, it was real. It was answered in kind as soon as I could develop the wit and words. We are, I hope, well on our way to being friends, and although he is still a devout Christian and I a struggling Buddhist, we have found some indefinable middle ground. I can see that neither he nor I are standing on quicksand and that, as I have always known, each of us will find, as with every other man and woman, our own way to heaven. I do not know if the time will come when he would stand at my back, nor do I know if I would stand at his, but somehow we are to each other no longer the enemy and may well become friends. Like my daughter, he is a child of mine by accident of birth, but will only be a friend by an act of conscious choice. Whatever will happen, I am thankful to accept and enjoy him as I enjoy all of the wonderful people life has seen fit to troop across the stage of life I have shared. I honor all of you, I embrace all of you, I love all of you, and I wish all of you all that can be, would be, and need be.

In the benediction of Tiny Tim, I join my voice
"GOD BLESS US EVERY ONE!!"

Chapter 10

The Disclosure Document and The 1991 Patent

God answers sharp and sudden on some
prayers. And thrusts the thing we have
prayed for in our face. A gauntlet with a gift in't.
—*Elizabeth Barrett Browning*

Larry could not, not work. There were some of our acquaintances who thought Larry was lazy and leeched off me, that I was the poor hard-working, set-upon wife. Little did they know! Of course, there were times when I wanted to believe that, times when I resented his apparent freedom … but I don't think I ever truly believed that misperception. Besides, I wanted to work, was born to work, would have died had I been denied the opportunity to work. And so it was with Larry. In my heart, I know that during his last night alive, when he discovered his fingers were no longer able to build the complex models of his tesseract, that was when he quit fighting to keep his fragile heart beating and let go, perhaps peacefully, I hope.

He had always worked. The tons of material—written, drawn, modeled—he left behind were a testament to his need and desire to work. That he did not become the millionaire he thought he wanted to be was irrelevant. He didn't want it for himself, he wanted it for me. He was planning on finishing his theory and selling it so he could get me a house … and this, two weeks before he died. But I was as much a gypsy as he was; what did we need a house for?

Kahlil Gibran (1958) said, in *The Prophet*, "Work is love made visible." Larry left a lot of love behind.

After China, Larry began a focused period of developing and refining his geometry, which he was to call by many different names as each new evolution appeared. First came the disclosure document called "Vallian Virtual Articulated Super Tesseract" (V-VAST) in 1990, which was 108 pages, followed in 1991 by the first geometry patent, called "Vallian Cubisphere System (VCS)." But before that was accomplished, life intervened on several occasions.

The Jill Scenario

Sometime in 1986, Jill decided that she was not cut out for college life—after all, her dad never went to college. Unfortunately, she posted her decision by falling in gymnastics class and nearly breaking her neck. Jill had always been kinesthetically skilled and very bright, but her first semester college grades had several D's, which she would have to make up to continue taking classes. While we didn't approve of her "passive hostile" methods of communication, we were forced to accept her decision—if we wanted to keep a healthy daughter, that is. I suspect she felt that if she didn't do something dramatic, we would put too much pressure on her to stay in school, especially since it was free for her as a daughter of a SJSU faculty. But, there were consequences. Earlier, we had made an agreement with her that as long as she went to college, she could live at home, rent free, but if she quit college, we would require a rent payment for her room. This was our way of encouraging her to get higher education ... unsuccessful as it was.

With her decision firmly made, Jill took several low-end jobs—waitressing at The Perfect Recipe, being a barista at Peet's Coffee, and clerking at Book's Inc.—and she paid her rent. But, as we expected, she soon blew off those jobs and instead got some training in massage therapy, setting up her own business. At about this time, she made another consequential decision: to move out! As Larry describes in his Christmas Sermon, we really missed her and were now confronted with the proverbial empty nest. As for me, even though I was working two jobs and pursuing a doctorate, I was devastated. She had moved in with a friend in Sunnyvale, and every time I drove by the freeway exit that I knew was near where she lived, I cried: this was worse than when she went to kindergarten!

To make matters worse, we had been saddled with my dad and his failing health for several years, but when he finally succumbed, he left Jill $5000 and my brother and sister-in-law the rest of his meager estate. We weren't even mentioned. My dad, with his usual paranoia, accused us of using his money to go to China; he seemed unable to conceive that I might be valuable enough that someone would pay me to go to China. But, my dad got even for our alleged theft. He managed to drive a wedge between our daughter and us by giving her that gift "for being such a good granddaughter." Larry was furious when he found out some time later; she had been to see her grandfather only once in all the time he was in and out of the hospital. For her part, Jill happily, but with guilt, bought a massage table for her new business; for our part, we became estranged.

But we survived this, even though I continued to cry every time I passed the Mathilda freeway exit. However, Mother Nature provided us with an unusual resolution to our Jill conflict.

October 17, 1989

At approximately 1700 on October 17, 1989, the earth began to shake, and boy, did it shake! The Loma Prieta earthquake was the largest the Santa Cruz-San Francisco area had experienced since maybe the 1906 earthquake that destroyed San Francisco. At either 6.9 or 7.0 on the Richter scale (depending on whom you listened to), the damage to both Santa Cruz (wiped out ½ of its downtown) and San Francisco (in addition to homes lost, a connector ramp for the freeways between Oakland and San Francisco collapsed resulting in lives lost) was severe and extensive. San Jose and the in-between peninsula cities also suffered various degrees of destruction.

I was in my office on the 4th floor of the Health Building at San Jose State University when I felt the floor moving under me. I looked out my window in time to see the water in the swimming pool across the street literally sloshing out; I ran to my doorway, looked down the hall, and saw my friend Kathy leaning out of the door of the next office. "I'm all right," we informed each other.

In short order, the campus police came by and ordered us out of the building—there were cracks in the foundation. Not known to me at the time, Larry had driven down to get me earlier than usual and had gone to the campus bookstore to check out computer books. He later told me that the floor started rolling, the lights went out, and he found himself scuttling about on the floor.

When the customers and staff were ushered out of the store, Larry found me hanging out in front of my building. Since it was still somewhat light out and the shaking had stopped, we decided to try to drive home. Larry had parked in our assigned space in front of a student dorm; students were sitting on our car, looking confused. As we told them we needed our car to drive home, one of the students looked at me curiously and asked, "Why?"

Without thinking, I responded succinctly, "Our cat." That seemed to satisfy them, and we reclaimed our car.

The trip home was an adventure. We discovered, as dusk arrived, that the power was out most everywhere. Because of the stories we had heard about people on the freeway thinking they had blown tires, and it was probably gridlocked anyway, we decided to take El Camino home. That route was 25 miles and slow under normal conditions—multi-phase traffic lights every mile or two. The trip was excruciating. Imagine, if you will, driving 25 miles in rush-hour traffic with no streetlights and very few functional traffic lights at major intersections. Since we were all in crisis, not knowing (and maybe not wanting to know) what we would find at our homes, we were all very civilized, polite, and took turns—but it was sooo slow!

After about 2 hours, Mother Nature, or maybe it would be better to say human nature, called, and we were hungry and had to pee. We hadn't seen a restaurant with lights on along this very dense main thoroughfare since we had left San Jose. Then, without warning, there arose a magnificent vision, or was it a mirage—I didn't think we had driven to the desert. It was a frankfurter restaurant on our right. Unfortunately, we weren't the only weary travelers who had spotted this most welcome oasis. But we joined the crowd, Larry and I taking turns going to the bathroom to keep our place in the food queue. We hoped to get one of those sacred hotdogs before they ran out. We did and being relieved—sort of —resumed our journey.

We crawled up the dark El Camino Real for several more hours, but when we turned the corner onto Mills Street, we were greeted with blazing lights in every house and apartment—amazing! We later learned that our street, and a couple of others nearby, was on a special electrical grid that seldom lost power. It probably helped that we lived only a few blocks from the USGS (US Geological Service). Speaking of the cat we had to get home to see, she gratefully joined us when we parked the car and went into our apartment. We immediately turned on the TV—only a fuzzy picture but good sound—since we had no idea how extensive the quake was. As far as damage to our home, it was minimal. Upstairs in my office, books were tossed on the floor, but most remarkable, our Tiffany-like glass lamp was sitting on top of an undamaged glass table and suffered only a few cracked panels.

We were horrified at what we heard on the TV of the damage, especially of the bridge connector collapse off Interstate 880 in Oakland—the Cypress Viaduct. We grieved for the loss of those affected. I discovered later that we were tightly ensconced in a cloak of shock and denial; the PTSD response came many months later. Our landlady Terry came to see that all of us in the apartment were OK and to make sure the building was safe for us to stay in. Assured, she joined us in "watching" the TV reports; she was surprised that we had power when everything for miles was dark. I don't remember any after-shocks, but there must have been some.

It was now about ten at night, but there was no way our adrenalin was low enough to sleep. The phone rang—we hadn't known it was "alive," just assumed the worst. We figured it was our kids or out-of-town friends—Eric was in Seattle, and Jill was in San Diego, the last we had heard; we still weren't in contact with her. I picked up the phone and heard this little, scared voice say, "Mom. Can you come get me, I'm in Oakland at a friend's apartment."

I handed the phone to Larry, and he said, "I'm not sure how we'll get there, but we are coming!"

The friend came on the phone and gave Larry directions. Larry got awfully pale when he heard where they were: overlooking the freeway connector that had collapsed. We got in the car and, after hearing which highways were impassable at that time (mostly wrecked cars or emergency vehicles closing them down), I mapped out a strategy of surface streets and back roads to get to Jill's location. No moon out tonight, so we carefully threaded our way to our destination. At about 1 AM, we arrived. Larry was further panicked—nothing visible, but I knew—when he saw said apartment building was on large posts (parking was underneath the actual apartments) that had deep cracks. It did indeed overlook the Cypress Viaduct. We grabbed Jill and her belongings and fled, encouraging her friends to do the same. After much hugging and crying and relieved chattering, we made our leisurely, dark drive home, retracing our route and hoping those roads were still open.

The next day (actually the same day, just later) we talked and talked, until all the mutual hurt was managed and we knew we had our lovely daughter back, and she had us.

The Aftermath

We recovered from the earthquake, though many were not so fortunate. Larry and I both went back to our somewhat frantic work schedules: Larry to his computer and geometry—as well as various writing projects—and me to my students and my doctoral studies. Larry spent a considerable amount of time and energy getting pre-patent materials to patent attorney, Alfred Miller; meeting with Roy, Miller's associate; meeting with a variety of other "experts" recommended by Mr. Miller, including a trip to San Francisco to meet with a possible financial source, only to be stood up. But no matter, Larry was having a great time; he felt like he was beginning to get somewhere, that he was being listened to. And I was making progress in the doctorate. We were optimistic about our work and our life. But ...

In January of 1990, Alfred Miller, Esq. informed Larry by phone message that his patent was too complex and that Larry would have to write it himself. Larry went into a blue funk. He fired off a letter to the associate, Roy, the next day.

Regretfully, Larry

Dear Roy,

In what now seems like centuries past but was actually about 15 years ago, I was using patent attorneys in Portland, Oregon on a project in which my wife and I ultimately invested over 50 grand, ten years of our lives, and a good many dreams. At one point, I found myself wondering how in the world patent attorneys ever made money. Certainly it could not be from inventors like me who just happened to wander into their very expensive digs.

During the course of many expensive (to us, that is) trips to their offices, I would arrive early and sit in a waiting room that included, among other things, a secretary at a small desk with two filing cabinets alongside. From time to time, the phone would ring. The secretary would answer, say a few words, look into the filing cabinet, read a few numbers into the phone, and hang up. This happened through several visits; she ignored me until she finally became relaxed about my usually early presence. I took to moseying around the small waiting room, looking at the art work and such, until one day as the phone rang, I happened to be in the position to get a look at the files from which she was reading the numbers. What I saw startled me and caused waves of nausea. There were folders, fat and healthy, with one word scrawled in what appeared to be three-inch high letters across the cover. That one word was, as I'm sure you know, ABANDONED! For this oversight of my "peeping Tom" behavior, the poor girl was fired, and for their later oversights, so were my attorneys. I wrote my own first patent.

I spent several years of my life as an orphan in a Catholic convent; believe me, I know what the word *abandoned* means. I do not care what it takes to run your office, and I long ago learned that neither the patent attorney nor the patent office is, in any practical sense, a friend of inventors. Ready or not, we, the inventors, are responsible to "prosecute" our patents. Prosecuting anything literally means the process is adversarial. The only break the inventor gets is a level playing field and some faith in the honesty and integrity of the law firm he is dealing with.

When Mr. Miller summarily stopped the preparation for filing my patent, without the courtesy to tell me face to face even though we had agreed that January would be the likely time for payment, I lost the trust I had in him. This dismissal was only a couple of weeks after he had given me the name of Arnold Wetcher, a proposed venture capitalist.

For two lost, frustrating weeks, I had tried to arrange a meeting with Arnold Wetcher, the first of which had me taking ten pounds of materials to San Francisco only to find that he did not schedule his own appointments and was in Cleveland?? There were second and third appointments re-scheduled then cancelled, by him, at the last moment. Finally he scheduled a fourth one at my office, to include a named mathematician. Two hours after the scheduled time, I phoned his office and got only an answering service, with no message for me.

I must tell you that I was not too surprised that he did not show up. The day before that last scheduled meeting, I received a phone call from Mr. Wetcher instructing me to fax him a business plan. Along with a rapidly scraped-together business plan, I faxed a letter in which I informed him that I had filed a Patent Office Disclosure Document (DDA) so that the patent would have some protection. Previously, he had expressed concern about my relationship with Miller; I thought this would settle his worries. In a follow-up phone call the same day, his response to this new information had seemed strange. The disclosure document should have calmed his unease, but I had the feeling it was not what he had in mind. It seems odd that so few people, apparently including your firm, want to see this patent in the patent office. At the end of our conversation, he reconfirmed the meeting, but then never showed up nor called to cancel.

Even if Mr. Miller were mentally incompetent, he would know that this patent is a money cow, potentially worth millions and needing years of patent attorney work. Gagging on $3000 dollars makes no sense at all. I had, and have, more avenues for investment. I did not need the likes of Arnold Wetcher. But since Miller had given me his name, I tried to work with Wetcher, but to no avail. There is no longer room for doubt: Arnold Wetcher is one of the biggest "flakes" I have *never met with* in some time!

I will try not to fault Mr. Miller in any way, but it must be clear: I have not a pixel of interest left in doing business with him. I want to make sure that it is understood that your firm and I are no longer con- nected. It is my intention to follow the disclosure document with a pro se filing, planning on new investment coming aboard. From all that has taken place, you may understand why I want no file of mine left with your firm, a folder with a final, non-revocable word scrawled across its cover: ABANDONED!

Regretfully,

Larry E. Wahl

On His Own Now

Larry's letter had the desired result. Roy called him to come get his materials shortly thereafter. It was unfortunate it had to be him doing the dirty work; Roy had been one of the "good guys." He had worked very hard to understand the ideas that Larry put forth in the material that had constituted the DDA (disclosure document). But Larry seemed destined to be invalidated by the mathematicians and not understood by the patent attorneys. Was this to foreshadow the tone of his inventive journey? I hoped not, and Larry was persistent in his belief that the Vallian Coordinates was indeed the future: the geometry of not just the 21st century, but well beyond.

And so he was good for his word as emphatically expounded in the last paragraph of his letter: on September 16, 1991 Patent Application 07 760513, The Vallian Cubisphere System was filed, but not without a lot of reflective anguish, which was overridden by the encouragement of a good friend.

After the debacle of Miller, et al, Larry became quite depressed. But being an interminable optimist, he pulled himself out of it and got back to work. Sometime in mid 1990, Larry received a letter from Jerry Walker, a long time friend of both Larry and Eric. Being glad to hear from him—it had been several years—Larry wrote back telling him about all the travails he was enduring and that he was dumping the whole geometric idea to focus on his writing. The response to that from Jerry Walker was a "You can do it, Larry," and offered his and his computer friend's help. This response so energized Larry that, on Labor Day 1990, he went to Portland for several days (Walker paid travel expenses) where he met with Jerry and Alex Halloran to evaluate a potential business relationship. By the end of their meeting, a tentative agreement was reached and signed. However, cold feet ensued, and in October 1990, the agreement with Walker and Halloran was cancelled. Alex felt he was more than qualified to do the programming but he did not believe that Jerry had the business sense to carry off that end of the deal.

So Larry was back to no technical and business support, but despite the inauspicious finish, Larry maintained the energy that Jerry had started. In November 1990, Larry filed the disclosure document for the Vallian Coordinate System—yes, he fudged a bit when he had pronounced to Arnold Wetcher that it already had been filed!

Now that Larry was recommitted to his geometry, in January of 1991, he tried again to promote the Coordinates, this time directly to Steve Jobs by sending him—now at Next, Inc.—a certified packet of materials and a letter, which follows. I noted that Steven Jobs signed the return receipt himself.

Try, Try Again

Mr. Steven Jobs
Next, Inc.
900 Chesapeake Dr.
Redwood City, CA 94063

Dear Mr. Jobs,
Several years ago, while you were still at Apple, I wrote you a letter about a new coordinate system. You gave a mathematician on your staff the job of figuring out what I was trying to promote. I believe his name was Mr. X. He explained that he was the one who got projects that "fell through the cracks." I remember thinking that if I could explain the basics of the system to him in several minutes, I might be able to interest you and Apple. Twenty minutes later, he and I were still talking. I felt very successful in communicating with this "voice" on the telephone, so well in fact, I believed I would be able to answer any question he might pose. I was wrong! The last question I remember him asking was, "How would you feel about my name being on it?" When I was finally ready to deal with this unexpected concept, you and Apple had parted company.

In the intervening years, I have modified and completed the total system and now have a Disclosure Document on file in the Patent Office. I am ready to file the patent. While being virtually transparent to the user because of the manner in which three different disciplines fit together in its construction, it is a complex system and the filing of a patent does little to avail anyone attempting to reverse engineer it. For these reasons, I am less and less concerned about protecting the trade-secret nature of the system. However, I will include a nondisclosure form, which I would like you to sign, primarily as additional proof that I have been working to "reduce the patent to practice."

Gordon French, of the old Home Brew Club, introduced me to the computer. From the beginning, as an artist as well as a scientific investigator, I was struck by the poor ability of the computer in graphics. This concern sent me deep into research on René Descartes and his Cartesian Coordinate System. He did not foresee the computer and, in fact, was not even able to work with (or religiously allowed to) irrational numbers. Thus, he was forced to work with the rectangular format instead of the cubic one he obviously understood and would have used had he been able.

A deeper mystery is why Buckminster Fuller, that genius of polyhedra, did not develop the cubic coordinates. It seems that he had a fundamental antagonism for the cube, feeling it was too simple for further development. Whatever Fuller's reasons for not arriving at it, I believe I can prove that I have. As the first new system in 300 years, it will usher in a complete coordinate system, set up from the start *for the computer.*

I have long had the feeling that I was meant to work with you. The naming of your machine "The Cube" makes me feel that this Cubic System is not just a dream but will come to be. As a seminal patent, this system will bear many children and is destined to change many ideas about the way computers are used.

Please do send me a note or call me for additional information should anything I have sent peak your interest.

Sincerely,

Larry E. Wahl

Inventor

Unfortunately, Steven never read this elegant letter: the package was returned, unopened, the victim of NIH, or not invented here.

The Elephant Revisited

Sometime in 1992, Larry and I realized we hadn't been enjoying humorous events as much as we usually did, and that was not acceptable. Never one to stay "down," Larry decided to make use of a funny happening and thought up a visual that we could use when our senses of humor became strained. I was so delighted with his "Do the Elephant" that I wrote up a description to go with Larry's drawing, and I even bought an large toy elephant, got it a collar and a name tag—we called him, Prince Val (Vallian). Doing me one better, friend Judy brought us some artificial eyelashes to complete Val's identity. From then on, I demonstrated and taught "The Elephant" to all of my students. I even have pictures with a group of my nurses pointing and laughing at each other. "Doing The Elephant" became a perennial favorite.

See pages 172-174 for the story behind the "development" of the Elephant.

Musing 108 by Larry

The Mind of Man

Wisdom is sometimes nearer when we stoop
than when we soar.
—*William Wordsworth*

The mind of man has its own rules, regulations, structures, advantages, and limitations. Cultural, social, and economic rules come about as necessities when individuals start to connect as families, tribes, cities, states, and nations. We now live in a multicultural mix of many colors and many nations. Thus, we have had to develop international commercial arrangements, contracts, and economic agreements. From the relatively simple single point of view of individual reality, combined human brains imagined and created greater complications in living social, industrial, and scientific bodies.

The physical and mental are more or less understood, yet there is still a third reality to the essential formation of mankind. This reality became the spiritual realm, and into this realm came the free form of imagination, producing structures that could not be directly seen. Instead, these brains imagined a substantial, but incorporeal, structure representing the rules of a God who prudently produced everything… except Himself! He apparently left that job to his creation, man. This third structural, non-physical, non-mental reality—in the sense that little about It could be proven—became the top of a pyramid consisting of Faith, Mind, and Body. These components, built only of imagined thought forms, could be collectively called FAITH.

Faith is considered by some, and I happen to agree, to be constructed of thought forms that can neither be seen nor understood

216

with any of the normal five senses and certainly resist analysis. In no way can these be proven, much less have any tenets repeatable in any scientifically controlled sense. They are called thought forms because they are agreements among people that this or that is true. These imagined structures produce actual seeable realities in the manner of activities, customs, and costumes.

Clothing, originally meant to protect persons from the vicissitudes of nature, became uniforms indicating position, rank, and social status. A group of individuals collects, ponders, and then selects one of their number to be a president, a pope, a tax collector, a head of the PTA, CIO, or CIA. Nothing about the individual has physically changed, but presumably his or her life has become richer, better, higher, more powerful, more exciting, and more satisfying. Supposedly it also means more responsibility. Far more than the characteristics given so far, the attempt to formalize these belief systems creates societies, nations, religions, and, of course, wars.

It is as if the thought forms become agreed-upon covenants between larger and larger groups until the plans and considerations become more solid as rules and regulations, and the necessary objects are produced to back up and make real the imaginary concepts. In just this way, a group of scientists imagined a theoretical concept that demanded the agreement of a whole nation to provide the physical resources, security, mechanics, scientists, secret locations, and the vast amount of real estate necessary to produce the atom bomb. The immense amount of technical know-how that this produced fit into the world of the real, the provable, and, unfortunately, the repeatability of the process.

Thus, the bomb became a tool of diplomacy—another imaginary quality—proving only that the unreal gives birth to the real, and vice-versa, and the realization that the conscious parts of our mind controlled by us are only a small part—probably less than five percent of all activity that goes on sub-rosa within our bodies. And some individuals have slightly more than five percent control, as has been demonstrated.

We believe in people whom we describe as charismatic, powerful, influencing, commanding, and we deduce that they are somehow superior to the average person. All we really can prove is that some of us have more control over our neighbors than others. The thought that these few people influence millions of other people and cause the death and destruction of whole countries is appalling. If their names are Alexander the Great, Attila the Hun, Caesar, Adolf Hitler, Osama Bin Laudin, they write their own lyrics and the music the rest of the world must dance to.

Chapter 11

Martin and the Birth of V-GHOST

Gazing up at the dark sky spangled with its signs and stars,
for the first time ... I laid my heart open
to the benign indifference of the universe.
—Albert Camus

After receiving the package of materials that Jobs sent back unopened, Larry decided to let go of that dream, at least for the moment. He resolved to continue investigating his geometry on his own since outside support was not much in evidence. Nevertheless, Larry filed the patent in September, then an extension in 1992, but believing the material was too broad and might interfere with future patents, he withdrew that application in 1994. But, it was not without benefit: he later turned around and submitted it—plus a lot more—as a disclosure document for the next patent.

While I had promised not to burden you, the reader, with too much complex mathematical theory, I feel I owe it to Larry to provide some example of what he had immersed himself for so many years: a brief glimpse, as it were, into this very unusual mind. To that end, the following are selected portions of that patent.

Serial # 07 760513 Patent Pending The Vallian Cubisphere System

Abstract: This invention is a computer method constructed for graphically and mathematically manipulating a Cubisphere in a computer producing drawn figures from which all pertinent mathematical and corollary data is indexed and extracted.

From Summary and Scope of the Invention

The cube in the abstract is known to be perfect. It is at Unity and has the value of the square root of 3 as the vector addition of its sides. With the use of these simple mechanics and the general pervasiveness of the ELF, the VCS cube can be proven to contain all of the necessary data, both mathematical and graphical, to allow infinite scaling, mensuration, and visualization of anything drawn on a computer that can "see" a hexagon.

The invention—the VCS System—automatically eliminates the Cartesian system's rounding errors in which the solution for one run in the sine-cosine cycle becomes the numerical data for the next operation. Thus rounding errors are produced that only vast amounts of memory can keep floating-point approximations to near ideal values, preventing disastrous degradation of data in this presently-used Cartesian system.

In the VCS system, only a relatively large pixel, which happens to be lit by virtue of contact with an infinitely small VCS point, is needed in any type of screen change. The VCS real number values that tickled a particular pixel into lighting up are single two or three vector values that may remain immutable and constant in a matrical system and do not change value; only the pixel locations tickled by a specific view will be in that view. Information does not need to be individually stored in multiple formats for subsequent translation, rotation, or other manipulation.

From Objective and Advantages

It will, therefore, be the objective of this patent application to devise a system for the computer that promotes, but is not limited to, the following ten goals, it:

1. Generates a system whose spherical and cubic nature is consistent and completely viable in all mathematical, graphic, algebraic, and geometric terms with all mechanics of spherical, circular, polar or other geometries, allowing for simultaneous use of spherical, circular, polar, cubic, and other geometries in identical-appearing objects;

2. Solves all problems of ambiguity and paradox in 3-D viewing;

3. Provides an immediate, completely graphic capability for mensu-

ration, but still provides for numerical input, if and when needed;

4. Provides a stable, absolute grid in 2-D or 3-D, which grid may be moved graphically about a cube with no operator concern for either primary or intermediate shape tables;

5. Allows the user to operate within an expanded, therefore transparent, cube whose limits do not intrude, thus negating any sense of claustrophobia or confusion;

6. Allows the user to pitch, rotate, or spin any object through over a hundred Vallian Cubisphere views, moving, transmitting, changing, and printing any view desired in plan, oblique, or axonometric form with easy control methods, while not excluding thousands of non-Vallian views by standard means, though these can not be edited;

7. Provides the user a universal and infinite scale both in maxima and minima, identifying each cube in terms of an extremely large number of subsets, allowing an infinite number of cubes to be considered;

8. Operates at unity so that all that is necessary for automatic numerical scaling is positive or negative scalar input;

9. Allows the user, to a degree never before possible, a virtual tablet or screen providing complete artistic freedom and transparent ease of drawing, viewing, and editing while simultaneously creating a completely useable numerical data base, available whenever and wherever needed;

10. Allows one of several formats (cubic, spheric, circular, hexagonal, planar, orthographic, stereoptic, hyperbolic, inverse, and mirror— to name a few) inherent in the system to be the descriptor of the objective measurements of given objects, while a differing format— spherical in this format—becomes the descriptor of the subjective, conditional, transportational, charactistic, molecular, reflective, mass, and other qualifying data.

Although the above descriptions, and any following, contain many specificities, these should not be construed as limiting the scope of the invention, but are merely to provide illustrations of some of the presently preferred embodiments of this invention. There is, for example, nothing to prevent this invention from being used effectively in database or word-processing applications. Since the VCS translates between implicit and explicit techniques, it may be seen that it is a natural bridge mechanism for language translative processes. The VCS, by its nature, converts and translates data between cubic and spherical realities. This translative construction would make it available for artificial intelligence applications, NMC, or various other control devises.

Confused or intrigued? If confused, thank you for your patience. If intrigued, view the granted 1999 patent # 5,982,374 online or in the Patent Office Abstracts. From the preceding sample, it should apparent why Larry thought that this would be too broad! When asked, "What is it good for?" Larry's response was, "It will replace the calculus"!

Printers' Ink Café

After the application was on its way to the Patent Office, Larry spent a lot of time at the café associated with the Printers' Ink Bookstore. It was within walking distance for him on California Avenue and, apparently, for many other computer persons as well. Hewlett-Packard and several other well-known companies were just up the road on Page Mill. Larry has described the California Avenue district of Palo Alto in a previous chapter (Chapter 7).

In the fall of 1991, Larry was actively looking for a programmer to make a prototype graphics program that would demonstrate the new geometry he was proposing. Many hours of the day, one could find Larry at Printers' Ink Café, talking earnestly to those he thought might be potential partners in his endeavors, explaining and clarifying his "non-Cartesian, non-floating point, triplet-based" computer graphics concept. I wonder if, at the time, Larry was aware of how much information he was freely giving out? And if that would have made any difference?

His active discoursing was successful; in December, he met and seduced to his cause a retired computer trouble-shooter and mathematics graduate named Martin Wilson. Christmas 1991 was a happy time.

The Group

On January 6, 1992, Larry and Martin signed a contract whose purpose was to produce a code for the graphics of the Vallian Cubisphere System. But Larry didn't stop there. From the many who had approached him—at Printers' Ink and as neighbors in adjacent offices at 415 Cambridge—Larry invited several interested people to meet with Martin, him, and me to form a working group. Please note that I was a reluctant participant, especially since I was in the key stages of my doctoral dissertation, but I never could say "No" to an exuberant Larry. And someone had to take notes of all the ideas that would be floating through that electrified atmosphere!

On January 23, 1992—not brimming over with enthusiasm, but the secretary nonetheless—I prepared a sign-in sheet titled "The 'Getting Up to Speed' Conference on the Vallian Cubisphere." Those in attendance were Eric Stensen, Frank Miller, Terry Nichole, Martin Wilson, Larry E. Wahl, and Sharon Wahl. I wish now I had done a handwriting analysis on those folks; it might have saved some trouble later on! I don't find any notes on that initial meeting, but I do remember it involved planning, as well as Larry explaining the patent and giving a pep talk to all participants, activities he excelled at.

By March 10, though, the group consisted of just Martin, Frank (lawyer), Larry, and me. A summary of that meeting was as follows: *Larry suggested Frank and Martin form a corporation, with Larry on the outside, licensing pieces of the patent to that corporation; Frank reported that he reserved the name "Vallian Cubisphere Systems"; Larry wanted to receive work salary and royalties and to assign the patent to Sharon; Larry asked for Sam Rock to be patent attorney (???), but Frank knew a Michael Waterman who would be cheaper; Martin was to work on six subordinate patent applications and be co-inventor with Larry; Larry would do trademarks.* I won't bore readers with all of the discussions around financing, office space, employees, equipment, etc.

The next recorded meeting was not until July 9th. I suspect that I had begged out because I was on a strict time limit: I had to complete my doctorate (Ed.D) degree before the San Jose State term began—about August 22—or I would lose my position at the university. I'm sure that by July, I had submitted my dissertation to my appointed readers, so I was able to give some energy to the project meetings. I have additional nicely written minutes from 7/21, 7/29, 8/4, 8/11. August 11th was the last of the minutes, but there followed a very complex "Project Development Agreement" signed by all four of us. These minutes make for interesting reading and, in retrospect, were prescient of subsequent conflict.

Sherry's Computer Program

During the March to July meeting gap, when Larry was working with Martin or seeking out partners or looking for appropriate financing or having meetings (and he called me the Energizer Bunny!), Larry was helping me with a project that was to be my dissertation and to secure my degree.

After seeing all of the errors that my students made when taking a test on "medication math," and many didn't pass the pharmacology course because of them, I decided to investigate the concept of girls/women and math anxiety, as well as to note what kind of errors my students made: calculation or problem set-up or various. Exploring these questions and finding most errors were due to an inability to logically assess the problem, select a correct formula, and insert the right numbers in the correct place in the formula, I decided to write a computer program to teach them how to do just that. I had access to a CAI authoring program, but I knew I needed help and an illustrator. So, my Sir Galahad came to the rescue. Together we produced a prototype program that received positive comments from faculty and student reviewers. After I included a conceptual model based on Gagne's (1979) "Nine Events of Instruction," *A computer–assisted instructional software program in mathematical problem-solving skills for medication administration (Wahl, 1992)* was ready to go.

I was so pleased with how well our collaboration had proceeded—it wasn't always so—that I was planning to have him help me complete the CAI project. Unfortunately, my program was done on a small floppy disk, and before I could even catch my breath, the authoring process bumped up a substantial level of complexity to DVDs. I just didn't have the energy to start over, and Larry didn't have the time.

A New Wrinkle in Time

Larry and Martin continued to work on the code for the program, but in late August, just as I was working all night pasting numbers—of all things—on the final, approved copy of my dissertation in preparation for mailing the next morning, Larry called 911 because of chest pain and was whisked off to Stanford. To this day, I don't know if it was my anxiety or his project that caused the angina, and I still retain guilt because I wasn't paying more attention to his complaints on that long night. But also, it may have been more of my famous denial when it came to his medical events ... or just my determination to send off the paper in time! At any rate, I mailed my precious package—and did make my deadline. Then I joined Larry at Stanford where, after an angiogram, it was determined his inferior coronary artery was blocked, and he should be scheduled for another coronary artery bypass graft.

The surgery occurred on the Labor Day holiday weekend. A recommendation: don't have major surgery on a holiday weekend!

The surgery itself went well, but because of the holiday, he was moved out of ICU before he was stable. That would have been OK except the step-down unit was bereft of regular staff, utilizing mostly temporary nurses. And, instead of being located near the nurses' station, his room was at the far end of the corridor. Having spent many years in hospitals on holiday weekends, I was not about to leave him alone, even though only an uncomfortable chair was provided for me. However, I'm very glad I didn't. The nurse assigned to his room had her own organized pattern for checking her patients and for giving care, meds, and all: she started at the room farthest away from Larry's and didn't get to him until well after 7 pm—he had arrived on the unit at the shift-change time of 3 pm. Though I went looking for help for him, even just to get some pain medication, it was to no avail. And Larry's roommate, scheduled for surgery the following Tuesday, was in a panic on Monday night due to similar neglectful care. I was running around trying to get help for him as well!

Well, we survived: Larry, the roommate, and me. But we were very glad when Larry could go home and recover there. I don't remember much about that autumn, except that I got my tenure and Larry came through his surgery without the complications of the first one, but with lots of pain. Because of the chest incision that had to be re-sutured when it was "coughed" open in 1983, the surgeon elected to access the coronary artery by a lateral approach, which meant removing part of a rib and spreading several others. If you have ever broken ribs, you know how painful that can be. But that too improved, given an appropriate time of convalescence. The only event I have documented for that period of time is a will that Larry signed, giving the patent to Martin and Frank if I predeceased him.

A New Adventure

A short respite, allowing Larry more time to recover, occurred when the San Jose State Pacific Rim Program offered me the opportunity to teach a nursing class in Saipan. Once again I was able to take Larry with me, though we did have to pay his airfare. Because Larry had spent time in Guam at the end of World War II (see book II), we arranged to have three days in Guam before going on to Saipan. Those three days were, without question, the most interesting of the entire trip. We arrived there on December 31ˢᵗ. Larry described our experience so well in two separate documents, I'll let him have the first say and I'll add more after.

To Guam and Saipan

It was strange to see the Island being "fetched" from the horizon as we flew, lowering to land on the North Pacific island of Guam. The island stood for so many things in my life, both wonderful and grotesque. As the sparsely loaded Airbus 8010 banked for its final approach, I wondered if it would still hold the mystery and intrigue that it had held for me when I was nineteen and the world itself seemed young, fresh, and dangerous.

I turned to my wife of 32 years and looked at her as she gazed out of a window seat behind me. She had heard so many of my stories of Guam, a whole series of would-be books compressed into the short four months I had been there. I wondered if I had oversold the place: Was it as beautiful as I remembered? Was the airport still as it had been almost fifty years before? Would I recognize Apra Harbor, Inarahan, the beautiful, deadly beach at Apra, or the capitol city of Agaña? How would Camp One look to me now and what shock would my psyche be subject to when I again saw the Naval Graveyard?

At last we landed, and luggage was unloaded into transfer carts. We walked to the large waiting room, and I found that it did not look much different. Then I realized we would have to show our passports. Unlike my first trip, when all of my identification papers bore the name of my particular contractor J. H. Pomeroy, Guam was now a point of entry to the U.S. When I had first arrived there, the entire Northern Marianas Territory was a U.S. protectorate. Now it was a contract commonwealth.

Guam, Saipan, Truk, Kwajalein, and many of the other hundreds of islands that made up this archipelago had been under military control in the late 40's and 50's. There were Army troops, Marines, Navy personnel, fliers, and support crews as well as builders and civilian office holders in the then mostly make-believe civilian government. The truth was that the entire area, legal and civilian, was under the control of the Navy.

Rear Admiral Powell was the successor to Admiral Halsey. Halsey, with his command centered on Guam, had been the architect for most of the battles in the North Pacific, including the masterful defense of Midway and the deciding, great Navel battle that followed. Because of his short and thick-necked physique and matching fierce attitudes, he was nicknamed "Bull Halsey." For some under his command, these were terms of derision, but for many more, they were a mark of deep respect.

As soon as the war ended, at least officially, Powell became the ranking officer on Guam, which now offered a permanent United States presence in the middle of the Pacific Ocean. There would be no more sneak attacks on the United States in this area, as there had been December 7, 1941; rules and regulations were quickly brought about to set up a permanent control by the U.S. military. Many hard political decisions were made, with many of them rushed through before the United States Congress would have a chance to water them down. In the intervening years, those decisions ensured that Guam became a very special place.

Though the island communities, especially on Guam, were listed as U.S. protectorates—supposedly under their own local control—great chunks of the island were off limits to local civilians and thousands of contract workers like myself. We were there as part of the many construction crews hired to build and complete the Apra Harbor Breakwater. This project was intended to, and succeeded in, making Guam a port area second only to Pearl Harbor.

The hulk of the battleship Oregon still resides 300 yards off Telefofo Bay. It was towed there at the height of the Pacific War as an ammunition barge, still in active service. In my day, the island had a beautiful rain forest with trees so large and vines so stout that an American convoy that had been shot off the road near Touman Bay was 30 feet off the road, but still 20 feet above the ground, tangled in the foliage.

Sherry and I puffed into a taxi, surprised by the heat and the humidity on this New Year's Eve of 1992. To my amazement, the cab rode on paved roads through the heart of a rebuilt Agaña and up into the neighboring hills, where the road turned into loosely graveled, great holes. At last, we were deposited in front of a large concrete building that gave the general impression of a basic, no nonsense automobile brake shop.

There was a parking lot that was simply an extension of a construction site, suggesting a new luxury hotel was being built. The half-built, skeletal structure served mostly to hide our hovel from view. There was no valet parking, no reception center with free coffee and cookies, no swimming pool, no restaurant, no bar, no lobby; there was only a makeshift counter and a file cabinet. Two concrete stories comprised "the compound," and there were jail-type bars on the few windows I could see. We had not been afforded the best accommodations because of late travel arrangements—not our fault—and the fact that we were arriving on New Year's Eve. We were later told that Guam was the playground for Japanese holiday celebrators and that all hotel rooms had been sold out many months earlier.

This part of town looked not too different from the kind of buildings I had been familiar with forty-some years before. Friendly but rough-looking young men took our luggage and led us to the second floor of this squat, armory-type building. Looking at this motley group of men, carrying side arms and rifles, the place began to feel more and more like a jail. At the very least, it was obvious we were not in the safest nor highest-classed part of the island.

Our room had only one pathetic window, eight feet up, for outside viewing; a bed that might have been all the rage in the 60's (the eighteen sixties); and sheets that were parchment thin, like covering ourselves with yesterday's bleached newspaper. The floor was covered with a rug of some faded, indeterminate pattern that had long since passed its useful life. The wallpaper bore numerous aborted, paint-over pattern decisions, apparently finally settling upon a seasick green. A single lamp provided light for the tiny room. Once it was turned on, we had the opportunity to see many multi-legged fellow renters scurrying across the floor for dimmer shelter. At the far end of the hall camped two men cooking lunch over a Bunsen-burner (they were there all night; we never figured out if they lived there or were to be our protectors!).

Sherry and I settled our few carry-ons, checking for truly empty spaces in the rickety bureau drawers, and then quickly made our way back down to the office and ordered a cab to take us back into the capital of Agaña.

My Take on Saipan

We rented a car and, over the next two days, we explored. Larry said the island was only 27 miles long, 8 miles wide, but we managed to put 300 miles on the car. As we toured, Larry showed me all of his favorite places, but he was appalled at the lack of trees—barren was not what he remembered. Since we had arrived in Guam about a week after a horrific hurricane had passed through, many of the trees that were still around the downtown areas had been decapitated. But that wasn't his main concern. Forests had been so thick on the east side of the island that abandoned jeeps were suspended in the trees, awaiting rescue. A lot had changed since 1945, and, as we were told by some of the locals, the Japanese had harvested an excessive number of trees to build their homes in Japan. Was this done after the U. S. had taken over control of the islands? No one knew for sure.

I was intrigued by the beauty of Guam, barren or otherwise, especially their elaborately flowered cemeteries, which splashed rainbow colors on the landscape. But these were not the Naval cemeteries that Larry mentioned. We tried to find them but were turned away at both Navy and Army gates. Oh well ... maybe that was better. I took many photographs of everything I found interesting, which was about everything. I almost had a too close encounter with a very large water buffalo as he approached me, perhaps wanting to help me get a close-up of him. I scurried back to the car, post haste!

But, alas, our time there—but not the accommodations—was over much too soon. I would have loved to stay there the whole four weeks, but duty called, and we were off to Saipan in a very small plane.

In Saipan, we were housed in a small one-room apartment over a restaurant. The apartment did have a bathroom and a counter at one end with a tiny refrigerator and a tinier stove. The rest of the room had a table (for my computer), straight chair, and double bed. Since the bed was really too small for a hefty Larry (he was carrying about 260 pounds on his 5 foot 11 frame) and we needed another chair to sit on, we asked for, and got, a recliner, which Larry preferred to sleep in anyway.

These accommodations had no protectors sleeping at the end of the hall; in fact, there was no hall, just down-going stairs leading to the outside and to what we were to call "our restaurant." We were served excellent food by darling, young, Filipino men, whom we came to know quite well since we were eating two and three meals a day with them. They told us that they came to Saipan to earn money to send back to their families; jobs in Saipan paid much more than they could make in the Philippines. It was the restaurant food and these young men that made an otherwise dreary stay palatable. The students and the environment were less so.

Regarding the students, they came in two flavors: intense (Saipanese) and laidback (Chamorran). None in either group was especially inspired by the curriculum (I was teaching nursing care for chronic medical conditions), but at least the Saipanese made an effort to learn what I was supposed to teach. The Chamorran students sat in the back of the room and chewed bettlenuts and spit the juice in coke cans, reminiscent of old men and their chewing tobacco. And to make matters worse, I developed severe laryngitis after a week and was put on complete voice rest for two weeks by the U.S. Public Health Service doctors. Trying to meet the expectations of my position, I spent night after night putting my lectures on overhead transparencies. Until ... I got smart and had the students divide the remaining content among themselves and present it to their classmates. At least this got the Chamorrans learning enough of the course to get a passing grade. If I had known, ahead of time, about the kind of students I was to have, I would have had them give presentations of the content from the beginning.

The environment was the other negative. As Larry pointed out, the whole island was a coral reef, and the roads threw up coral dust; the dust also arose from the construction sites we drove by daily. That dust was most certainly the cause of my laryngitis; we wondered how it also might be affecting the construction workers. We encountered another problem when we tried to go for a walk on the beach in the moonlight (intended to be romantic). Apparently the beach belongs to whoever owns the adjacent land, and dogs are kept on the property to reinforce that notion. After we had been chased down the beach by two snarling dogs, we limited our strolling to the few yards allotted to our restaurant/apartment.

There were some beautiful areas mixed in with the leftover horrors of war. The beautiful was the grotto, which I visited frequently, and the ocean: indigo blue on one side and luminous blue-green on the other. One side was the Pacific Ocean, the other the Philippine Sea; I don't remember which color went with which body of water. I took many pictures. The horror was Suicide Cliff from which hundreds of Japanese and Saipanese men, women, and children jumped to their deaths when the imminent arrival of the American "captors" was announced. They had been led to believe that torture and other mayhem would be would be their future under the Americans. The site of the cliff was memorialized by means of a sign explaining its significance to the people of Saipan.

A usual activity in every town that Larry and I travelled to in the U. S. was to seek out a local bookstore. Saipan had none! There was a library, but its collection comprised only copies of the books we had provided for the students and a shelf of paperback romance novels that the librarian ashamedly showed us. In my mind, that was the coup de grâce! There was one extenuating event. Since it was still Advent—a Catholic holiday persisting until January 6th—we curiously stopped by the local Catholic Church one midday. Larry could hardly contain his laughter as he listened to the sermon being solemnly delivered in a broad Irish accent!

For the rest of the story, Larry adds his brief comments.

Sherry was posted to Saipan in (writing this in the middle of the night and don't have all the time sequences yet... that's what Sherry does). Anyway, San Jose State sent her, under contract for the United States Public Health Service, to teach young and not so young nurses on Saipan. While Guam had been a US protectorate before the war, Saipan had been under Japanese control for several decades. While we were spending our month in Saipan, we never saw any U.S. service people. Guam on the other hand was full of Navy bases and Operation Centers.

The "local" police on Saipan were mostly Pakistani and Indian enlistments. Due to Saipan being a port of entry and the head of the Northern Mariana Territories, it consisted of tribes from formerly warring islands who, at one time or another in their history, fought each other and, in some cases, ate one another!

The USPHS hospital was unbelievably modern and up to date, but the nurses who worked there did not go out on home visits, though that was what the San Jose State program was preparing them for; everyone went to the hospital. In some cases, if a nurse wanted to go to a village that had natives who were hostile, the people would simply be gone when they got there. It was a most depressing place. All the more for the beauty of the island, especially at night... but it is full of ghosts.

So after for what was to have been our respite, more for Larry than for me, we were particularly glad to get home and back to our usual, well-known routines.

I recently found some writing Larry had done about Saipan that I was not aware of. It gives a little different twist to the Guam story—a little more reality—that I knew about but had not shown up in the previous writings included earlier in this chapter. I think this is an appropriate addition.

I do not ever remember traveling so far to see so little. The original idea of this trip, for me at least, was to symbolically bury two young Japanese officers I had been ordered to butcher, with "great prejudice," in a cave on Guam, almost 50 years earlier. While spending our scheduled two days on Guam before beginning our extended trip to Saipan, in an absurdly simple manner, it became abundantly clear that the two young Japanese liaison officers, their deaths, and my history on the island were all equally irrelevant.

It turned out that on the island of Guam, there was "no such operation at this location" as the one I remembered … and could not forget. Certainly, five decades later, the scenery was even more beautiful than I remembered. However, in the time since I had been there, the whole island's reality had quietly slipped from the 19th century into the 20th, with neither warning nor any apparent intervening history. I found myself on an intimately remembered Guam I now barely recognized.

I was sitting in bewildered wonder and great cognitive dissonance, eating Snow Shoe Crab at a local Sizzler Restaurant in air-conditioned splendor. Besides all the Stateside fast food outlets, there were cars and new hotels and work projects everywhere, indicating wealth and growth. At least that was the observed situation, if you didn't look too closely. In this little island, connected by history and blood to the United States, the American stock market crash had reached across thousands of miles to strike all of the far-flung American outposts. There were abandoned building sites, restricted water usage, "For Sale" signs, abandoned and neglected roads, and a haunted look of disbelief in the eyes of the recently unemployed, all of which rang of the certain new, raw "reality."

Previously, I mentioned the blindfolded-leaps off Suicide Cliff in Saipan, but there were similar mass suicides on Guam by Japanese troops and civilians when the end was obviously near. American troops, with public address systems, attempted to convince the Japanese trapped in a large cave to surrender, trying to assure them that they would be well treated, but to no avail. Thousands were found at the mouth of the cave, killed by their own bayonets.

As telling and dramatic as these places of death and destruction are, somehow their history seems bogus. It is not what is said or written by those now living in the islands as much as it is a kind of attitude, a sort of tongue in cheek, mock reverence that seems to slyly infer … "or perhaps none of it took place at all." It is as though the Walt Disney Company was given the assignment: "Now, since we are building Karaoke bars and first class hotels for all the Japanese tourists, whose yen hold up the island economy, we don't want to upset their having a perfect vacation experience. Certainly you have to tell them the truth, but do it gently: no pictures of thousands of crushed bodies, no rivers of blood and guts … keep it kind of … well, you know … clinical."

So, in this particular island "Disney Park," you see thousands of extras leap off the cliff, but only onto an unseen ledge, out of camera frame, laughing and queuing up for the next showing of the "Saipan Suicide Plunge." Die? Of course not. No one really dies at Disneyland. So with a little revision, I can see my two young Japanese cadre officers sitting around drinking Saki. They are just awaiting the cues for the next performance that features them having their throats cut. And, that's show business, folks!

Back home, many months later, this chapter of my life with its guilt, self-loathing, illness, mystery, hopelessness, rages, and suicidal episodes was finally and gently put to rest.

In the immortal words of Porky Pig… "Da…Dee…Da…Deee… dat's all folks!!!"

LOVE

By Larry E. Wahl
11/26/95 3:35 AM

It is a strange and varied menu we have chosen
my friend, my dearest love, of this life's bounty
of feast or famine, pestilence and tear

But through it all, we both have baked together
rationed life and dined on laden larders,
mixed love with chaos and with fear

And so it's thought that this time is the rites for ending,
that life is slowly winding down for us
and we must save our strength, our breath, our joy

For the time of reckoning comes too soon to be ignored
but dying is a process to the two of us
that works into an Other Creatures' ploy

Guessing Whom or What, He, She, or It is
is a wonder for each thoughtful moment?
and wonder is the very salt of life

But I will tell you many times, my loved one,
I would not share with kings or wizards wise
the endless banquet that is an amazing wife

For you have been the Summer of my Discontent,
the Autumn of Hope and Vital enterprise,
seeded with the toil and endless trying

You have been the Winter blowing with the cold
and fierce winds of change and moving
through random things aborning and of dying

You have been the master chef of life for your life's choice
of mate who often did not do you honor
in your own land or his misbegotten home

But through it all you have sustained and carried
your love, your gratitude, your caring
you have not given up your need to own

You have managed somehow to be all things to me,
to help me see the errors of my ways
and helping me to help you to help yourself

You have been a provoking devil and tiresome foe,
a scourge, a whiner, and a nag, yet at the same time
a saintly rock, a heroine, and an elf

You found me bent and broken from the beginning,
set on death and waste and killing,
more interested in death than in surviving

You have turned what could have been disaster
of selfish, greedy sorrow and of hate
into a semblance of a life of "lifting"

Into an endless of Spring of wonders large and small
that you have shaped in loving care
within "Your Kitchen" homeland
You have always, somehow, managed to connect "the dots,"
the right ingredients for your students
and now believe me, one of them is me

You have always tough-loved everyone you met, confronted,
left them bruised, confused, and shaken
then gently taught them how to see

You have filled "each unforgiving moment" with full distance run,
you have filled my life with music, mind, and laughter
and which is more, much more … have made a man of me.

Chapter 12

Slap Dab in the Middle

I may not have gone where I wanted to go,

But I think I have ended up where I needed to be.

—*Douglas Adams*

A curious title for this chapter, but this was a strange period of time. In *Chasing the Tesseract: The Complete History of the Vallian Coordinate System* (Wahl, 2011), I identified these years as "The Middle Years." So much had happened that I had to summarize the ensuing events in brief, bulleted paragraphs. However, from the time we returned from Saipan in 1993 until June 1996, I have little first-hand experience of what occurred during those years. My excuse was that since I was now a tenured professor, my workload tripled because I was "encouraged" to take on more leadership and administrative roles in addition to my teaching commitments. That encouragement also included the necessity to increase my publications in order to be promoted to the next level, the one that would be desirable for eventual retirement. It seems ridiculous to me now that I had to be concerned about retirement so early in my teaching career, but hey, that was academia, and I had signed on to it. So, most of the information about the goings-on in these "middle ages" of Larry's work came to me mostly through our pillow talks.

Work, Work, Work

The original VCS working group drifted away until only Larry and Martin were left, with other people popping in and out of communication. I do remember typing up a number of documents and business plans as Larry reached out to leadership folk at Sun Microsystems, Hewlett-Packard, SRI, etc. So while Martin worked on developing code for a beta program under

Larry's tutoring, Larry also schmoozed with people at Printers' Ink and other computer people he met or that Martin recommended. In December 1994, Larry once again tried to engage Apple by sending a package of material, showing examples of the developing program as well as other copyrighted, descriptive material. Larry had taken the main information from the abandoned 1991 patent and added new concepts and drawings, using that as a new disclosure document (DDA), which he filed in 1996. We sent the material to Apple "return receipt requested," but the signed notice never came back, and we were never able to locate anyone who had signed for the package. After many phone calls to people who mysteriously became "no longer worked here" on subsequent calls, Larry finally gave up his pursuit of Apple. In retrospect, perhaps that was the beginning of his personal battle with Apple and Jobs.

During one of his coffee conferences with people at the café, an attractive young woman who had recently returned from France where she had worked on a computer graphics program called Ray Dream sought him out. She was very interested in Larry's VCS; he gave her a copy of the to-be DDA, having her sign a confidentiality agreement. A friend, having met this woman and knowing Larry's interest in Ray Dream, brought to Larry's attention the cover on the Ray Dream Program box: it shouted "No Floating-Point Needed!" and mentioned the use of "triples," two essential concepts of the Vallian system. Larry became concerned since the group in France that developed Ray Dream was under the auspices of Apple.

Abandonment

Larry and Martin seemed to have a love-hate relationship, though I got the impression that Martin liked and respected Larry. I assume that Larry may have been difficult to work with because he knew what he wanted in the program, even though he was not able to do the code himself. And of course, his ideas so violated standard mathematical principles, they were often met with skepticism. I heard a lot of grumbling! Larry had offered Martin a partnership, which Martin refused. But in June 1996, just as the code had resulted in a successful prototype program to be used to acquire funding for their business, Martin abruptly quit the project, saying that Larry would never file the patent. Larry later discovered the code Martin produced was "spaghetti code"—as described by subsequent programmers—and missed some of the basic concepts to make it Vallian.

Larry was determined to go on, on his own if necessary, but still be looking for programmers who could make him a marketable product. Why didn't Larry just go to some group of programmers and hire someone? Money! We had only my salary to pay for living expenses and my leftover Ed.D bills, as well as his office, patent expenses, and equipment. So, Larry had to use the barter system, offering a piece of the action for help. Larry was persuasive. Over the next few years, he attracted several different programmers, which he attempted to train in the theory of Vallian but never was practically successful. Martin had been his best prospect.

Larry wasn't trying to create just a new computer graphics tool, he was looking at the same multiple dimensions that the "big boys" of physics were exploring: the multidimensional geometry derived from string theory: " ... that geometry of hidden spatial dimensions might be the universe's Rosetta stone, embodying the secret code of nature's fundamental constituents." (Green, 2015, p 24). But, because Larry didn't have a Ph.D, or a masters, or any college degree, his ideas were discounted by lesser mathematicians in the competitive field of particle physics. That dismissive behavior is deemed unseemly by Brain Green (2015) as he states, "Yet, the history of science has also convinced us to not dismiss ideas merely because they run counter to expectations." (p. 27)

Without the mathematical acumen or language, for the most part, Larry relied on his geometric models to explain his theory. He also thought a practical application in computer graphics might help.

In October 1996, Larry copyrighted the code as the Vallian Virtual Articulated Super Tesseract and then set to work pulling together the new patent. Since I had been awarded a full professorship in August 1996, I was able to relax a little and help him by organizing and editing his writing: he knew the language, I knew the punctuation! We made a good team.

The Crises

During this period from 1993 to 1996, Larry was also coping with several medical problems. September 1993, as he was walking the few blocks from his office to Printers' Inc, he heard what he described as "a popping in my right leg." Later that evening, because he complained of pain in that leg, I checked it out and was horrified to find his right calf red and swollen! I had visions of more pulmonary emboli. So he was off to the hospital for a two-week stay at bedrest and with an IV of Heparin dissolving his clot. This was just a year after his 2nd heart surgery, and he had been receiving the anticoagulant Coumadin all during that year. Larry apparently has a strange body chemistry; there was no way he should have gotten another DVT (deep vein thrombosis) while on Coumadin.

He got through that potential crisis without major damage, only to find out six months later that he had prostate cancer. Fortunately it was caught early, but still major surgery was involved, sapping his energy. That was 1994. Then just a week before Martin resigned in June 1996, Larry had more surgery, this time a meniscus repair of his right knee. The Universe seemed to be trying to tell him something! After that, his health settled down, he got back his energy, and worked hard on the patent. But just as we were preparing to celebrate our 37th wedding anniversary, another problem arose, only this time it was mine.

My Turn

As you have probably figured out from my narrative, I don't get sick very often, and my only previous adult surgery had been a tubal ligation. It seemed that it was now my turn for a lesson. I had noticed a small lump in back of my right knee (popliteal space) that had been present for close to a year, but recently had begun to grow, now having an irregular shape. There was no pain, but I did think it wise to have it checked out. The day before our anniversary, April 9th, the lump was removed; the day of our anniversary, I got a call from the orthopedic surgeon to "come to the office and bring your husband." I knew what that meant. The diagnosis was a liposarcoma (cancerous tumor); the doctor had scheduled me for surgery with a Stanford orthopedic oncologist.

I was scared; Larry was wonderful. We talked and talked, and he even bought me a "Daffy Duck" toy since we had to cancel our anniversary plans (I still have Daffy in my kitchen). After the surgery, Larry told me that while they were waiting to get started, the doctor said he hoped Larry wouldn't have to get me a wheel chair: there was the possibility that my leg might have to be amputated … How Larry must have suffered, waiting for the outcome. He told me later he liked being the patient better than being the family member.

Well, I still have both legs, but the right leg is missing the gastrocnemius muscle, several nerves, and lymph nodes. I was very lucky. The tumor was mostly encapsulated, but the surrounding tissue was removed to be sure it was all gone. I didn't need follow-up radiation or chemotherapy. I just had to relearn to walk correctly since the proprioception (position sense) in that leg was altered. "Don't limp," Larry advised me, "or you'll never walk without a limp." I didn't limp.

There were a couple of incidents, still fresh in my mind, that occurred while I was hospitalized at Stanford on the orthopedic unit. My friend Judy came to visit me the day after the surgery. As she came through the door and saw me, she gasped. "Sharon, you have two black eyes!" I didn't know anything about this.

She handed me a mirror from her purse, and there I was, looking for all the world like I had lost a heavyweight boxing match. My eyes were black from below my eyebrows to my cheekbones. An explanation came later from Dr. Cohen, the surgeon. He related that it is easier to operate on the back of the leg with the patient in the prone (face down) position. Given that I frequently take a lot of Aspirin for headaches and was a redhead before I started blonding my hair, lying several hours on my face during the surgery had resulted in the delightful periorbital bruising I now possessed. When I asked Larry why he didn't tell me, his response was that he didn't want to upset me. I countered with, "I'd rather have known than discover that the staff had been laughing about the raccoon in room 220!"

The next incident occurred when an oncology psychologist came to visit me. I was in good spirits and laughing with my roommate, Julie, who was laid up with a broken leg, when this small, somber-looking doctor entered our room: the atmosphere chilled immediately. He began talking to me in a low, despondent voice about what a terrible experience cancer was and that it was all right to be sad and cry and there were a number of support groups available to help me through this and to prepare me for future negative consequences (I assumed he meant death). While he was droning on morosely, out of the corner of my blackened eye, I could see my roomie trying to suppress her laughter. I had been adamantly assured that all of my tumor had been removed and would require no further treatment; why was this man talking to me like this? His manner would depress, not soothe, any potentially terminal patent. I thanked him, and he left the room, but he was just barely out of hearing range (I hoped) when Julie and I dissolved in laughter. We unkindly—after all, he was just doing his job—christened him Digby O'Dell after the "friendly undertaker" on the Jack Benny Radio Show.

The last incident wasn't as amusing. I am not one to pay attention to pain; I just take my Aspirin and then ignore it. So, when I did have pain that was harder to ignore, I acquiesced and took the Vicodin they offered me. But I hated to ask for the pills, so I would take one and hide the second one under my pillow so I could take it when I next needed it. Dumb, I know, but that is who I am—a control freak.

Then the day came when they wanted me to get up—it was about day four, post surgery. My right leg was in a cast from groin to lower calf. The physical therapist, a pleasant young man, came in while Larry was visiting; Larry was anxious to help with the procedure: the sooner I could get up, the sooner I could go home. But none of us had thought about the muscle loss that occurs after only a few days of inactivity. When I stood up, the cast dropped to my foot, accompanied by the most intense pain I had ever experienced (and I've had two children). Down I went, in a total faint, caught by the PT and Larry. They got me back in bed promptly; that was the end of my ambulation experience for the day. Later that evening, another pleasant young man came in with a buss saw to carefully cut off the cast. I was most grateful. However, after that experience, it took a lot of coaching and supporting from Larry and the PT to get me to walk in the newly acquired Bledsoe brace; not only was it painful, but I was afraid of falling. But they prevailed, and I finally took a few tentative steps so that I could go home—with crutches and a walker. You can bet that I didn't hide the second pill under my pillow during *this* phase of my convalescence.

I must note here that all of the Stanford health care workers, from my doctor to the janitor who cleaned my room, were the best of the best. I recovered without any disability, which they certainly contributed to in great measure—even Digby O'Dell. That event has given me many chuckles over the years.

I suppose many women in my occupation, who are used to being the caregiver, wonder if, when the time comes, will they be taken care of. I did have that concern. Because I was in a brace for several weeks before I was allowed to get up by myself, I needed a lot of caretaking. But I needn't have worried, Larry was a champ. Yes, he grumbled sometimes and got upset with me when I was irritable and didn't think he was doing things fast enough, but he was there. When I had been particularly exasperating one day, he reiterated that he liked being the patient better than being the family member!

But it wasn't only Larry who took care of me: friends from school visited often, brought food, gave advise, sent cards, and even "bought" me a housekeeper for a month. And because I was scheduled to present a research poster in Portland in early May, Larry, one of my faculty friends, and the student I mentored took my materials and did the poster presentation for me, while another friend took care of me in her home. My lessons from the Universe were to not only gain awareness of how many people would put themselves out to care for me, but also to learn to accept that care. It was a very important, life-changing lesson for this "caretaker"!

The Beginning of Paranoia

Now, with most of the major crises resolved, Larry continued trying to figure out ways to get the code translated into a product that could be beta-tested and used to get financing for setting up a business. He wasn't against having some other company pick it up—anyone but Apple—as long as they would hire him to direct the development process. But the companies that he contacted would, first of all, hook him up with their staff mathematician, and that would be the end of the communication; these mathematicians apparently couldn't believe this man with just a high school education could have discovered a new geometry! Larry explained over and over his basic mathematical concept of unity $1 = \sqrt{2} = 1/2\sqrt{3}$ that, when programmed properly, would lead to an extraordinary computer graphics system, but also had unlimited applications in other fields. But, even from Martin, he was unable to get understanding of his thesis.

In addition to not being able to get acceptance of his theory, Larry was concerned that someone would get hold of his idea and develop a product that used part of his innovation but would neglect the important theoretical aspect: the geometry. The resultant product would be incomplete, lacking the aspects that made it unique. When he was shown the cover of Ray Dream's box, he then believed that was what had happened: someone had used his material to "invent" a product that encompassed only a small portion of what was possible. But it was still stealing! In the monograph of the Vallian history (Wahl 2011), I wrote the following:

> While we don't know what edition of "Ray Dream Studio" had the stated, "No floating-point needed," the history of that product and its relationship with VCS, possibly seen as coincidental, is very suspicious. The following information is from Wikipedia, the free encyclopedia.
>
> *The history of Carrara starts in 1989 when a group of individuals moved from France to California and founded Ray Dream, Inc with the idea of creating graphic software for the new Mac computers with color displays. Two years later, 1991, the first version of their new 3D graphics program, which they named Ray Dream, was released. In the years that followed, Ray Dream Studio became a successful product, having at one time over 200,000 users. In 1996, Ray Dream Inc. was sold to Fractal Design Corporation, and was in turn acquired by Meta Tools, given a new name MetaCreations. http://en.wikipedia.org/wiki/Carrara_*
>
> As discussed by the Wikipedia article, the program went through many evolutions and companies, ending up in 2006 with DAZ 3D acquiring three different companies—Enovia, Carrara, and Hexagon—who made some form of the original 3D graphics program, Ray Dream.
>
> Consider the following: Larry's talk with the Apple consultant/ Stanford professor was 1981; Apple had connections with France

through one of its executives who was back and forth through France in the 1980s; Martin Wilson began conversations with Larry July 1991 and worked with him through 1996, only to abandon him when the code had produced a successful beginning prototype program. Even though Martin, under Larry's tutelage, produced code, it missed some of the basic concepts to make it strictly Vallian, or a new geometry. The basic constructs of VCS could easily have been transferred through several different "routes" to the Ray Dream, Inc group, one being Helen Jones who talked with Larry in the 90s and reviewed the disclosure document in 1996. She had been on the developmental team in France. Because Larry had refined the VCS, which became the final Wahl patent, this refined, copyrighted material could have been used by Ray Dream, Inc in their further editions in order to have arrived at the use of "no floating-point needed and triples." That Larry's system encountered no infringing patents during his patenting process indicated that Ray Dream, Inc., under any name, had not filed a patent!

Larry gave PowerPoint presentations to people referred to him as interested in the Vallian concept. He made the mistake of showing his program (his demonstration disk) in comparison with other graphics programs, only to be questioned as to why his was needed when these others existed. Because his program was primitive, he could only counter that there were infinite possibilities and other applications as well as the advent of a new geometry. But, these alleged "interested people" weren't convinced of its value and had little interest in a new geometry. And if he mentioned ease of use for graphic designers, that didn't seem important to those audiences either. When I wondered why he wasn't presenting this to graphic designers or engineers, Larry would point out that the mathematicians stood in the way!

Larry firmly believed that his invention had been stolen, probably by Apple, with help from Martin and even the patent attorney. And from then on, everyone who talked with him, offered help, or seemed interested was not above suspicion. I found that a hard concept to swallow; I couldn't believe that everyone was trying to take away his project. But thanks to a friend, recent information that has come to my attention brings me to a point of believing that Larry wasn't just paranoid: This is Silicon Valley! I laugh as I remember him saying, "You aren't paranoid if someone is out to get you!"

After the several fiascos with Apple, which started in the early 1980's, and especially when his material went missing somewhere in the bowels of the Cupertino Apple campus, Larry bad-mouthed Steve Jobs every chance he got. Our publisher of Book II encouraged Larry to use caution, reminding him that Jobs was an icon in Silicon Valley, a guru to many. Fortunately for our Vallian Book III, Walter Isaacson (2011) blew open that tight compartment, and Malcolm Gladwell (2011), of "Blink" fame, said the things that many people secretly wanted to say. Gladwell exposed the real genius of Jobs: marketing, not innovation!

The concept that stealing ideas is not new was explored by Gladwell who noted that during the industrial revolution, Britain dominated because it had " ... resourceful and creative men who took the signature inventions of the industrial age and *tweaked* them—refined and perfected them, and made them work." (p. 10)—a rethinking of the original. And so Gladwell applied the *tweaker* nom de plume to Jobs. According to Gladwell (who cited frequently from Isaacson), "Jobs was someone who took other people's ideas and changed them." And referring to Isaacson's information, noted that Steve Jobs kept the architecture of *his* products closed because he didn't want them changed. "The greatest *tweaker* of his generation did not care to be *tweaked*." (p. 28)

Larry may or may not have been able to document (his empirical information probably would not have held up in a patent court) that Jobs, or a compatriot, had stolen, e.g., *tweaked*, Larry's computer graphics application of the Vallian Coordinates, but at least Larry knew for sure that it worked. As he would tell people who questioned its practicality, "Go check out Ray Dream."

While it would have been fortuitous for Larry's claims about Apple and Jobs to have been fully confirmed during his lifetime, a 2015 movie *Steve Jobs: The Man in the Machine* by Alex Gibney, the acclaimed, award-wining director who brought down Enron, graphically validates what Larry knew. In the Mercury News article by Karen DeSousa (Sept 4, 2015), Gibney notes that he "wonders what all the emotion [about Jobs' death from cancer] came from, given Jobs' track record of cruelty and betrayal with the people in his life." (p.E3) Gibney expands his contention by noting that " ... Jobs fancied himself a Zen monk, but he got his first job at Atari by passing off his buddy Steve Wozniak's work as his own," and frequently lied to Wozniak's about how much money was received on joint projects, giving Woz only a fraction of the total as his share. (p. E3) Jobs' genius was that not only did he give people what they wanted, he made "... an exciting and seductive pitch that this machine wouldn't just be an extension of you, it would be you." Gibney indicted us as being addicted to the power and beauty of Jobs' machines.

As Gibney implied, Jobs may have created a culture, and though he may have been at the right place at the right time, I think Larry was ahead of his time. Whereas Jobs fed the needs of a glitter-crazy population, Larry was appealing to the intellectual, geometric elite. There were many more recipients for glitter than "dull" geometry.

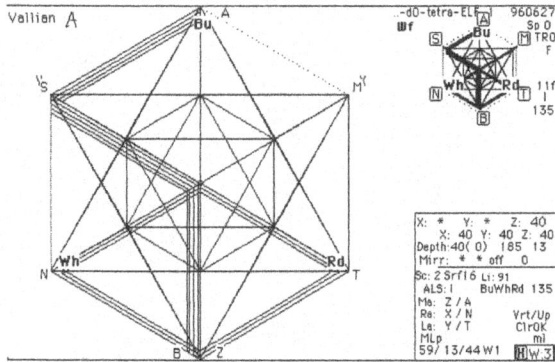

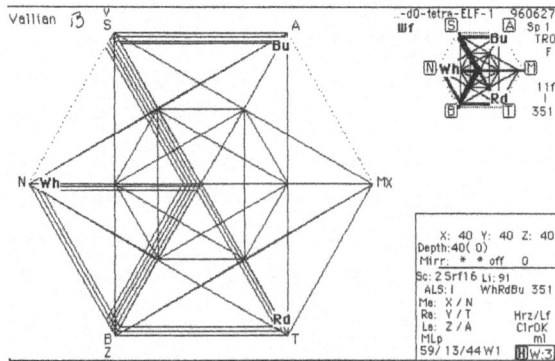

Vallian GHOST Program Sample Screen

Chapter 13

The Master Patent

Hope is a thing with feathers that perches in the soul
And sings the tune without the words and never stops at all.
—Emily Dickinson

During 1996 and early 1997, Larry and I had been actively working on the patent application that would incorporate the dismantled 1991 patent and add new theory and illustrations; Larry hoped this would be the beginning of many other patents, applications of this, *The Master Patent*. Even though life intervened in the form of unforeseen disruptions, he worked diligently, especially on the drawings, while I asked the "why" and other clarification questions.

When my cancer episode interrupted the flow we had going, I believe that Larry, to maintain his sanity, worked on it, all the while encouraging and supporting my progress back to full health. After the acute phase of my episode had passed, and I had a lot of spare time on my hands (I was on six weeks medical leave from SJSU), I helped him with the final organizing, review, and editing. On April 30, 1997, patent application # 08845807 was filed.

Since I included excerpts of the 1991 patent, I'll include similar selections from this application. I'll leave it up to the reader to make the comparisons. From my prospective, the 1991 patent was a "walk in the park" compared to #08845807! I have yet to encounter anyone who, having expressed interest in reading the patent, didn't walked away scratching his/her head, admitting it was "out of my league."

The following is "The Claim," written as one *very* long sentence (and read without taking a breath?). "The Claim" is the most important part of the patent application since it is what the patent office grants him. All of the other 33 pages and scores of meticulous drawings are just "details," explaining and supporting the claim. Larry wrote the claim in the manner that you see in the following because he wanted to cover all perceived (at the time) future applications from his seminal patent. I can't remember exactly how many hours of writing, erasing, and writing again that it took Larry to make sure he used *le mot juste*, just the right word(s)! So here, word for word, semi-colon for semi-colon, is "The Claim."

I claim:

I. A data-stream manipulative method for the computer, constructed for graphically and mathematically manipulating a Vallian/Geometric Hexagon Opting Symbolic Tesseract, comprising:

(a) a method which accepts general input data from which all pertinent mathematical and corollary data-base material is indexed, extracted, and displayed using;

(b) a non-Cartesian system which has three, mutually perpendicular axial surfaces creating a usable, mensurable space figure which, in fact, does not exist in normal 3 dimensional space;

(c) which said system is locked to a virtual internal pegs, based on integer locations which allow for common indexing of multiple attached features and added characteristics, whereby;

(d) a said Vallian/Geometric Hexagon Opting Symbolic Tesseract computer method enables the user to interface and interphase with AI, graphics, data-base, engineering systems, architectural detail, systems analysis, note-taking, CAD/CAM, and internet type communications. *(Wahl--United States Patent # 5,982,374)*

Although we celebrated the filing, that event was restrained because we knew this filing was only the beginning. It isn't enough to research and develop the innovation, the inventor is required to defend his offering against the "prior art." If the inventor did his homework—and Larry did—he will have a good idea of the type of patents that his new filing may be seen as infringing, and he will be prepared for that inevitable day when the letter comes from the patent examiner. That day arrived in June 1999, more than two years after the application was filed.

The prior art consisted of five previously granted patents. After carefully reading all of the referenced patents, Larry dug in and went to work. The following is an example of his responses:

Simpson 5,268,998. Simpson seems to be occupying a large amount of facts not in evidence, because he makes the assumption that this will be done in standard techniques (Cartesian) and nowhere explains, claims, or utilizes cubes constructed mathematically from a cubo-octahedron working out of a hexagonal footprint. Further on, in column 17, lines 13-19, Simpson describes "/LOOK/TOUCH mode for 4-D Euclidean Geometry." Euclidean Geometry is not the subject of the Wahl patent.

(I know, I don't have a clue either!)

Along with 15 pages of rebuttal, Larry sent "several pounds" (his term) of supporting materials, ending with the conclusion, "The Applicant believes the Vallian patent proves a novel approach."

About the time of my birthday in November of 1999, the phone rang and a foreign voice asked to speak to Mr. Larry Wahl. I handed the phone to Larry and ran to pick up the extension. "Mr. Wahl, this is Mr. Singh, the patent examiner." I held my breath. He continued, "I have some questions for you about your application # 08845807." Before he could say any more, Larry launched in to a detailed explanation of the materials he had sent.

"Mr. Wahl, I wanted you to describe …" More explanations from Larry. "Can you just send me …"

As Larry caught his breath to make another comment, I said, in my best teacher voice, "Shut up. Larry. He's going to give it to you!"

Mr. Singh tried again, and this time Larry kept quiet. "I need a definition of the word you used on page 33. When I get that, your application will be complete. Your patent has been deemed novel and useful for the arts. Pending receipt of the requested material, your patent will be granted. Congratulations!"

Larry and I went out for steak dinners and champagne.

The Search for Computer Programmers

Now, with patent in hand and his previous programmer out of the picture, Larry began actively looking for help to transform his ideas and the previous code into a useable computer graphics application, a GUI (graphics user interface). One of his potential programmers was a very talented young Ph.D. who had developed an array of computer graphics that Larry found very impressive. As Gerhardt sought to understand the spaghetti code (from Martin) Larry presented to him, the two men also spent considerable time working on an encryption system. While their relationship was rosy for a couple of years, it ended in flames when Gerhardt dramatically disavowed their partnership, declaring that what Larry wanted to do was not possible, the mathematics did not work without some derivative formulas.

A not surprised, but sincerely disappointed Larry spent the next few years trying to teach several industrious, but mathematically inexperienced followers, his geometry. He even started working with a hypothetically university-educated Latino man, who, when Larry discovered he was undocumented, was encouraged to return to Mexico. The young man had promise; Larry was almost as dismayed as he had been when he lost Gerhardt. But Larry was an optimist: he kept seeking the perfect programmer. In order to attract and teach new associates, Larry developed a number of materials as instruction manuals or for on-line teaching. These beautifully illustrated essentials were shared widely. Chapter 14 has some examples of the instructional material Larry put together for his web pages. There is more description of our web page difficulties in Chapter 14, as well.

Larry provided detailed drawings with all of his written instructions. But despite all of the energy he put into explaining and clarifying and illustrating and modeling his geometry, most of these efforts were dead-ends or met with mathematical ridicule; this happened over and over. For the next section, I am including Theory 203 Background and Foreground, which he wrote in early 2000, a discussion that I find particularly enlightening. There are a number of places where the insertion of his drawings would be useful, and I will attempt to match those to some I have in the files. One of the many reasons I wish he were here while I'm writing on this is that I have numerous documents without drawings and equally numerous drawings without documentation.

I need him to coordinate the words with the pictures. I'll do my best.

Life on the Edge

I don't mean to imply that all of these years were grim; they weren't. Neither of us would tolerate doing the same thing day after day, week after week, so as the designated social director, I would plan events, trips, visits with friends, and interesting books to read together at home.

Larry and I loved to take trips in our little, gas-conserving Prius; he calculated we had driven to the moon and back several times. At about the same time we got the first Prius, on our way home from Long Beach, Washington, we stopped by Seaside, Oregon for lunch. We noticed a new resort on the primary dunes, called Worldmark at Trendwest. They had a sign announcing tours of the vacation property; curious, we wandered in. A very effective salesperson guided us through the one, two, and three bedroom apartments that were beautiful and pristine, and they were "living" at the ocean that we loved. It didn't take much to convince us to buy into the project, especially after we learned there were several more proposed properties designated for the Oregon, Washington, and California coasts.

These were to provide enjoyable, weeklong vacations for many years to come. Thus, our timeshare (now called Worldmark at Wyndam) became the location for the tradition we had developed for our Christmases, with or without the rest of the family: Victoria, BC; Discovery Bay, Washington; Depot Bay, Oregon (we only went back to Seaside one time—it was too much of a party town for our tastes); and San Diego, California were some of our favorite destinations—and we drove to every one.

When we weren't traveling to the timeshare, we roamed our beloved, adopted California: Santa Cruz, Monterey, Carmel, Big Sur, Cambria, San Luis Obispo, Solvang, Long Beach, San Diego, Sacramento, Grass Valley, Lake Tahoe, Bodega Bay, Mendocino, and Fort Bragg to name a few! And we took trips on the train to Sacramento, often with computers and books, staying overnight at a local hotel, exploring old town, visiting the Railroad Museum, and eating at River City Brewing Company.

One evening at home, when a windstorm knocked out the television, we discovered the fun of reading together. I found some interesting mystery novels and would read until one or the other of us got tired. I would read, and Larry would listen; that worked well because if Larry read, I would fall asleep. One of our favorite authors was Elizabeth George: we read everything she wrote and even went to a book signing at Keplers Bookstore. This evolved into a rest-of-our-lives pleasure. Other favorites were Ian Pears' art mysteries, Jacqueline Winspear's 1920's British mysteries, and Daniel Silva's spy series.

Occasionally I would get ambitious and decide we should have a party. Though our little apartment couldn't handle too many people, I went ahead and invited a lot of folks from the neighborhood and friends from work, assuming many wouldn't come. I was wrong on that most of the time, so people guzzled wine and nibbled on cheese and crackers while milling around shoulder-to-shoulder and even on the patio. I love seeing people enjoying themselves.

A couple of these parties stand out in my memory. For one, we had a very urbane, elegant, British wine "salesman" put on the party for us; we just invited the guests and provided enough wine glasses. Working for several German wine distributers, Doug brought a variety of reds and whites and gave enlightening lectures about these wines. Oh, those German Rieslings! I fell in love with their sweet, but crisp mellowness (not really an oxymoron) and prefer them to this day. I'm sure he and the companies he represented were delighted when all of us bought cases—or split one with a friend. I think he went home with an empty car. Unfortunately, we were unable to repeat that delightful experience; the next "wine master" not only lacked the elegance of Doug, he actually seemed bored with the whole process.

The second remembered party was Jill's idea. Larry, Jill, and I were all born on the same decade that ends with a 7, so Jill suggested we have a decade party and invite only 7's. I put out the word, and all of us 7's had a wonderful time. There were a few interlopers, but we let them in because they were accompanied by a 7.

I'm including all of this because, while there was a long period—years, actually—that was stressful and difficult, we saved our sanity and kept going by enjoying life with many interesting activities inserted between episodes of intense work. Even though I was working at San Jose State and Larry had his offices outside and inside our home, we spent a lot of time together working on either his or my projects. So to have these periodic time-outs were essential to our health and the wellbeing of our marriage.

Musing 109

Who-Rah!

Let us, then, be up and doing
With a heart for any fate;
Still achieving, still pursuing
Learn to labor and to wait.

—*Longfellow*

When I was in high school, one day my English teacher was talking to the class about being a writer, emphasizing that writing was excruciatingly hard work but did have its rewards. Mr. Jones looked over at me and said, "Tell them, Larry, how hard it is to write."

"Oh, I don't know," I said, "I think it is quite easy." I'll not readily forget the sour look I got.

Writing is harder work now. I remember when I first decided to be a writer: that event was easy to remember because it coincided with the first time I had a thought. Thoughts came out pell-mell, tumbling over one another, quickly making room for those behind. My laser eyes would fasten on an object, and it would be dissolved, magically, into words, sentences, and paragraphs. Writing was easy and direct; it was automatic. When I looked at a toy bus, the operator would ask for my ticket, and words flowed over and over and took on the form of the lady I sat behind on that bus. All that was necessary to leave the bus was to shift my gaze somewhere else. Then a new jumble of words flowed like water from a pump. In high school, I effortlessly wrote a few special pieces for the school paper, as well as two plays, short stories, and poetry.

Suddenly one day, I was twenty and I no longer wrote. My life became deadly, miserable, threatened, and futureless. All this would produce a wealth of experiences to write about, but I didn't have enough wit to know this at the time. Then at about thirty, after three wives and having sired several children, I awoke to a new wife and a new life. She was a hardworking, dedicated, no-nonsense lady, ten years my junior but a couple lifetimes my senior in character and wisdom.

I had set up an art studio and spent more and more time working on inventions. I started a patent; I started with no experience and totally unrealistic hopes. My first attempts took more time and energy than I had ever conceived giving to anything. Seven years and three complete patent applications later finally culminated in an attempt that was successful. I was listed in the Patent Official Gazettes as Wahl Pat. #5,982,374. But, it wouldn't have happened if my petite warden had not kicked my recalcitrant tail down the bumpy, formally-framed, paragraphing niceties of patent writing.

One long evening, we had a fierce, neighborhood-rousing, verbal battle over the precise distinction between the words "comprised" and "composed." It turned out that comprised, for example, represents the reality of a vanilla ice cream, chocolate syrup-covered, nut sprinkled, cherry-topped congeries, e.g., a random group, a combination generally producing bad news from the patent examiner. Composed, on the other hand, is like two atoms of hydrogen that when connected to one atom of oxygen results in H_2O—water. There can be no water without these two integral and necessary elements present. Probably more than anything else that ever happened to clear my foggy thinking was the understanding that the words in a patent must describe the picture in your mind: good enough, or close, will not do! If your language is indistinct or your descriptions flawed, you will receive tense missives from the Patent Office, splattering polite, formally-phrased venom all over your wretched attempts at immortalization.

A granted patent is a special kind of immortality, even allowing for the grudging granting of an acceptance, closely balanced by your knowledge of the multi-year insanity it took to complete. Long before you have a copy of your granted patent, complete with its cute little red ribbon seal, you will know your concept has likely been pilfered, used, manufactured, and sold by five different companies who have had access to every word you have wrenched out of your fevered brow.

You did the work ... they get the money, but you have that beribboned piece of paper that attests that YOU are "really" one-in-a-million of the forgotten throng of men and women who have lived and invented in the United States since 1776. I, in particular, am the five millionths, nine hundred eighty-two thousandth, three hundred seventy-fourth person granted a valid United States Patent.

WHO-rah! WHO-rah! Yah!

Theory 203

Foreground and Background

Preface

An attempt will be made to fit many years of often seminal research and development into a few paragraphs in order to interest the reader in further information about the Vallian Cubisphere System.

Vision and Mind

For the purposes of this discussion, the term art and graphics will be used interchangeably. Art or graphics will be described as any non-alphanumeric character or any process that makes an unspecialized mark on the computer screen.

Mathematics is well known to be the infrastructure of graphics. What is not obvious is that the reverse is true: graphics can be the infrastructure or background of mathematics. The mind, like the computer, is capable of functioning both in the background and in the foreground. Usually we are conscious of one level while the other operating level is invisible, or barely visible.

Art is generally considered to be intuitive, spontaneous, and natural, while mathematics is conceived to be deductive, cerebral, analytical, and mechanical. If mental operations could be programmed into a computer graphics paradigm, the field of psychology could be a bridge between art and mathematics. However, several layers of meta-structure separate what we *look at* objectively from what *we see*, in both subjective and objective reality. Many of these layers involve hardwired mental trapdoors and slight of hand, fuzzy-logic secrets because they are very difficult to observe in operation or to make logical when analyzed. I call these "paradoxical anomalies." They are mind-bending optical illusions that must be solved, unequivocally, for both the operator and the computer.

The mechanical aspects of the Cartesian Coordinate System are almost totally unable to handle these occult visual processes. Descartes saw the road in his Cartesian octet. This was a perfect cube to sphere, one to one system he was never able to implement, and so he settled for and saddled us with the inherently faulted Cartesian Rectangular System instead of the Cartesian Hexagonal System.

Individual realities are filtered through certain obvious, and not so obvious, processes including visual, proprioceptive, auditory, and various other sensory mechanics. These all feed into a gestalt input that mediates all physical and mental responses, which are elastic and sensitive.

All of the above are normally time-sensitive in some settings. At no speed per hour, we can drink coffee, answer the phone, and daydream and still be mentally planning a trip to the city. If instead we are actually driving to the city at 60 miles per hour in "real time," we should concentrate on the driving and subordinate extraneous time-sensitive actions. Even though real experience on the highway may place us behind a driver who is actually answering a phone call, drinking coffee, and possibly combing his hair, if a 20-ton truck suddenly cuts in front of him, his actions must be appropriately swift and decisive. If we are to avoid similar accident situations, we cannot *think* about a response … we must simply respond, immediately.

Stated another way, if we decide to cross a street in heavy traffic, a mechanical part of our brain may be functioning at tremendous speed to determine (1) if we should take this body across the street or (2) if we should continue to wait on this side. We may, in fact, perform this decisive and dangerous maneuver with one part of our specialized brain while our consciousness is firmly fixed on an entirely different agenda: What are we going to have for dinner, what are we going to do an date, or how are we going to present ourselves in an upcoming business meeting. We will cross that street routinely and usually with success, without troubling or interrupting that part of the brain concerned with food, dating, or peer recognition. The actions related to unconscious decisions while crossing the street safely are *background*, while the conscious part of the mind works on dinner, date, and business meeting in the *foreground*.

Generally speaking, then, design is an art form that is, in the beginning, almost totally foreground activity: it is what we wish to accomplish. Dimensioning is usually background: how we intend something to be scaled. In the usual course of working with art and CAD/CAM programs, we are forced to jump back and forth between the design parameters (foreground) and the mechanical plan (background), such as measurement, tolerances, limits, and production restraints.

Using the previous analogy of driving while talking on the phone—or is it talking on the telephone while driving?—the driver should be schooled in both in order to do either successfully. However, one function will be seen to be forward of the other, e.g., the subject is talking while driving or the subject is driving while talking. In other words, one function will be in the foreground, while the other will be in the background. Ideally, any person—even a non-engineer—should be able to switch back and forth as there is a need, instinctively and intuitively. The human mind is designed to do this but the computer, with contemporary hard and software, is not.

Let us say that an engineer has a mental picture of an item needing to be built. This engineer-creator is trying to accomplish this goal using concepts like form, mass, volume, color, and shade. The creator may thus formulate cunning and complex structures, all sections of which can be completed without straying in any way into the field of formal mathematics. But as soon as this representation must be measured or mensurated, the whole "picture" literally changes. This representation must somehow transform from a drawing to become a plan or blueprint for an *actual* object.

Because the engineer has been grounded in some mathematically rigorous, ordered, and controlled system of design or engineering, this transfer project is possible to complete. It is, however, difficult and consistently time-consuming because, although the engineer may want his mathematical data to remain uncorrupted, the same cannot be said for his graphic representation.

The problem is no fault of the engineer; it is inherent in the Cartesian Coordinate System. In this system, numbers describing graphics go through constant variation and changes because of inherent rounding and averaging formulae operating through the multiple movements, transfers, scaling, etc. that must take place in describing pixel locations on the computer screen.

René Descartes built upon the constructs of Euclid, Paracelsus, and even more ancient and unsung geometrists for formalizing the mathematical system that bears the Descartes name. It is the general Cartesian Rectangular Coordinate System designed for mensurating all 2-dimensional and 3-dimensional graphics. Three hundred years ago, Descartes was restricted to pen and ink representations on paper of his 3-dimensional constructs by the mathematical limits of his era. He had no imaginary numbers, no computers for high-speed calculations, and no ability to manipulate immense amounts of data. We are still using some of these outdated paradigms, although even Descartes knew of better algorithms and proposed them in his octet.

If art and mathematics were connected in graphic computer systems in the same way background and foreground processes are in the brain, it would be possible to stay with one or the other of these modalities. Constructing an "object' would spill out upon demand since all the other computer system data necessary would have been carefully recorded in the background, out of the way.

As driving is background activity, so is mathematical data processing. This processing takes place automatically in all sentient life forms. A squirrel crossing the street (for whatever reason they cross streets) has to unconsciously calculate, at extremely high speeds (computer speeds?), the comparative analyses of vehicle (or cat) size, speed, angle of attack, safety zones, velocity of squirrel at flank speed, incremental movements, etc.—just to get across the street. And all of this must be kept out of the hands of the ponderous, meticulous, and easily confused conscious foreground, to be retained firmly in and to be speedily executed by the subconscious background. To accomplish this task successfully, for either man or rodent, is to get to the other side of the road. To take the time *to think about it* is to become instant road-kill!

Because it is intuitive, coupled, and comprehensive, the Vallian Cubisphere System allows engineers, artists, or anyone having basic drawing skills to transparently cross mental roads of real or imagined structures without getting lost or run over.

LXV

Chapter 14

Publications: Articles and Other Writings

Words fly, writings remain

—Latin Proverb

After many nonproductive meetings resulting in a plethora of failed possibilities, Larry grew weary of staring into disbelieving eyes and speaking into non-comprehending ears. I grew weary of hearing Larry's brilliant ideas dismissed so casually with comments like, "Why do we need that when we have so-and-so?" or "What is it good for?" Even Larry's understated revelation of "It will replace calculus" didn't appease the doubting Thomases. Thus, together we decided to try an approach in which we both felt comfortable: writing.

Larry had no dearth of written material: writing about his geometry was almost a daily activity. There are a few of these expository manuscripts scattered throughout this book, but my next project will be to gather all and put them in a book of their own. However, we had never selected any one of them to prepare for publication as a scientific article.

Our first step was to figure out what would be the best recipient for Larry's geometric focus. I thought about *Scientific American* or *Science* or *Mathematica,* but figured that they were so popular—especially the first two—that our chances of it even getting off the bottom of the pile were limited; Mathematica would probably agree with what the mathematicians always said, "What you are doing can't be done!" So, I went to Keplers' Bookstore to browse their magazine section, and voilá, I found a possible candidate in *Knowledge Magazine, UK,* a new science journal from London, England. Assessing their publication requirements and a sample of their articles, I thought they did seem to be directed more toward the interested layman. But I decided, "Why not?"

When I presented my findings to Larry, he concurred. I was to discover, in the years to come, that he would leave the whole publishing gauntlet to me.

I guess it was time for me to learn a new discipline; after all, Larry seemed to explore a new one every few years, why shouldn't I. Believe me, if I had, at that time, had any idea of what I was getting into, I would have gone running down the street screaming, "No way!" Fortunately, I guess, I have a tendency for involving myself in things that, if I had given them even a moment's reflection, I would have discovered I was terminally unqualified. But that reflection never happened, so in I went, into this new and mysterious and scary swamp called self-publishing. I do have several nursing articles and a number of book chapters to my credit, but someone else always invited me, mostly approved what I did, and took care of the publication details. I was not prepared for this new universe we had clambered into; well really it wasn't we, it was me 'cause Larry didn't care if they got published, he just wrote 'em.

OK. Ready, set, go—the race was beginning. I looked through a number of the post-patent documents Larry had written in an effort to bring the content to a level that I could understand. My theory (not his) was that if I could understand it, anyone could. But then, he always did hold my mental abilities in higher esteem than I did. I finally picked an article that seemed to flow more easily than the others—I could almost understand most of it.

After a thorough editing, adding new material he wanted included, and formatting it as the journal required, off it went, certified and return receipt requested. Then we sat back to wait. This was 2008. But before we sent "my baby," and they were all "my babies," I got an ISBN number to assure that it would remain in his name; both of us had experienced our written material being "borrowed" and published under an unauthorized name.

Since I'm a very poor "waiter," while the article, *The Elephant in the Room*, was moving through the publishing mechanism, I decided to have my printer friend Duc Vu make a monograph of it. And before I did that, I had another bright idea: include the "Talking Points" document that I had prepared for Larry to help him keep his dates straight when talking to interested persons. I expanded the content from a bulleted outline to a full narrative and named it, *Chasing the Tesseract: The Complete History of the Vallian Coordinate System* (which name I plagiarized from another article Larry had written). So actually we could say that this was the first Vallian publication—not counting the patent—proudly complete with its own ISBN # 978-1-4507-6638-8.

I seem to have a skewed sense of publishing ethics: until I received a positive "No" from the journal to which it was first sent, I would not send it elsewhere. Well, forget that! We waited and waited and after six months, in February 2009, without even a letter acknowledging receipt of our manuscript, I suggested that we assume that they weren't interested and see what else we could do with it. Since we were treated so non-professionally, I wasn't encouraged to try that again. So next, we sent it to the research department at Microsoft—twice—and again received no notification that it was received, let alone a rejection letter—even that would have been welcome. Larry decided that NIH again raised its serpent head. The recipients of Larry's intellectual property could have absconded with it, especially in England, though I do think Larry had applied for foreign patent protection.

Since Duc had made several copies of the joint publication, Larry decided that he would just hand them out to people who approached him at his "office," the local Starbucks. Since he spent a lot of time there drawing, writing, and working on improving the theory, he often held the attention of the "regulars" and attracted new folks to his project. His offerings were graciously accepted, but not by people who could help him with what he needed most: converting his geometry into a usable computer program. While he gained a reputation for being "that brilliant mathematician," no one affirmed that they understood what he was projecting, even with his illustrations. In fact, the people who saw Larry on a regular basis enthused more about the human figures and faces that he drew, as he used up many of the available napkins.

Larry received numerous suggestions from his Starbuck's colleagues as to how best to sell his ideas. One suggestion was to *expect to receive a million dollars* for the theory, but Larry wasn't open to that. As Larry tried to sell his technology, he would present himself as not needing to be wealthy, but rather wanting to be able to help develop the applications for his patent, demonstrating the full potential of his ideation. Many "advisors" told him to not say that; Silicon Valley venture capitalists would want Larry to *want to be* a millionaire.

In 1968, Douglas Englebart (Sousa, 2015), who invented the computer mouse, hyperlinks, and video conferencing, had voiced the same consideration that Larry had 30+ years later: Englebart wanted his invention to help solve complex problems; money was not that important. Englebart had more *formal* education (Ph.D) than Larry, but they went down similar paths. Englebart gave one demonstration and dazzled the computer community, but was soon forgotten when Steve Jobs came on the scene. Englebart never received any royalties for his mouse, nor did Larry for his innovative geometry. Perhaps the path they walked is one that inventors of important concepts usually do, and maybe that's because they don't sell themselves at the real value they are worth.

Never one to be stagnant, when his project seemed to be going nowhere, Larry took up writing his autobiography again, filling up zip discs at a rapid rate. It was from this current writing and material previously done (some also on napkins or lined notebook paper) that I was able to extract, organize, and edit the books that we eventually auto-published. Along with his life story, he interjected essays that conveyed his philosophy of life, death, and many other beliefs. Some of these essays are scattered throughout this book, as well as his poetry and letters. If I had just one word to describe Larry, the writer, it would be "prolific"!

Larry had a joke that he repeated often because it exemplified his distain for ideas being presented without context or illustrations. It went like this: When teaching about chairs, the (your choice of ethnicity) always removed the chairs! He had tons of "chairs" in his classrooms.

In *Chasing the Tesseract*, I called the years from 2000 on, The Older Years. Because events seemed to happen at such a rapid rate, like a reckless driver trying to beat an express train to the crossing, the perception of our lives through these years often seems time-scrambled. I don't suppose the reader will argue with me about when exactly some of our life activities did occur, but I *care* about some sense of timeliness. Except for what I can abstract from my saved datebooks and calendars, I'll just have to let go of that form of perfectionism. With that said, I'll now proceed with our story.

During this period, Larry had several physical problems that kept him off balance. In 2000, he fell and sustained a non-serious, but very uncomfortable back injury, and in 2002, he had cataract surgery of both eyes, with much improvement in his far vision. I was glad to see that happen since I had been reading road signs to him for some time. In 2003, he was diagnosed with cellulitis in his left lower extremity; thank goodness there was no evidence of blood clots.

After a few, busy, but uneventful years, along came 2006—not a good year for his physical health. May 2006, he and his chair fell backwards onto our friends' brick patio and fractured the 7th thoracic vertebrae (don't think it hurt the chair). That was breath-holding time, but he just had more back pain and no paralysis. Whew! That same year, we went to Las Vegas (our first and last time) for a spinal cord conference related to my work. We weren't that enthused about the whole experience, but I was even less so when he became very ill and jaundiced in November and was diagnosed with Hepatitis A in early December. The timing was right for him to have acquired the infection from the salad bars in the Vegas hotel where Larry ate and I didn't. He was out of commission for several months; it was very fortunate that he survived at all. I wasn't able to work at the hospital until it was verified that I didn't have the disease (I didn't); it was just as well because I needed to take care of him, full time. Also, during this year, Larry had several incidents that took him to the emergency room and for a few days of hospitalization: atrial fibrillation, a cardiac arrhythmia, and fainting in Cosco-maybe also due to the arrhythmia. What we didn't realize was that this year was foreshadowing future events we really didn't want to know about.

I formally retired from San Jose State in 2005, but continued to teach one class a semester until 2007. However, needing a little extra financial support, in 2002, I started working at the Veteran's Administration Medical Center in their Spinal Cord Injury Unit (SCIU). I worked two days a week at their convenience, which was usually weekend evenings; that was all right with me since Larry and I usually liked to go places on weekdays when there were fewer crowds. Most of my previous non-teaching work had been in home care and ICU, so the slower pace and the longer-staying patients were very enjoyable. I continued that schedule until 2013 when Larry became increasingly ill and I needed to be at home with him.

Larry and I spent one whole summer trying to set-up our web pages. The assistance available, unless you wanted to spend big bucks to hire a Webmaster, was written in computer-ese, which Larry said he understood; I knew I didn't. As it turned out, he either didn't or it was so poorly written that following the directions helped not at all. After at least a month, we managed to get a start of a learning module on the web, but then found we couldn't make corrections without cancelling the whole thing and starting over. We even tried several different web-designing programs, but with no more success. Finally we hired a man who set up web pages for recreation—we did insist on paying him something—and over several weeks we did see some written material on our pages. Unfortunately Larry's illustrations were apparently not compatible with our Webmaster's computer software. We only had his help for a short time because he was moved up the corporate ladder and thus had no more "recreational" time. The two pages he put up are still there ... unchanged.

I think I became panicked with doing anything on the Internet, but later on, I investigated an EarthLink free website and a web development program. Probably enough time had passed to have considerably improved hosting materials. Thus, I was able to set up pages for both Larry and me; I still have that page active, and I add to or change it whenever I have time, which is not very often. The following material is an educational program Larry designed during our earlier efforts and that never was "launched."

Vallian.com
Home Page   Index

√3 · Vallian GHOST

Lewis X. Vallian Associates
Presents The
(After 300 + Years)

THE Vallian/GHOST (Geometric Hexagon Opting Symbolic Tesseract)

Twenty-five years (and thousands of dollars ago), we began work on the Vallian/GHOST. We have received the patent titled in the headline above.

It has been a long, but fruitful journey, and we are anxious to share it with the rest of the world. Many have aided in the development of this new coordinate system. It is now ready to be written-up, published, and hopefully, used.

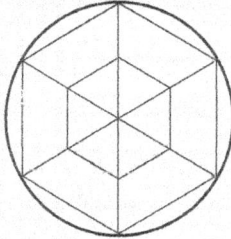

This drawing appears in the official "Patent Gazette " publication as : Patent #5982374 .

5982374

This patent has taken seven years getting through the patent office, and almost 25 years of research proceeding. It is a landmark patent, and we are in the process of seeking financing.

I n t r o d u c t i o n

1

Vallian.com

√3 Vallian GHOST

I
n
t
r
o
d
u
c
t
i
o
n

History Of

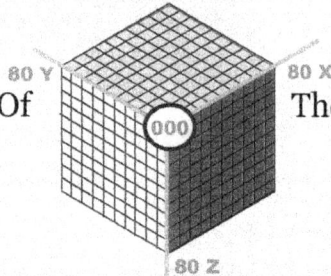

The Vallian
Cube

80 Y

80 X

000

80 Z

Up to this moment, the world has been using a coordinate system de-signed by Rene' Descartes over 300 years ago. It was used to describe 3-D objects. These objects, normally seen in space, must be presented only on a flat 2-D surface. Descartes tried to use the perfect hexagon as a base, but because of multiple problems, mathematical, political and even religious, he failed. Now with Vallian, it is possible avoid the use of Floating-point math, allowing the use of a single, even-integer base for all operations.

This Vallian material was developed over a period of many years. In all of that time, there were many false starts, and although the main concepts were far from easy to track down, they are relatively simple when finally seen.

The main thing that the reader needs to understand is that the Vallian Sys-tem and the basic physics concepts of light and sight are put together in such a way that the mechanics forming the foundation of these systems are, for the most part, almost always hidden

The reasons for this are many, but one example may serve to illustrate. Our eyes roll around in their sockets on an almost continual basis, but the lack of nerves in the sockets, makes us unaware of our eyes turning. It is not informa-tion which we can use, and notice of it would only confuse us.

The body does not tell us <u>most</u> of the things that it is doing, as long as every-thing is all right. It is only when something malfunctions that pain usually lets us know something is amiss. This lack of information is nowhere more prevalent than in the machinery of vision.

2

Vallian.com

Introduction

The Vallian Tesseract *Uses* the Optical Illusions that consistantly confuse the field of Computer Graphics.

These optical illusions, pictures and sketches will be self-explanatory and their importance to the understanding of the Vallian /GHOST system will be explained as we go through the lesson plan. You will be expected to use only common sense, and a smattering of novice mathematics in order to fully and expertly understand the nature of how we see, what we see.

Illustrations, like the one below, will appear in all of the lesson material. Hundreds of computer drawings done over the years will help you, as they have helped me sort through all of the half-digested material which makes up the former knowledge of coordinate systems.

In the illustration, is "a" the top of the box? If it is, then "b" is the front.
But, if "b" is the bottom of the box, then isn't "a" the front?
Answer:
There is no definitive answer, the box will continue to change...forever !

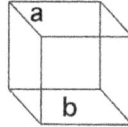

a

b

One of the first Palo Alto California attorneys I contacted five years ago, after hearing my "song and dance", asked me,
"Yes, but what is it good for?",
I will admit to being taken aback, but after a long pause, I answered,
"Well, for one thing it will replace the Calculus."
It was his turn to be taken aback.

Another, specialist attorney from a San Francisco office was sent to talk to me. After we had talked for two hours, he gave me his opinion. It was too complex for them to take on, on speculation. I should try to patent it myself.
So, I did!

3

Vallian.com

I n t r o d u c t i o n

The attorney's question did not come as a surprise, because I had spent over20 years on the research. The problem is that this system is a full and effective GUI. GUI stands for a Graphic User Interface, and as such is simply the plan or method by which the computer translates the numbers, (which are the only things it actually processes) routinely transfering them to pictures. These pictures can be anything visible from alpha-numeric entries to tables, to drawings, and even to literal programs. Because of the "program" consideration, Vallian, standing alone, could easily be developed into a simple operating system.

The computer screen, is a two dimensional creature, and as such cannot generally portray 3 dimensions, but then neither can our eyes. The third dimension is something that is created in the MIND of the observor. It happens so often, and so quickly that we do not even know that we are doing it. In the midst of a compelling story line, on the TV or in a movie theatre, we can become fully involved with three(and more) dimensions, without considering that we are looking at a bunch of pixels on the TV, or the flat, serial presentation of single photos in the case of the movie.

This picture of a light bulb would not make any particular sense to our early Indian  populations, but, then it would not make sense to the new settlers looking at it. It assuredly does not exist forever, but only within a time and space in which the picture is a facsimile of a known object, an idea whose time was now.

4

Vallian.com

√3 Vallian GHOST

I
n
t
r
o
d
u
c
t
i
o
n

It was while teaching at Oregon Polytechnic Institute, that I decided one fateful day to draw a J.P. 57 jet engine in isometric(a 3-d appearing drawing system) from memory.Immediately I came accross the problem of ellipse perspective. The standard way of dealing with all these types of 3-D drawings turned out to be the Cartesian Rectangular Coordinate System.

When I realized how complicated the system was, and how much memory and computer energy it took, and how inefficient it was, I knew that there had to be a better way to do it. This was especially true since DesCartes had invented his basic tenents over three hundred years previous..pretty unlikely system for modern computers, but then, there it is.

It has been truly said of explorers, in every field of endeavor, that they stood on the shoulders of giants. This is certainly true of the 30 years of work that has gone into producing the Vallian system.

Some of the shoulders I found and was able to stand on were Jan Gullberg, John Casti, Olive Wicher, William Stanley, Buckminster Fuller, Einstein, and myriad of other sources.

While the shoulder quote is assuredly true, and nobody is successful alone, it should be rememberd that these shoulders are extremely high, and it takes a lot of Faith, Trust, and a hell of a lot of energy to get up there!!

© LXV
2000

5

One of the first writings Larry did for his autobiography—which he published on one of the web pages—he called Chapter Zero: In the Beginning. Since this present chapter is called Publications, it seems appropriate to include it here.

Chapter Zero
In the Beginning

Most books start with Chapter One and proceed numerically. But in my case, there is a question as to when the beginning of my narrative really started. I liken this to birth. From the time that I first drew breath, there was a BS detector in my nature that seemed to come with the basic package. Generally, this was exemplified by a total unwillingness to share anyone else's values.

Certainly I was, from the beginning, ready to listen to information and data. I came in seemingly very sure of what it was I needed and was determined to get it wholesale. I wanted no dealers and no "middle men." This attitude is obviously a character flaw, as I have been told more than once. Experience, that great but obscenely expensive school that so many are forced to attend but fools may never avoid, made sure that following my own lead would take me to and through the other side of every life experience that I even vaguely wished for. It was not until late in life that I learned to be careful of what I wished for.

Consequently, I drove through passion, obsession, lust, and anger to serially become one or more of the following: a thug, a liar, a thief, a murderer, and/or a wicked, violent, self-loathing devil. Driven by insatiable sexual desire for its own sake and ignorant of any real constraints, I crashed through life with total abandon for my fellow men or women. However, because I lived long enough and had the good fortune to meet someone with even more raw power than I had, I was given the opportunity to leave the "dark side." I became enmeshed with the master rules of a neutral but loving Earth and the real human properties that drive the planet, with all the creatures on it, including we miserable humans, supposedly masters of the earth.

It was clear to me from day one that I had lived before. Saved from a quick and dirty death by a life that would not give me a "free ticket to ride" no matter how firmly I struggled to believe that it had, I was saved from death again and again with nothing that resembled any kind of order or sense, and certainly did not foster any reason to believe in the ultimate "reign of fairness coming." I heard from endless gentlemen and ladies that sometime, usually sooner rather than later, there would be such a "coming," and Truth and Justice would reign.

Though I had no sense of either place, I knew instinctively that heaven and hell did not exist, but with the most tortured of logical concepts, could be seen to exist only in the here and the now of the individual soul. A case in point in my past-lives' history was the unbelievably detailed and richly textured views of former places and former things.

As a ten year old Christian, I knelt in the middle of a large clearing, surrounded by a dozen or so men, women, and other children, trying not to hear the thousands of voices filled with excitement, frenzy, and palpable hate. We had come through a barred door in the rocky twelve-foot wall. We were frightened but somehow or other knew that in the end things would work out, if only we believed. There was a general stink about the place that had filled the deeper cells in which we had spent a few days. But, though we smelled as bad as the place, we did not seem to bear the stink of fear. The older men, lead by a biblical father figure with a long beard, soiled toga, and numerous orange/blue scars from the scourge and whip, walked firmly upright to the center of the clearing; all of us at the same moment knelt and prayed.

There was no question as to why we were here. In some ways we were as excited as the crowd, even though I understood that all of these people were going to be able to go back home when the show was over. It was equally clear to us that the view of the Coliseum would be the last thing any of us Christians were going to see. The crowd noise rose to a crescendo as something happened somewhere in the periphery of my consciousness: I heard them before I saw them.

There were six lions, four males and two females. They came lop-ing slowly towards us and then stood and just looked. Finally, one of the females trotted past me on my left, and I remember that its huge feet made little dust puffs in the dirt but no sound at all. Then there was a short, truncated scream, and I saw a severed leg spitting blood to my left. More gasps, screams, and tearing sounds assaulted my ears. Then I saw him: a big male. He ambled up to me with almost a friendly demeanor and stared deep into my eyes. I could not look away. He opened his mouth and his fetid breath overwhelmed me. However, it turned out that he was simply yawning. I thought perhaps God has saved me. The male shook some of the dust from his mane and passed me on the left. Yes, that was it, somehow in the middle of all this horror, I was going to be saved.

I closed my eyes and started a prayer of thanksgiving, but I had only murmured a few words when the breath assailed me again. The male had walked around me, opened his mouth wide, and casually split my skull laterally, as he turned his maned-head sideways and crunched.

There was no pain. There was the sense of suddenly being blind, as the large canine teeth tore into my eye sockets. And then there was only anger. How dare that big, bloody, bastard let me think I was saved and then attack me from the back. It was so cowardly, so unfair, and just so rude!

This might explain some of my feelings about formal religion; also the thought of lions makes the hair on the back of my neck stand up!

Another example of my past lives: One night, before I had less reckoning of time than I now have, I had this feeling of flying. I recognized that I was out of my body, somehow, but still was able to feel the air rushing past my ears and that cool stream rustling my curly-headed locks. It was a feeling of pure exhilaration, motion without concern and with neither time nor destination to be considered. Then suddenly there was a momentous jolt, and I was somewhere, but barely conscious. I smelled bad. I was a middle-aged man dressed as a trapper, with a bundle of furs under my head; I realized that I was just waking up. I roused myself and looked around. I was in the middle of a dense evergreen forest, and the only sound I could hear was the gurgling of a nearby stream. I got to my feet and was surprised as I found long gnarled fingers extruding from my heavy shirtsleeves. It was the hand of a man who had been working in the wilds for most of his life.

The hands spoke of battles with life, battles with death, and worst of all, battles with myself. I was not a happy being. The scarred and callused hands found the belt at my waist and fingered the axe enclosed in a leather sheath. I didn't know who I was, just what I was, and I froze as I heard stealthy but rapid steps coming towards me. I raised a rifle--I had done this many times--and held it at port, as a figure appeared out of the soft fog that lay like a wreath around me.

Standing in front of me was a small Indian warrior, who looked the worse for wear. He was younger than me by a span of years and looked pathetic enough to assure me he was not a threat. He made gestures towards his mouth, indicating that he needed something to eat, and he certainly looked like that was the case. I stood back a little way and then reached for a leather bag that had some berries and some hardtack in it. Making a gesture of open-handedness, I offered the bag to him. For some reason, the flick of his eyes towards my wrack of furs did not tip me off in time; perhaps I was still partially asleep. As he reached for the food carefully with one hand, as though afraid I was going to change my mind, he had a scalping knife in the other. He held the knife underhanded: I felt it before I saw it.

The short blade dug into my bowels and stopped as it hit my spine. I looked at him uncertainly, as my musket clattered to the ground. He did not look angry, but simply like a person doing a job that needed doing. The blade twisted laterally, with his entire hand within my gut. I didn't lose my balance but simply sat down, as he stood above me. Satisfied that I was dying, he gathered up the food bag, retrieved the musket and horn, wiped his bloody hand on the top of my shirt, and finally took my beaver hat from my balding head. He put it on his own head with just the trace of a guilty smile.

I, of course, had completely lost interest in him, his plans, and his future. Unbalanced, I rolled over on my right side, and, as my eyes became fixed, I felt an oddly comforting, cooling wind blow through my brain and body. My last view of him was an out-of-focus sideways picture of his stealthy retreat with my spoils, my food, my hat, and my life.

I was flying again, this time over the Seven Hills of Rome. It was home, but not really home. I realized, dully, that I was never going to be at home.

To continue our publications, the next logical one would seem to be to include Larry's actual autobiography, but that is not going to happen because it is already published; you will find it as Book I and Book II of this series. Rather, the next chapter will describe the process of getting that autobiography ready for and finally published.

Musing 110 by Larry

Extremely Toothsome

Adam and Eve had many advantages, but the
principle one is that they avoided teething.
—*Mark Twain*

Considering myself extremely fortunate is relatively easy for me since abundance is all around, but the fact that I am having my face lengthened was not even on my priority list. My wife saves up and saves up, works hard and plans in secret to extend my life. If extending my life was all that she did, I am not sure I would be either grateful or compliant. But, the things she does and the things she arranges are all so sudden and so wonderful that they fall within the prevue of things I would do for myself if I had an unlimited fortune. The old joke goes: when you are up to your arse in alligators, it is hard to remember that you only intended to drain the swamp. Sherry's gifts and processes seem to say, "The hell with the alligators, full speed ahead."

The last time I got a new set of fangs, I was 40 years younger. The process then was simple and direct: I told the "operator" exactly what I wanted, and in return, he gave me exactly what he had on hand. I didn't imagine there was any kind of a return desk, nor even a policy, so I just shoved the damn things in my mouth and went on about my business. The tab as I remember was nearly two hundred and fifty dollars.

When Sherry makes up her mind to do these sorts of things, she just goes and puts in her order on the innocent belief that the person giving the service does not understand the word "service" to have any relationship to what the term means on a stud farm. She realized that the prices had probably gone up ... some ... and so expected a bill of about 2000 dollars and change. For my part, when I first arrived at the doctor's office, I realized that I was in the high rent district. The office was in Atherton, which is a millionaires' area of over-sized and over-priced castles.

It turned out that my former toothy experience and this one were as far apart as night from day. Not only was my feedback desired, there were more decisions to be made than I had concerned myself with in the sales office of my local Toyota new car dealership; I was given control of a great number of parameters, and, in order to make all the proper decisions, seven visits were necessary. The Queen Mary (the ship) probably had fewer measurements taken in her construction than the number of metrics recorded on my face, jaw, and general physiognomy. It was not long before I began to think of this "simple" process as a close relative to plastic surgery. The jaw is not a simple structure and much of the general appearance of the completed face is controlled by it.

Humans, like dogs, are often innocent of the results of their random rutting, and it is all too often that a Great Dane will copulate with a female the size of a Dachshund. The end products often look like something square has been forced into something round. In my wife's case, her teeth are set into a jaw that was not designed for them. She is cute for all of this, and well loved and well adjusted, but my lovely lady orthodontist would positively drool to get her hands on my adorable little dachshund! However, my wife letting anyone mess with either the teeth or the eyes that God gave her is akin to the likelihood that people in hell will be allowed to go ice skating.

The doctor made clear at the beginning that the $2500 I originally told Sherry about was only half the bill, but Sherry was not listening. When she recovered from the sticker shock, I gave her some idea of all the metrics, fixtures, and assessments that had been made on me and allowed as how the cost looked at in that fashion was miles from exorbitant. How this regal woman orthodontist can stand with her fingers stuck in my mouth holding an awkward appliance or setting some sticky PVC material for as long as ten minutes at a time indicates the nature of just the physical effort of her job.

When I arrived at session four, I found that it was necessary to put a metal contraption on my head that had two prongs that were shoved into my ears and had a spur that threatened to enter my sinus cavities without benefit of hard drink or pain killers. Parts of the apparatus were clamped onto the molds parked on my gums, and it was not long before I started to think seriously about the "Man in The Iron Mask." Then I was relieved of all the hardware, my mouth was filled with my own good old teeth, and I was given my reward. The doctor approached with racks of front teeth for me to pick from. I started with a set of front teeth that would have done good service to the average gopher. She did not try to dissuade me, but kept gently saying, "is that what you really want?"

Oh, the giddiness of the almost unlimited choices. I realized that, with this initial choice, my jaw line would be about an inch longer than it had been (read Lurch!). I settled for a little smaller version of the teeth, but still a truly respectable set of gleaming dentures. I asked for the brightest white available, and the tech, after allowing that they didn't come quite that bright, came and took the set I had picked— now safely married to the fixture that I had been concerned was going to give me a prefrontal lobotomy. This "tooth fairy" disappeared from the office with my new face, entered a panel truck parked in the back, and drove off with my smile. I had the sinking feeling that I had made a serious mistake, but the doctor, understanding my concern, explained that when I next saw my dentures, they would be set in wax, still in the fixture from which they could be removed and tried in my mug. A mirror would then give me the final decision as to whether my choices were both wise and good enough to be cast in permanent form.

I sure hope that Sherry likes the results, and I have the feeling that she is going to enjoy my new teeth as if they were her own. She lives a good deal of her life in me, as I live a good deal of my life in her. In a very real sense, they are going to be OUR teeth.

The doctor and I became hearty acquaintances, and since I spent so much time with her, I gave her chapter and verse on my three previous marriages (hard to do without teeth) and the one that Sherry and I have shared for 42 years. The doctor felt sufficiently aware of my character to promise that if I ever even thought of leaving Sherry, at the very least she would see to it that Sherry repossessed my $5,000 dollar smile.

Larry's New Smile

Chapter 15

The Books: From Zip Disk to Publication

Writing is a record of the practice of life, of history experienced.
A record written through windows of choice, however narrow,
Where we remain culpable and permeable and alive.
—*Valerie Miner, The Low Road*

I have no idea when Larry first conceived of putting his life to paper; I don't even remember how I came to know there was a book to be published. Larry was very forthcoming about his activities, and he had requested my grammarian's assistance with many of his publications, including his patents, so I'm sure that he mentioned writing an autobiography. I do know I had some of his initial writing, dating from the 70's. He refused to call it a memoir: he insisted that the events he wrote were not remembrances; he was *there* as he wrote his life experiences. In Book I, he talks about having eidetic memory (*marked by or involving extraordinary, accurate, and vivid recall of visual images*): his experiences were relived as they originally had occurred. I find this fascinating since my memory, especially of my childhood, consists of a paucity of occurrences, actually only those that were in some way dramatic or life-threatening.

I do have one advantage over Larry regarding past events in that I can attach a timeline to mine: he identifies "what's" and "where's" but not "when's." Looking over the material on his zip disks—where he had attempted to organize his writings into a book—I noticed that his chapters went from "I was born" to an essay on "discipline" to working for the CIA to high school. This would not do! Our first task was to sit down together, and, starting with his birth certificate, we would date his ages and list possible locations. The research to verify those would come later. By the way, he had two birth certificates with two different names and two different birthdates; on the real one, Larry admitted to having changed the date to make him older so he could join the Navy. He also ended up with two social security numbers—his mother had gotten him one that he didn't know about. You can imagine the fun we had trying to get him a passport: Jill and I had to vouch for him! Larry used to joke that he was set up perfectly for a life of crime, except he would probably forget which name he was using.

Larry *was* a storyteller; thus, I had heard many of his anecdotes. As I read what he initially called "The Vallian Chronicles," I jotted down the events I was familiar with that were not documented in his current writings. I developed a strategy to deal with those omissions: I would wait until we were in a quiet location and had space in our schedules, then I would say, "Can you tell me about the time you worked at Westinghouse or North American or etc.?" That was all it took: out poured the tales, complete with excruciating details, comprehensive conversations, and descriptive locales. My main problem was being able to write fast enough to keep up with his narratives; it wasn't too long until I began to type "the dictation" directly into my computer. And in the process of spinning out the particulars, he added enough other tidbits that would help me to locate that story's position on the emerging timeline. If I fell behind and didn't remember what he said, I could count on him to repeat it accurately—a talent, unfortunately, I do not have!

To begin the organizing prior to editing, I gathered up all the napkins, pieces of notebook paper, and typed material from a dot matrix printer—these I would later type into Word—and, thank goodness, several Zip disks with the events, written in no particular order. The first thing I did with the Zip Disks was print out everything so I could try to order the episodes in a way I thought would make sense to our potential readers.

In an egoistic and unwise bout of poor judgment, I minimally edited the contents of one of the Zips, which I then proudly presented to a couple (friends) for their evaluation. In retrospect, I should have heeded the unknown author who said, "A manuscript, like a foetus, is never improved by showing it to somebody before it is completed." I don't know what I expected, probably glowing approval, but the writing, while of good quality, had not yet been optimally organized, and there were still many grammatical errors and typos … Boy, were Larry and I in for a dousing of ice water! I learned from that self-esteem damaging experience that you never share less than perfect, complete writing to friends—at least not if you want to keep them as friends.

I thought a lot about how to start the book to catch the reader's immediate attention. At one point, I thought about beginning with one of his more dramatic CIA assassination incidents. I tried out that idea on another friend whose partner was an editor and had heard Larry's stories first hand, but they discouraged that. And I didn't really want to start with "I was born at 1:00 in the morning. " I finally decided to use the brief, poignant episode when he was first taken to a Catholic children's home, where his mother dropped him off because she felt she could no longer care for him. Then it was easy to transition to his birth story. From there, using the timeline we had developed as a guide, I was able to order the rest of the stories in a loose chronological order. However, he had included a number of essays that I took out, saving them for another book—maybe this one?—and I hadn't even begun to review all the handwritten material. Fortunately, Larry had so much duplicated on the Zips that was very similar to the handwritten stuff, I didn't have to do too much there.

When I finally had a first draft organized and edited—it was over 500 pages—I gave it, with much trepidation, to my friend's professional editor partner. He read the whole damn thing and made written comments; then he sat down with us over coffee and gave us some superbly useful suggestions. He was very gentle, and he wouldn't accept a dime for his work—we later took them out to dinner. His help was a vital turning point: I began to learn how to be an editor.

From what I have described of our process so far, it sounds like I did it all by myself—where was Larry in all of this? The truth is, in my usual, control-freak style, I did try to—do it all myself, that is. But with this initial draft, Larry taught me another lesson in the art of editing. As I previously described, Larry has many words, sophisticated words, and many more than I do, but he has a tendency to use *too* many of them, especially adjectives. So part of my editing process was to trim down the wordiness and limit the number of adjectives assigned to any noun. I also would sometimes change some words if I thought a sentence was not clear. This was me not being a good editor!

Remember, Larry had an eidetic memory: he knew every word I eliminated or changed! And, that I had not consulted him. After he called me on the carpet, to coin a phrase, I realized that I had literally taken over his writing project. Not only was I correcting punctuation and some grammar, I was rewriting his stories. Not OK!

From then on, with his permission, I continued to correct his grammar and put in and take out commas, but when I wanted to change something or remove adjectives, I asked permission. Even though we occasionally got into shouting matches over something I wanted to change because I couldn't understand his particular description, after the dust settled, I would ask him to continue explaining what he was trying to describe until I could paraphrase it in a way that was acceptable to him. And I read every chapter to him as we proceeded. This took longer, but ended up with a much stronger and mutually satisfactory document. Either of us could discover sections that didn't flow or had gaps between ideas. Not only did I learn to be a much better editor, our already "not bad" relationship, grew from this intense, but actually fun, interactive time; it created a new kind of intimacy. We had never thought that we could work together—too headstrong—but there we were, not locked in combat but dancing a graceful waltz of mutual love and respect.

Silently reading what he had written was one thing; reading it out loud had a very different effect: dramatic! I would find myself having trouble reading some of the passages to him because the pathos was so powerful that I would cry. It's hard to read when you're crying. Then other times, specific sections were so painful for Larry that he would have me stop reading partway through. But, Larry also had a well-honed wit that frequently graced his pages; this humor delighted us both. Sometimes his metaphors were so deliberately absurd that I would have to quit reading because of our laughing-tears. So, while the reading out loud was very useful in catching errors or missed punctuation or incomplete sentences, it was a mixed effort, slowing down the editing process. However, that technique, developed as a result of our working together, has provided an excellent strategy that I now use with individuals with whom I'm editing; that and asking permission before making changes are now valuable tools in my professional repertoire.

It was 2007 when I undertook this project. Like the article that we published and with which we tried to get his work noticed, if I had had any idea how long the going-for-publication process would take, as well as how terrifying it would be, I doubt I would have started it. But I'm good at lying to myself about the time and energy any unusual or not-previously-experienced activity would take. I was immersed in fear when I finally confronted the reality that I was exposing our private lives to anyone who cared to look. On the eve of publishing the first book, I wrote the following:

March 2, 2011

Where is my so-called courage? I am about to move out of my comfort zone into unknown territory, and I am fighting it. I expected Lulu [our first self publisher] to do all of it, but what I didn't let myself know was that this situation is much different from my previous publication experience where I was sought out and solicited to do the writing, in my professional field. Now I'm doing the soliciting as an unknown and in an area I have not a semblance of knowing what I am doing. Friends have tried to warn me off, noting this is not where I have expertise; I have felt insulted and refused their suggestions.

They certainly are right about my lack of knowledge in publishing (and editing!) an autobiography, a manuscript not in medicine or nursing. But I am right about not being deterred, of moving ahead despite the risks and cost, because I believe so strongly that Larry's story must be out there. I'm setting up a budget to manage our expenses so that I don't have to depend on the book to pay for my time and energy. These books are to be a gift to the Universe, and I cannot expect recompense in the form of money; when it comes, it will be as something more important. I've always known that. So I will proceed against the odds and get it out there, one way or another.

Right now I have to gather my courage and use Larry's support to—what is the Rosicrucian term?—Jump the abyss and go through my dark night of the soul? (Probably not their way of expressing it.) There are several factors that comprise (or is it compose?!) that abyss: fear of rejection, having to ask others to help (what happened to the lesson from 1997?), the exposure of our private lives, and losing the hard-gained respect of people when they discover we aren't who we seem (project) to be.

Am I up to the job? Can I suspend the fears and let go of long-term needs—those that I don't have but want? Buddhist teachings are helping, but they are not yet strong enough in me, not enough engrained to consistently override the programmed negativity and expectation of rejection acquired over many lifetimes. However, I haven't turned down many opportunities that Life has offered me, and I'm not about to turn this one down, either. So I will bite the proverbial bullet (also the physical one Larry gave me during my doctorate studies) and move forward.

Another issue that I'm just becoming aware of is the need to manage unfairness, injustice—the books move right through that.

How naïve I was! There is more self-introspection, as well as practical aspects I pondered, but I'll save those comments until I get to the actual preparation for publishing, after the editing is completed (Is it ever? I discovered: not!). Some time during those preparatory years, we realized that Larry had too much material for one book, so we split it into two and then into three where it became The Vallian Trilogy.

The Vallian Trilogy: An Inventive Life. Part I: The Engineer

Now back to the project. As Larry and I were putting together his timeline, we noted places and people he wanted to include, but we needed more information. In April of 2008, we took our first research trip—to Portland, Oregon and Vancouver, Washington where Larry had spent much of his childhood.

The Portland Jewish/Italian ghetto was where, until he was six, Larry had lived for several years with his "evil" stepfather and frequently absent mother; at our visit, it was no longer there. Being subject to a big city's gentrification project, out of that despicable dump there arose a marvelous, beautiful civic center and high-end condos. We were disappointed, but then realized that my graduation from the University of Portland, with Larry present, had been held at that very same, then-newly built civic center. Larry had shown me the mom-and-pop grocery, which was still there, where he had an accident that transported him to the hospital and out of the "evil" stepfather's reach. But, another coincidence (we really don't believe in coincidences), I had served my public health clinical experience in that ghetto before it went away, and we think I may have even been in the house where he had lived for those miserable years.

Because we couldn't visit the ghetto, as such, our next best options were the library and the historical society. At the Portland Historical Society, we hit the proverbial pay dirt! Larry had written about a fire that occurred during his stay in the ghetto; a large lumber mill on the bluff below the ghetto had burned to the ground as he watched. The society had old newspapers that detailed the fire and its outcome. From those facts, we learned Larry was in the ghetto at 18 months old (and some say that babies don't have memories??). That validated another piece of his timeline.

Our next stop was Vancouver and the Catholic Providence Academy, where he had been the lone live-in orphan in an elementary school and a girls' boarding high school. It was now a series of small shops and business offices. I wanted to get some photos of the building—one such picture currently adorns the cover of Book I. We talked to the proprietor of a beauty shop, asking if we could tour the building, but she referred us to the owner (and original builder), Hidden Bricks. We found the grandson of Mr. Hidden, who had built Providence and many other brick buildings in Vancouver. After Larry had shared our project, the young Mr. Hidden willingly gave us carte blanche to troll the Academy. He even called the property manager to clear any obstacles for us.

The next day we went back to the Academy, had lunch in a small on-site café, and met the property manager. I had brought a copy of one of the chapters (well-edited!) that covered Larry's time there and presented it to a very interested office staff. Being curious about its history, they quizzed Larry regarding the building—Larry performed superbly for an appreciative audience. Then he toured me, pointing out places I had read about. This was an enjoyable stroll through his history, even though living there had not always been pleasant. And so we validated more of his timeline. We had accomplished a lot but knew we would need at least one other research trip: it ended up being two more over the next two years.

2009. The objective of this trip was to revisit the University of Portland (Columbia Prep, in his time), which was also my alma mater, to explore the places he remembered and find the names of some of his teachers. The campus was still as beautiful as we remembered. With help from the campus librarians, we achieved our goal and walked away with some great pictures and important information.

Larry and Blossoms at the University of Portland

Because we had a favorite hotel, the Red Lion and its superior restaurant overlooking the Columbia River on the Vancouver side, and, with time remaining in our trip schedule, we spent the next two days finding Larry's adoptive homes—one block apart—and the airfield where, at nine years old, he saw a Russian flyer, having crossed the Pacific Ocean alone, land to the applause of an excited crowd. We also visited the public library and again, with help from supportive librarians, got more information documenting local events

Larry had written about. During this trip, we found the Vancouver Historical Society and got a copy of Larry's graduation photo from the yearbook: he
excitedly showed me pictures of his high school friends. And while we were
there, the librarians found the death notice of Larry's adopted grandfather.
We left, well nourished with validated data, as well as a new understanding
about Larry's young life.

The next and final research trip we took in late September 2010, which
we combined with a trip to one of our favorite timeshare vacation spots,
Discovery Bay, Washington. On our way northward, we stayed for several
days in Vancouver. Here we saw a memorial located on the land of the Kaiser
shipyards that turned out many a military ship throughout World War II.
Larry spent some time during the summers of his high school years scrubbing out the insides of the huge, dirty hulls of ships coming in for repairs. He
joked that, at the end of his shift, he came out the same color as his Negro
co-workers; at that same time he wrote an editorial for the Vancouver Sun,
exposing the awful conditions in which these co-workers lived and rebuking
the city fathers because some of these grown-men earned less than he did as
a teen. The article was published.

I wanted more pictures of Larry's memorable locations: the train station,
also where he worked; his grandparent's home with its famous tree; the home
of a high school first love; Battleground Lake, where they often biked for a
day of swimming. Larry also wanted to find the mural he had painted for a
long-gone bakery/restaurant/bar, but we couldn't find the location where it
was supposedly stored. This was a disappointment because he had not had
the foresight to photograph it at the time it was installed in the bar and just
wanted to take a picture of it now.

Larry did not have much energy during the trip because of an exacerbation of his heart condition earlier that year, so we tried to pace ourselves. We
also spent some enjoyable time resting in our hotel between explorations. I
was satisfied that we had accomplished most of what we wanted to do. From
Vancouver, we drove to Discovery Bay on the Olympic Peninsula and across
the straights from Victoria, Canada and spent some quality time with our
Seattle friends.

After a thorough re-edit, of the "First Book," with pictures inserted, it was time to find a real publisher. My first try was with Lulu.com who, for a $300 down payment, would publish a first draft. I am not the most savvy computer person, especially when it comes to sending off a manuscript to an online company. My previous comments about not operating out of my strength definitely apply here. But I dutifully followed their instructions and, holding my breath, sent off "our firstborn." I waited and waited for acknowledgement of receipt, but none came. So I sent an urgent email seeking the fate of our book. They responded that they didn't have it; I was to send it again. I did. No acknowledgement. After the second email, I received a response: they were glad I wanted to publish with Lulu, and if I would just send the required $300, I could then send them my document ... In my vulnerable state, no way was I going to send more money and certainly no "document" again. They had lost our treasure, and I had lost any faith that it would ever get published there—maybe they stole it! Not likely, but we decided to write off the $300. I kept copies of our and their emails, thinking that someday I would consider legal action. I never did. While writing this in 2016, I wonder if, with my mixed feelings about going public, I screwed up the process myself. We'll never know.

But, I was not going to quit. I started searching the Internet for publishers, self-publishers. I had long ago given up any thought that I could send it to literary agents and it would be scooped up by some big publisher; I had heard too many stories, and even the publishers who knew me from writing book chapters offered no help. Expecting it to get found is like a potential actress expecting to be discovered in a local drug store at the fountain counter—possible, like winning the lottery, but unlikely. This is not the 1940's; the world and the volume of books have greatly expanded.

My next bright idea was to take it to Duc Vu, who had published our monograph. I was very familiar with his work from several projects he had completed for me over the years. Duc agreed to do it, but after asking his advise about marketing—I was going to peddle it at all the local book stores—he brought up a point that the innocent me had not considered. He said, "What if they want a hundred copies, and I couldn't handle that; what would you do then?"

"Oh ..." was my intelligent response.

He then continued by suggesting that he make one copy so I could see what it would look like, and I was to check with the bookstores about publishers. Or, I could try looking on the Internet. I set out to follow his advice.

First I went to the major local bookstore, but all they had to offer was a book on marketing (which further terrified me) and no clue about publishers. OK. So I gritted my teeth and went to the Internet again, starting with the company where I got the earlier ISBN number. They did publishing, but no marketing; what I learned from the bookstore experience was that I would want someone else to do the marketing. Finally, what came up from the Google search was an auto-publishing agency that was a close relative of Amazon: CreateSpace. Bingo!

After Lulu's $300 cost, I now planned on spending about $500; once again, my ignorance raised its noxious head. The total cost, with advertising sent to all major journals and newspapers, came to $1500, give or take a few cents. Maybe the problem with Lulu was that it was too cheap; don't I know that you get what you pay for? I mulled through the money concern by realizing that if we had good enough credit to get a new car (my beloved Misty Plum Corolla was totaled by a tree falling on it), we had enough credit to pay for the publication of the books.

After I requested information about the program, I received an email that the CreateSpace manager wanted to talk with me to explain the program and answer any questions. So, on Monday, March 14 2011, I had an 11 AM phone conference with John Mark Schuster. I suspect he may have eventually regretted taking me on because over the weeks, I know I was a pain! But he was an angel, patient and supportive throughout. At that first conference, he explained the costs, that I would have a design team, that I would be instructed on how to load and digitally transmit my Word document, and that I would have total freedom as to what was published—the latter after it was ascertained that the work was not pornographic! He also reminded me that the package price he quoted would not include any editing--that was additional. I was OK with all of the conditions; I did my own editing. (Much later, when preparing it for an e-book, I found out how useful an editor might have been—the errors and mistypes were legend.)

With the preliminaries out of the way and the contract signed, now the headaches began. I received, via the Internet, a long form to complete before any manuscript changed hands. Besides the standard demographic data, they asked all sorts of questions that sent me into deep discouragement: I was being asked to brag about our "product." I don't brag—which is why I almost didn't get promoted at SJSU; my friends had to tell me what to write to the president to present my worthiness case! Now, you are probably asking why bragging was a problem—the book wasn't written by me. Couldn't I brag about Larry? Yes, but it wasn't that simple. I had invested four years of my energy and love into that book, so it was just about as much mine as Larry's. In fact, Larry and several friends insisted I put my name on it, but I knew that wasn't right so Book II was sans Sharon. Bragging was a problem. The following were my notes as I was considering this aspect of publishing.

March 25, 2011

I really felt threatened by the questions I was being asked by my design team: how was I to put in words such a long and complicated life story. What scares me are all the decisions—what if I really screw up? But, what about my history of decision-making? Haven't I made good ones? And I have used help from others to get there, especially when I was disinclined to go, e.g., going to get the doctorate and on the tenure track when advised by a mentor. I have plowed ahead despite fear and discomfort.

Enter Buddhism: "It is what it is" and "Don't trip over your ego!" Pure and simple, this book is for the universe and not merely a display of my editorial (and writing) talents. This is an opportunity for readers to share Larry's unique life path and his hard-won philosophy of life. Through his stories you can see him and that life evolve—a look into the mind of a recovering genius. (Note, these last two sentences ended up on the back cover description—I was composing as I wrote!) I think I can put together some pertinent ideas of what this book is about.

I don't stay scared very long—I make decisions and take action. When I made the commitment to throw our resources into this project, I knew it would be tough and would take much of my aging stamina. But, as I usually do when I take steps bigger than my 17-inch gait, I hide the effects and consequences until

I'm grown enough to accomplish the task. So it is now, and I do freak temporarily as I confront the reality of what I have gotten us into.

And there still looms vividly the privacy issue. I find myself wanting to warn our friends, "don't read the book; it is too revealing!" Won't they wonder why I took up with this "monster," and isn't that my real issue: What does it say about me? I blush for my self-centeredness. Am I strong enough to let them "see Sharon"? I'm reminded of the women who take up with murderers in prison—how am I different? Maybe they could see what I saw in Larry: the soul within the crazy individual and the belief that, that soul could be saved. I did, but I have to wonder how much of that was my doing rather than just realizing that he was a special human being who only needed an opportunity to grow into what he really was. And wasn't that what happened to me as well? Larry gave me the chance to grow into who I am. I could surmise that might be the difference between the prison spouses, and me but we can't know what is in others' hearts or their needs. I did allow myself to change as I assisted him. We became catalysts for each other—and that is what shows in our relationship. So telling of that growth and change, and all the factors that facilitated them ... that is Larry's story. He gives credence to all those who participated in his evolution, both knowingly and unknowingly. What do I have to be ashamed of; I'm one of many who had a say in his transformation.

I've been ashamed of my life, all my life, and now I have an opportunity to redeem that life by putting it into the proper context.

Handling the emotional realities of this publication was not the only concern I had. Being a Mac person when the rest of the world is PC presents untold difficulties. I was told to click on a button that wasn't there or to send to a location that was not identified. And to make matters worse, help was in South Carolina, three time zones away. This went on and on, and even with John Schuster holding my electronic hand, the process just did not work. But finally, after much thrashing and screaming, I settled down to seek and utilize the help of my "team." Chris told me how to "zip" (shrink) the material so it could be transmitted easily, and Lindsey helped me with what was missing and what wasn't working on my screen. But most helpful was her calm and supportive manner. And then there were Tereza and Larry. Tereza helped me put things in perspective and gave me a special name I was to use to comfort myself. Larry provided the ballast that kept me stable. When it became obvious that the Mac just wasn't going to work, Larry brought out a previously purchased Dell computer and together we problem-solved the process to get the materials sent. (I'm sure Mac users can empathesize with how difficult *that* was!)

And sent they were! We completed submission at 7:20 PM on March 31, 2011. Now, Phase I was completed—with the help of a community. To paraphrase Ms. Clinton, "It takes a community to raise a book."

Of course there was still Phase II—the edit of the first proof—and Phase III—the dreaded marketing. One humorous note in the re-edit was not my error: the phrase, Larry "lived in Al Capone's brothel" came back as Larry "living with Al Capone's brothers"!

So that I could go over the manuscript page-by-page and word-by-word, I printed out the entire pdf file and took it with me to work at VA. I don't think I took a break or ate a dinner there for several weeks while I was looking for needed corrections. And once I found what I thought were all the errors, they had to be documented on CreateSpace's form with page number, paragraph number, line number, and what the original was and what the correction would be. What was really sad was that, I as an Intuitive doing Sensing work, missed a lot, and at that time, I hadn't yet met Annie and was oblivious as to the grammar error I was making: the comma and period go inside any quoted material, whether a dialogue or a single word. Fortunately, I was able to do many more corrections when I later submitted it for an eBook, but still did not get all the commas in quotes correctly!

Duly edited, our "baby" was born on June 15, 2011. The author copy they sent us had all the pictures in full color, whereas the bought copies were not—too expensive.

They did write a marketing letter for us that was so insipid, I promptly rewrote it. I had sent them tons of ideas that were ignored. In retrospect, I could have saved the $498 for marketing since the only responses I got from the multitudes of letters that they said they sent out were offers to be in a company's newsletter for a (large) fee and an invite to be interviewed on some underground-type radio station, also for a (large) fee. We were "fee'd" out, so we eschewed the offers. If I was any kind of a marketing person, I would have trotted around to all of the local newspapers and given them copies to review. (I may do that with all three when this book is published.) I did leave a few at local book stores, but one in Half Moon Bay I never heard from, and the contact person at a bookstore in Palo Alto got very upset, saying it was a novel, not a memoir. I have no idea what button of hers got pushed. A savior was Bookshop Santa Cruz that took books on consignment and put my marketing letter on their website. Even still, we only sold a few. But, I shall be eternally grateful to them because they told me about Annie and Dave, publishers of Book II and III.

The Vallian Trilogy: An Inventive Life. Part II: The Learner

Much of the second book was already written since we divided the original 500 pages into two, with the third part to be added later. Thus, as soon as the first book was published in its final form, our next job was to begin the first edit of Part II and identify what Larry and I felt might be missing. One strategy I use to help in beginning the organization is to make a table of contents with chapter names and brief notes as to the content. I had done that for the very first copy, so it was easy to pull together all of those chapters not included in Part I. With this as a guide, we started the read and edit activity that had worked well for Part I.

During the time I was agonizing my way through the mechanics of publication, Larry continued to work on his geometry and his daily sketching at Starbucks. I was working two to three days a week at VA, so whenever I was at home in the evenings, we agreed to work on the book together. I was able to edit in the computer as I read to him. This enabled Larry to notice errors in the narrative, and for me to identify grammar or punctuation mistakes. This was slow, and sometimes painful, as I mentioned before, but we pushed ahead, even adding chapters when Larry noticed he had left out important episodes. We took our computers along when we enjoyed short vacations in Half Moon Bay or Carmel or Sacramento. The writing and editing were often fun, so it was easy to incorporate it into vacations.

Finally, near the end of September of 2011, we met with our new publisher *River Sanctuary Publishing* in Felton, about 10 miles north of Santa Cruz in the mountains. Annie and Dave worked out of their lovely home and had requested we come for an interview; they didn't publish just anybody. Their publishing focus was spiritually based. I had polished up a couple of chapters and brought a copy of Book I as our credentials. We needn't have worried: it was love at first sight! We shared life stories all around, and Dave and Larry discovered similar Navy backgrounds and their mutual love of sailing. We went home with a tentative contract and a lot of happiness.

Annie told me she would make suggestions for punctuation or grammar changes in just the first few chapters, after which I would be on my own. Since I was very much alone during the CreateSpace publishing, that was OK with me. But the work that she did was so significant: it went right to the heart of my writing weaknesses. It was Annie who taught me to put the commas inside the quote marks, and it was she who encouraged me to not use so many semicolons or colons. In one of our more humorous punctuation exchanges, I wrote to her, "Don't you mess with my beloved colons!" But it wasn't just the punctuation and grammar suggestions, it was the loving support that we felt right from the beginning of our relationship. Annie and Dave are very special people.

I don't have any notation on my calendars about when we submitted the completed manuscript, but I think it was sometime in late November or early December. I do have notes about working on the re-edit in March, and then on September 7, 2012, we presented Annie and Dave with the signed book and a bottle of champagne. So, mission accomplished! However, in October of 2012, I started a table of contents for Part III.

As I now contemplate the strife I endured—mostly self-caused—I could have used the following quote from *The Spirituality of Imperfection* (Kurtz and Ketcham, 1992) to have lightened my internal load.

The self comes clean when it is most exposed, most vulnerable to its own imperfections. Welcome the imperfections! (p 40)

Musing 111 by Larry

The Flying Bridge

Everything flows, nothing stays still.
—Heraclitus

Today is April 17.

This has really been a weird day. It has certainly had its highs and its lows, and it is not over yet. The work is reaching the point at which all of the many streams of my life seem to be flowing into a mighty river. At some point, this massing river is going to come crashing and tumbling into the giant ocean from which, in the distant corridors of time, it all began. First it was just a little trickle of water, welling up from a fertile field. Then gradually it was joined by first one and then another and another, until it was a freshet, cascading down a mountainside, and finally it became the swollen and mighty force it now is.

Of all the stories I would like to have woven around me, the mysteries, the loves, the hatreds, the intrigue, the promises usually kept but often enough broken, none is stranger to me than the one I find myself in now. On the one hand, it does seem as if all of this has happened before, and yet ... I find in these so-called later years that it is almost impossible to acquaint the me I know, with that strange fellow who is either glaring at me in the mirror or else looking at me quizzically, as though I had just been in a head-on auto crash and came away with out a scratch.

Certainly, truth be known, I have way more than my assortment of dings, scratches, broken bones, surgical scars, healing wounds, and displaced or missing organs. The opportunities for me to cease to exist have been fulsome and well documented. Yet somehow, here I still am, heart beating and occasionally still able to breathe flames.

There is a long litany of friends won, loved, lived with, and transported by. Yet, at some point with every one of these experiences, there is the bitter end, diabolical dissonance, and complete dissolution of each and every one of these arrangements. Women, as well as male friends, assumed that in some way, I would always be there for them. All, to a man or a woman, felt a deep sense of betrayal as one by one they reached the point where, as Richard said, "Well, you've just met Larry."

It was always as if my truth-telling, my attempt to make them understand what it was that I was seeking, where the roads were, and where the mile high cliffs at the end of those roads were located would help them understand that there was no place left to go. Then, just as they waited for me to turn around, smile, and embrace them, I simply stepped off the edge of the mountain road, and walked slowly but deliberately off into space, where I didn't miss a step, walking carelessly on the air. I always remember that shocked look, the vituperation, the dismay, and, oh so often, the curses fading off in the distance.

There were a handful of exceptions. They were always people who, like me, lived a secret life and were prepared for an even more secret death. These were the people whom you recognized as kindred spirits, as brothers or sisters. We were members of a very special band of individuals. We were, and are, a certain kind of ghost, ephemeral and tied to the Earth by the slimmest of tethers. Among this distinguished group, there was always the gentle but firm tension on both of these tethers: one anchored to earth and the other summoning to the boundless aromas and tastes of the "Otherness."

From the beginning of my "watch," standing on the flying bridge and looking at the distant horizon, there was always the feeling of responsibility that could not be easily shrugged off. The questions of whom I was answering to and whom I was standing watch for were all non-questions. I was here because I was here. I was standing watch because it was my turn. The rest of the ship could be filled with people sleeping (their favorite pastime), gamboling or gambling, lying, cheating, and doing the lairds' or the Lords' work, as they would see it.

They could die of rust, but they did not have to stand a watch. What was it I was watching for and why was it that I could never see the faces of the officers on the bridge a deck below me? Indeed, not only could I not see their faces, I could not see their bodies either. The wheel seemed to be constantly adjusting for course; the inclinometer and the compass registered a course for a destination that was not up to me to approve or disapprove. I could hear the whirr of the radar and see the pitch and roll of the ship showing up on the various instruments.

Why would anyone put up with this kind of automaticity? I didn't have an answer and even doubted that there was an answer that would make any kind of sense. I heard the ship's bells ring 1, 2, 3, 4! The end of my watch, and I could climb the ladders down to the main deck. I could find myself back in my fo'c'sle as I laid me down to sleep, with no idea if the morrow would bring me one step closer to the ship's destination, or mine—if it happened that they were both the same thing.

When I signed on for this duty, gave them my papers and my Z number, I forgot to ask where we were going, how long the journey would be, and when and where we should be paid off. I was listed as an able-bodied seaman, which I thought was strange since I had lost a few valuable parts along the way. Able-bodied? ... maybe it was meant to be a joke. I decided to laugh, and if I couldn't laugh, I would just smile a lot.

Perhaps the captain has the answer, but even if he did, I have never seen him and doubt that I could make an appointment that he would allow. Perhaps he does not make appointments. Maybe he is running the entire ship by remote control. I just don't know, but here comes someone I do know: It is the boson, and I realize that it is fifteen minutes to midnight and time for me to get out of my bunk, get dressed, brush my teeth, and make my way back up to the flying bridge.

I always stop and look into the round port on the door to the bridge and nod to the captain, the AB of the watch, and the quartermaster— even though I have never seen them. I continue climbing until I am walking across the flying bridge to the center of the coaming, directly above the quartermaster's station below, where my repeating compass is pointing to 270 degrees. It seems to me that it is always pointing to 270, although for as long as we have been at sea, you would think that we would have strayed off the face of the Earth some time ago.

Maybe we did stray that far, and the trip is much like the night I remember when the Marine Wolf was anchored in the middle of Lake Chelan. I had walked up to the bow, past the anchor chain wench, and stared down into the smooth black water, where there was no water to be seen. Instead, below me, as above me, there was nothing but stars. There was no water at all: we were sailing on a sea? Was it a real sea? I DIDN'T KNOW THEN, AND I DON'T KNOW NOW. It may well be that I will never know, and if that is so, then that is so. I will keep rising up to take my place on the flying bridge, checking the binnacle, and searching the endless horizon with the 7-50 binoculars for some other traces of life. Maybe they are out there, and maybe not. I guess it doesn't matter. It is only a matter of time until I am relieved again, and one of these times we will make port.

Chapter 16

Lewis X. Vallian Associates, Inc.

The very least you can do in your life is to
figure out what you hope for. The most you can
do is to live inside that hope, running down its
hallways, touching the walls on both sides.
—*Barbara Kingsolver*

The active time spent on editing and publishing the books transpired from 2007 until 2012, but during that time both Larry and I had additional lives. I had retired from teaching at San Jose State, but had not retired from nursing. In 2002, I applied for and got a job at the Veterans Affairs Medical Center in Palo Alto in the Spinal Cord Injury Unit (SCIU) as a staff nurse. It was suggested that I might apply for my friend Pat's education director position when she retired, but I didn't want that: I wanted to take care of patients. My position was called intermittent, so I had no specific days to work; in general I worked the evenings they needed me, mostly weekends, but would cover for other staff when asked. I thoroughly enjoyed this work, both the patients and my staff colleagues. And, though I didn't know it at the time, what I learned about rehabilitation would be very personally useful later.

Larry, I think to keep his sanity in between his geometry and search for programming helpers, increased his involvement with art, trying out new techniques and approaches. He even bought a large easel, several canvasses, and acrylic paints, intending to resurrect his skill in portraiture in acrylics. He had an old partially completed canvas of me that he planned to update; I made him promise "no grey hair." But he still continued to fill sketchbooks with faces and figures, using pens and pencils (sometimes colored) as well as experimenting with formal art on the computer, rather than only commercial or geometric drawings.

Pretty Woman Coffee sketch   *The Monk Oil on canvas*

On Monday nights—a slow time for most cafes—we would go to GC Tasting Cafe, a delightful, local, wine and cheese bar. I would bring my computer and work on the books, while Larry would sketch, to the delight of the other patrons, often giving mini-art lessons as requested. I think it was here that Larry first started painting with coffee. He would ask Gerald, the proprietor, to brew him up some strong coffee (I don't know why he didn't use espresso) and, using special soft, blunt-tipped applicators, would proceed to paint faces, between sips. Gerald always managed to keep Larry's cup filled. As Larry filled up watercolor sketchbooks, he often gave them away to interested parties, including one to the café owner.

Larry, friend, and me at the café with one of the coffee paintings he gave to the friend.

Much to our dismay, GC Café went out of business. If it had not, I think Larry would have been able to set up free coffee-drawing classes; there was much interest in this new technique he was demonstrating, and it would have boosted the café's business.

The geometry was never far away from Larry's interest. It was during this time that Larry wrote so many of his treatises on the Vallian geometry—and did hundreds of drawings—in an attempt to get some understanding from the people he was still trying to convince to help him. As previously mentioned, we also put some of his writing on his web sites. *The Elephant in the Room* was written and published in this interlude, as were some of the articles included in this book.

In 2008, Larry decided we needed another corporation, partly for projected book royalties, but mostly in an effort to again pull in investors. My take on the new corporation? To paraphrase one of Larry's similes: We needed another corporation like a whale needed peanut butter! But if it made him feel more secure during this difficult time, I would go along with it.

We hired a recommended lawyer to draw up the paperwork for a sub-S chapter corporation, and on March 3rd, 2008, we had the Organizational Meeting of Lewis X. Vallian Associates, Inc. The corporation consisted of two officers: Larry as president and me as everything else; and two members of the board of directors: Larry as chairman of the board and me as everything else. We funded it from our personal accounts in exchange for stock, but we were able to deduct expenses for tax purposes. As corporate "everything else," I kept the books and wrote up legally correct minutes of all meetings.

Larry enticed one interested person by giving him stock to help search for programmers and to find an early Apple computer on which to run Larry's beta program. Unfortunately the correct computer was never found. Nor were any programmers. In 2010, Larry met with another friend, and providing the friend with a box of theory materials, offered him the patent, hoping that he could find funding to get it programmed. In 2012, the friend turned down the offer. Larry's comment to me was, "Well, it's just you and me now. We'll have to do it."

We kept the corporation viable as long as Larry was alive. I finally shut it down in 2014, saving the yearly $800 minimum tax payment to the State of California. What more can I say about this period? It was a time of hopes, then disappointments, of more hopes and more disappointments.

Larry's health was reasonably stable during this time, though he did get periodic colds, some of which progressed to bronchitis if I didn't get the Echinacea, Vitamin C, and Zinc pills to him soon enough to thwart the nasty bugs. His main concern was his legs: his knees were painful and he couldn't walk more than a couple of blocks without pain throughout both legs. He quit walking with me fairly early on because he said I walked too fast for him and it would limit my getting exercise to slow up for him. Shots of cortisone in the knees helped that problem, but nothing seemed to consistently improve his legs. When a test showed that his leg arteries were somewhat narrowed, in 2008 we applied for a handicapped sticker; this helped a lot when we wanted to go places that might require having to park too far away. He could get to the desired activities, like the Cirque Solé, but not without several rest stops. I don't think it ever occurred to us that this might be related to his heart, or maybe we didn't want to. In the past, Larry had joined and regularly attended an exercise spa or gym. I usually preferred walking or biking as my exercise, though I did do core exercises with weights at home after I was diagnosed with osteoporosis. In 2009, Larry gave me a membership at Gold's Gym for my birthday. However, we didn't do similar activities there: As he usually did, Larry swam and exercised in the pool while I did a half hour on the treadmill.

Larry had been an active Rosicrucian in the late 1940's and professed being a Buddhist—in philosophy and spirituality—most of his life, but some time in the early 2000's, he began to practice the Kabbalah. I think this stemmed from a 2004 Rosicrucian retreat where we attended an excellent presentation on the Tree of Life. From then on, Larry read everything he could on the Kabbalah, studied the meanings attributed to the Tree of Life, and attended several more conferences on that subject. At one Rosicrucian conference, when the expert explained, in depth, the meaning of the Hebrew letters, after about an hour, Larry became ill and had to leave the workshop. We have always had the suspicion that one or both of Larry's biological parents may have been Jewish; the contact with the symbology of that religion may have been too much for Larry's psyche.

But that experience did not disrupt Larry's ongoing practice. Every night before we went to bed, he would sit on the edge of our bed and mentally recite the Tree of Life, noting, he told me, what areas he tended to forget and subsequently needed to look at more deeply. One of my most precious memories is that when Larry had finished his Kabalistic examination for the night, he would call me in and envelop me in a warm, loving bear hug. I certainly did not lack for hugs from Larry, but these were special: they had a numinous energy.

During a discussion at the first meeting with our publisher, Larry mentioned his work with the Kabbalah and how much it was helping him cope with the past life events he was writing about. Dave, who also practiced the Kabbalah, gave Larry a book that further enhanced his practice: *The Power of the Kabbalah*. It did not surprise me that Larry put a copy of one of the tenets he copied from this book in a place where I would find it after he died. This Kabalistic concept of Certainty was Larry's gift to me; from it I found the strength, not only to go on without him, but also to launch myself in a new tutoring and editing career.

ערל

*TO AROUSE TOTAL CERTAINTY
IN ANY SITUATION*

*There is only one way to render all the tools and
principles of Kabbalah inoperative and worthless. It is
called uncertainty. If we are doubtful or uncertain
about any aspect of Kabbalistic teachings, we literally
pull the plug and shut them down. "I'll believe it when
I see it," must be replaced by, "When I believe it, then
I'll see it!" In life, certainty is not about receiving what
we want; rather certainty means recognizing that we
are receiving what we need for spiritual growth.
When we face situations that ignite our doubts
and uncertainties, these letters will awaken
certainty, conviction, and trust.*

—Yehude Berg, The Power of the Kabbala

Musing 112 by Larry

On the Ropes

Life is like playing a violin in public and
learning the instrument as one goes on.
—*Samuel Butler*

It is a fact that I annoy the hell out of people, with a very few exceptions. I am now passing my 80th birthday and, only now, do I realize all the reasons for this fact. I have been studying human nature from the very beginning of my life since it was necessary for basic survival. In the process, I have come to realize that I came into this life thinking of myself as some kind of angel, here to help the people of Earth improve themselves. It was, and still is, amazing to me the numbers of them that do not feel obliged to accept my help. More importantly, they often refuse this help immediately after they have specifically asked me for it. Nonetheless, I am always at the ready to give until it hurts … either them or me.

Such self-suffering punishment comes in the buckets of grief these would-be participants give me. But it is well worth the joy that is mine when one of these marvelous connections is actually made. Often, and most easily, this takes place after I have just saved someone from being blown up, run over, burned up, or cut to ribbons. Thus it would seem that people don't mind having you save their bodies, but staunchly resist having you look, much less try to make them look, into the habit of their falling down the same psychic manhole they have plummeted down time and time again.

No amount of signage, warnings, or barriers will prevent them from inventing more ingenious methods for gleefully and, with forethought, dropping into the abyss. The reason that I am so damn smart is that I have spent half my lifetime falling into those same types of holes and only now can recognize them … in the fog, in the middle of a pitch-black night, from several hundred miles away. I have no hard-wired connection with some special galactic wisdom, just the intelligence that comes from surviving enough of these holes to recognize that if I don't go away, the holes won't either. It is almost a rule of thumb that usually the same kind of behavior will result in the same kind of results.

Starting with my first organized attempt to find a map for life by studying the early writings of L. Ron Hubbard, I found a very compact set of plainly organized, exceptionally rugged, and dependable rules for getting through this life, while carrying experience from the last that would give reliable hints on what to concentrate on in the next.

Unfortunately, Hubbard, being more human than his perceived Thetan—just like the rest of us—went into the routine exercise of setting up his organization that (more often than would be desirable) proceeded to defeat, confuse, and eliminate many of the most important principles he had just laid down. The ever-ready temptation of the always-rebellious human ego is there for us to fall into. We do this with disgusting regularity.

In my eighty years so far on this earth, I have had the amazing good fortune to meet an unbelievable array of the dull and brilliant, lucky and damned, happy and miserable, as well as thousands of the permanently sleeping persons who are blissfully running our world through the middle of an unconscious siesta.

Chapter 17

The Last Hurrah: My Karma?

Everything that has a beginning has an ending.
Make your peace with that and all will be well.
—*Buddha*

While Larry had been plagued all his life by one form of illness or another, he always bounced back, often better, wiser. However, starting in 2009, Larry's health began to slowly deteriorate. I noticed that he was not fully recovering his energy and enthusiastic approach to living during one of our Christmases at the timeshare in San Diego.

Larry was recuperating from a cold as we were preparing for that trip. Resting and watching the news, I had my head cuddled against his chest when I noticed he seemed to have crackles (ráles) as he breathed in. Alarmed, I got my stethoscope and took a listen; yes, he did have some inspiratory ráles. I shared my discovery with him, but he said he was fine—it was just leftover from his cold. I had listened to many a breath sound in my nursing years and those sounds weren't from his cold; I insisted we see our family doctor to get clearance before we left for San Diego.

When Dr. Young checked Larry the next day, he found no evidence of fluid or exudate in Larry's lungs. I listened also: he was completely clear! So maybe Larry was right and I was losing my "ear." Even though he had been given the OK to go, I packed a stethoscope, blood pressure cuff, and two bottles of medicine left over from a previous incident: Lasix (diuretic) and Potassium (to offset the loss of that electrolyte in the urine). Just in case! I'm glad I did because when we stopped at a motel along the route, Larry became very short of breath while bringing in our luggage. I made use of my stethoscope and noted the rales had reappeared. I don't know how he did it, but Larry got rid of the fluid long enough for us to get on the road.

Over the next ten days, I listened to his lungs and fed him the Lasix as needed, which seemed to keep the fluid in check. We enjoyed a subdued holiday, except for one incident where we got in a shouting match over him not letting me get us a taxi back to the light rail and him insisting on walking the longest route back to the station. I was so mad at Larry, I got very snarky and wouldn't wait for him as he stopped frequently to rest. Obviously, I didn't help the situation. If I had gotten out of myself and thought about it, I would have realized that he was trying to exert some control over his body, to feel strong and able. Unfortunately his body was not cooperating.

Larry always loved to drive and usually did most of it, even on long trips, but when we were preparing to start home, he asked me to drive. And when we got to our overnight lodging—unfortunately it was on the third floor, no elevator—I smiled my best smile and got the maintenance man to haul our luggage up the three flights. The rest of the trip was uneventful. I drove.

As soon as we got home, about 8 pm, I checked him and then said, "Let's go to the emergency room." Of course they admitted him, and the next day he underwent several tests that demonstrated heart failure and a small posterior myocardial infarct (heart attack). Larry had always bragged that because of his timely heart surgeries, he never had any heart damage, except for what the docs did to him: "You'll have to beat my heart with a club to get it to quit!" So, this was a new and sobering event.

Throughout most of 2010, Larry and I worked at our respective jobs; he was monitored periodically by our physicians. In April, we celebrated our 50th wedding anniversary with 3 days at our favorite place to stay in downtown Carmel: Carriage House Inn. This was a special time because, in 1960, Larry had promised me 50 years, and we made it!

Sharon and Larry on their 50th Anniversary

We continued to take a number of short and long trips, but shared the driving. Larry was generally more fatigued and walking was increasingly difficult. A friend at work gave me her father's walker and offered his wheelchair, but Larry wasn't ready for a wheelchair; canes and the walker would do very nicely.

In early August, during routine blood work, we discovered the reason for Larry's increasing fatigue: his hemoglobin was down to 8.5mg% (a healthy adult male will have 14 to 17mg%), and his renal function tests were abnormal. A referral to a kidney specialist and an order for 2 pints of blood fixed him up. The kidney secretes a hormone called erythropoietin that facilitates the maturation of red blood cells in the bone marrow. When the kidneys are not functioning well, erythropoietin decreases and a severe anemia results. The apparent cause of the kidney problems was the decreased functioning of Larry's heart. And so the major systems of the body work together and, unfortunately, fail together. When his cardiologist did an echocardiogram, he was not surprised to find that Larry's heart's ability to pump blood was only 30% of normal; this was a radical departure from previous tests. To maintain an adequate level of erythropoietin, Larry received injections of the hormone when his hemoglobin went below 12mg%. All of these interventions made it possible for Larry and me to take our book research trip to Oregon and Washington, though Larry was exhausted when we got home, and again, I did most of the driving.

On January 1, 2011 at about 9 pm, a gigantic tree fell in our parking lot and killed my beloved "misty plum" Toyota Corolla. I worked the evening shift, getting off at midnight, and because he wanted to, Larry always drove me to work and picked me up afterwards. On this night, near midnight, I was surprised to see Larry and our neighbor sitting in the hospital family room.

Bye Bye, Misty

The neighbor explained—apparently Larry wasn't sure how to tell me about the accident—that none of the cars could get out of the carport because of the tree; he happened to be parked on the street so volunteered to bring Larry to get me.

We didn't get much sleep because the tree folks spent most of the night cutting-up and removing tree parts. The next morning we reported the accident to our Allstate insurance company; they promised to fetch the crippled car before the day was over. The next day, we drove to the car repair place, I collected whatever I could safely get from Misty, and I kissed her goodbye (I have always had a personal relationship with my cars!). They presented me with a check for $5500 for the totaled car.

After our car farewell, we went to Safeway for groceries. While I shopped, Larry often stayed in the car and listened to the radio, without incident, but this time our 2nd car, the blue Prius wouldn't start. We waited at least 45 minutes for the tow truck and had the driver take it and us immediately to the Toyota Service Center.

I had read recently in the newspaper that Toyota was having an end-of-the-year sale of 2010 cars. I remember thinking it might be nice to get one of the new Priuses with the beeping, back-up camera and a CD player…

The mechanic had just informed us that the problem with the car was a dead battery (the small auxiliary one), a problem easily resolved, when—I swear it was psychic communication—a salesman appeared at our side. He invited us to come in and look at the cars they had in the showroom: 2010 Priuses (Priui?). What the hell, I thought, we've got fifty-five hundred, unanticipated dollars stuck in our pocket, so why not! Larry nodded his agreement, and a few hours later, we went home with a brand spanking new, pearl white, 2010 Prius! We didn't pick the red one that parked itself; we wanted to maintain some control over our driving. The new car was for Larry; the blue Prius was now my car. Larry loved that car! It was a little bigger and easier for him, with his arthritic neck, to get in and out of. Much later, after I inherited the white Prius, I wished we had gotten the parking assistance: I embarrass myself whenever I try to park it.

The new, bigger car seemed to alleviate Larry's driving concerns. We made frequent trips, sometimes staying a day or two. We celebrated our 51st anniversary by taking a several- day trip to the delightful Danish town of Solvang. I had learned my lesson from San Diego, so now I asked for a handicapped room or at least one not too far from dining areas. In Solvang, we stayed again at our timeshare, but this time we had our room inside the main building with an elevator. When we went out to eat or visit a favorite bookstore, I would drop Larry off at the door and would park the car wherever I could find a place; we did have a handicapped placard but those parking places were often hard to find.

In July, we had a Sherry-caused disaster trip to Carmel. Our room was all right, but Larry didn't want to do much outside of it, preferring to work on his geometry proof or watch TV. In order to prevent myself from becoming stir-crazy, I took long walks with my camera, photographing the interesting scenery and houses. But, I could feel the loneliness building up inside me—I wanted company on these excursions, someone to share the beauty surrounding us. I tried to suppress those feelings of abandonment. It didn't work.

When we went out for dinner, Larry wanted to go to an Italian restaurant we had previously enjoyed, but I insisted on a new one that had been recommended. Since I wasn't sure of its exact location, I parked in the vicinity and we walked, two blocks farther than Larry could tolerate, as it turned out. Then when we got to the restaurant, I discovered that the entrance was up two flights of stairs. I said I would go up and check it out, but similar to San Diego, he insisted on climbing the stairs with me. When we got to the front door, we were turned away: they had a private party that night. So back down we went; Larry was obviously distressed. I did go get the car, making him wait by the stairs, and then we went to the restaurant he originally wanted. Our dinner was a silent affair.

My Norwegian aunts and grandparents refused to acknowledge illness or disability; it was considered weakness, and weakness was not tolerated. I don't know if that mind-set was buried in my DNA or if my meanness was part of my Scorpion inheritance. I would behave, at times, like my aunt Minnette (also a Scorpion), who represented the epitome of callousness in the presence of illness. Although I harbored that attitude, it seldom emerged when I was working as a nurse but, with sick family members, I often omitted the soothing hand on the brow. After my own bout with a serious disability, I lost much of that negating behavior; however, "my Minnette valence," as Larry called it, popped up from time to time, and this trip was a prime example of its appearance. Unfortunately, it was to come out again as his illness progressed, only in a different form. In my journal, about this incident, I wrote:

But the fact is that I was Minnette, and I had zero tolerance for his illness that day. Selfishly, I wanted to have our trips to be fun again. So I am guilty of all that he said [that I hated him and could have killed him], and I have to acknowledge that I did, but not because I hated him, but because I hated his being ill. And I'm so tired of always considering what we can and can't do. No excuse, but I can now see that as the "caretaker's syndrome."

I still feel shame for my inability to empathize, to understand how difficult this was for him.

Fortunately, I learned to manage my needs and disappointments a little more effectively, and I know Larry went places and did things that he was too tired to do, but he did them for me.

One of those activities that he endured, but was very enjoyable because of adaptations by both of us, was staying at the JW Marriott Hotel in San Francisco for three days and visiting the art museum for a Picasso exhibit. It was my birthday present to him, and we were treated like royalty. I do have to take some credit for managing the whole experience. Our room was located conveniently across from the elevator (by request), but because the distance from the elevator to the dining room was extensive, I requested a wheelchair; one was provided for the duration of our stay. We took taxis to and from the museum, where I again requested a wheelchair, which enhanced the art experience for both of us. People would move out of our way so we could get close to the paintings, where Larry would then provide me with artistic knowledge, increasing my appreciation of the paintings; I stood behind him, my hands caressing his shoulders. We were surprised by a young woman saying to us, "You two are so precious. I can't wait until my husband and I are your age so we can be like that!"

Our room in the hotel was on the 16th floor, so in addition to excellent food and service, we had a superb opportunity to observe a gorgeous sunset over the ocean. And, as an added bonus, we saw our team the San Francisco Giants win the World Series—on the television. We vowed to return and would have had not an acute exacerbation of Larry's heart disease intervened.

Steve Jobs died on Larry's birthday! In my journal on 10/6/11, I noted, *I'm trying to suppress my fear of losing Larry after Jobs' death, because I am afraid if he doesn't have Steve to hate* … I was struggling with my emotions through much of this difficult period. One book that helped me conquer my need to go away somewhere, anywhere to be free of the grief I was beginning to recognize, was the previously mentioned Kurtz and Ketcham (1992) *The Spirituality of Imperfection*. The authors cited Richard Rohr (1987) as stating that spirituality involved letting go of " … the need to be in control, the need to be effective, and the need to be right." (p. 173). Trying to achieve *that* level of "spiritual imperfection" was to be my struggle for the rest of my life!

While Vallian (his geometry patent) hadn't recently seemed to be in Larry's focus—he was spending much of his free time sketching—in early 2012, it emerged from the background and became a single-minded, frantic burst of his mental energy. After a three week bout with bronchitis and antibiotics, he stayed up one night sorting through 30 years of the geometry—grieving the unrealized at one moment, planning on giving it away the next. A friend or Eric or even I was targeted as a potential candidate to carry on with the Vallian tradition; I was to learn it so I could explain it. I knew that never was going to happen. Larry would get all fired-up about doing something with it, even would have me start writing a page or two, but then seemed to forget about it—even what he had written. He would talk about getting his easel operational so he could paint again, followed a short time later by "I have found the geometry proof!" And he seemed to be reverting to what I perceived as "magical thinking," deciding, despite all of the evidence to the contrary, that he was going to sell his patent to Apple and Jobs, and they were going to pay him "big bucks." Then we could buy a house on one level (going up and down stairs was increasingly difficult for him) or we could cruise to Australia. Thus, our existence had become a roller-coaster ride.

Was this Larry struggling with his losses? That bronchitis brought him down a lot. Or was all of this part of the mental aberrations I had begun to notice. In my journal, I commented, *I almost feel like I don't know him anymore—but did I ever truly know him?*

From reading my extensive journal notes, I seemed to be sensing a pattern of erratic thoughts and behavior. However, I tended to lay the blame on myself: I wasn't giving him enough attention or understanding. But from a present-time perspective, I do wonder if this was not the beginning of some subtle—and not so subtle—mental alterations, which became more obvious as his renal functioned worsened.

I began verbalizing to Larry that I didn't believe that he could let go of his "child" and that was why all of his "deals" fell through. I told him I felt we were wasting so much time on essentially futile meetings that would never go anywhere. He would tell me that "I will quit working on it any time you want me to ..." He had said this many times over the last few years, but would then forget saying it by the next day. However, deep inside me somewhere, I felt that it was his geometry that was keeping him alive, that if he quit working on it, he would die. I didn't know how prescient that thought was.

On August 13, 2012, a Sunday, Larry arrived at VA to pick me up and told one of my colleagues that he urgently needed a bathroom: he was bleeding. Apparently I was with a patient and didn't know of his arrival, so this caring LVN went with him to check out the problem, got some heavy surgical pads for him, and took care of him until I was located. I took him home and assessed what was happening, discovering he had been bleeding from hemorrhoids. The bleeding had stopped by then, but I noted that his legs were again swollen and he had several large bruises on his thighs.

An hour later, the bleeding started again so I whisked him off to the emergency room at Mills Hospital. After they discovered that his coagulation factors were severely decreased and his weight considerably increased (fluid retention), he was transferred to Peninsula Hospital. During the four-day stay, he was given several units of fresh-frozen plasma to increase his coagulation factors and massive doses of Lasix to get rid of the unwanted fluid. During the process of doing multiple tests, it was noted that most of his body systems were compromised. I stayed with him, sleeping (occasionally) in a bed thoughtfully provided by the hospital staff. This episode ushered in the beginning of a number of subsequent health crises.

After this latest incident, Larry seemed somewhat depressed, tired, and fragile. I had to coerce him into walking outside, although he enjoyed it when he did. We set a lot of short-term goals. Larry apparently was aware of how close to death he had been; he told me he experienced this event as an "Oh My God, I'm shot!" This remark came from a joke he told me many years earlier, one that we would reiterate every time reality slapped us in the face. The story goes like this: An actor who had a reputation for "phoning in his acting," i.e., not imparting a sense of reality about what he was supposed to be portraying, was to say the line: "My God, I'm shot," when a fellow actor fired a fake bullet at his leg. Through many performances, he woodenly said his one line. Finally, the director, exasperated with the man's "non-performance," actually put a real bullet in the gun. He got the desired response from the passive actor when, after the gun was fired, the actor exclaimed, "OH MY GOD I'M REALLY SHOT!!!"

Even though Larry had been told that his heart was only pumping at 30%, it took the experience of a multi-systems failure to bring him to that bona fide place of "OH MY GOD I'M REALLY SHOT!" I was beginning to feel more and more that I wanted to cut back on work, to be able to spend more time with Larry. But I was concerned about finances since we still had a lot of credit card debt; however, I did request to work only every other weekend.

By September, I began to transfer more of my time and energy to being Larry's nurse. I became disconnected from my feelings, and perhaps from my compassion; I began nagging Larry because I thought *he is not trying to get well, he won't even get dressed.* Larry may have gotten "Oh my god, I'm shot," but apparently I had not: *By god, he was going to get well!* I was blaming the Vallian project for his "cripple" behavior, all the while recognizing *he was brighter and happier when working on it. Maybe he didn't think he had much longer to do so.*

I had begun to be concerned about our being able to write Book III of the Vallian Trilogy. He had made several starts, but they were all repeats of what he had already written in Book II. I noted in my journal that I shouldn't interfere with his plans for Vallian *because it seems to give him a sense of control when he doesn't have much.* I also recorded in my journal that he began telling me what I should have done to improve my appearance, like had my teeth straightened, got contact lenses, grown my hair long. At the time, I was hurt, but looking back, I believe he just wanted to assure himself that I would be OK without him, thinking maybe he wanted me to be more attractive for other future partners. Did he not understand that he had spoiled me for any other man?

Throughout this period, I struggled with wanting him to get better, trying to control him, even forcing him to do more than he was capable of. It was like I was treating him as if this were simply a temporary setback. He was giving me ample clues otherwise.

I was nervous about taking the trip we had planned for the end of September, but Larry assured me he would be OK. The trip was important because he planned to formally offer the Vallian patent to a colleague he was to meet during our trip.

We took that trip and fortunately stopped to see Eric; it was the first time Larry had seen Eric in many years, though they had been corresponding by mail. It was a happy reunion, but it would be the last time they would see each other.

I did all of the driving because Larry was too tired and felt he was unsafe. The trip did have many enjoyable moments, but Larry's colleague turned down the offer to take on the patent. Larry seemed to accept that decision, but I noted that by the next day, Larry started retaining fluid again, his legs so swollen he had difficulty walking from the car to the hotel or restaurant. I have a picture taken of us by the dining room staff on his birthday that should have reinforced, in me, how very sick he was. But by now, I was in total denial: I told myself he had eaten too much salt on this trip. In that picture, he looked 95, not 85—his face was drawn and haggard, his smile forced. Despite his comments otherwise, I believed Larry's health deterioration was related to "a broken heart"; he saw the refusal of his offer of the patent to the colleague as his last opportunity to leave something important, something valuable, behind.

After this trip, Larry tried to continue some normal activities like driving me to and from work, but as I noted in my journal on 10/15/12:

...he continues to be up and down, often just "goes away" and seems withdrawn and depressed, eating little and resisting my attempts to encourage him to eat more. He hasn't touched his art or sketching for several months now; he hasn't done the jumbles in the newspaper, which he always enjoyed. I really feel like I'm losing him—that he doesn't want to live if Vallian doesn't. I'm getting more and more discouraged that I can't help him anymore. Just standing by while he gradually kills himself is almost impossible. Personally, I feel abandoned, but that is my selfishness. I must get into the "one day at a time, one moment at a time, there is only now" mode. But I grieve.

At some level, I think I recognized Larry's withdrawal as dying, and I was beginning anticipatory grieving. According to Kubler-Ross and Kessler (2005), "Anticipatory grief is the 'beginning of the end' in our minds. We now operate in two worlds, the safe world that we are used to and the unsafe world in which our loved one might die. We feel that sadness and the unconscious need to prepare our psyche." (p. 2) Yes, I was in anticipatory grief, but at another level, denial intervened, and I wasn't accepting that his heart and kidney failure caused his abnormal, apathetic behavior. I tightened my control over his health and life. This was to cause much guilt later since I became so harsh with him, reinforcing strict changes that I was sure would bring back "my Larry."

My next "mental stop" was to decide that Larry was just putting on a performance, i.e., manipulating me so that I would learn more about Vallian and go out and sell it. I told him I would put much of what he had written about his theory in Book III, but that didn't seem to be enough. My thought was that if I couldn't go out and peddle our books, how on earth would I be able to sell a process (Vallian) I didn't understand or really know what it could be used for—besides replacing the Calculus! I wrote:

I know he thinks it will change the world, but I am of two minds: the world has already passed it by or the world is not yet ready for it. I would like to believe the latter, and if that is the case, no amount of putting it out there will help. Another factor is that he had many opportunities to let it go, but wouldn't—possibly because he felt it wouldn't be developed properly.

The next day I felt ashamed because of my reaction to what undoubtedly was his psychic pain. But that evening, he fell in the bathroom; I had to call

911 and have several husky Emergency Medical Technicians (EMTs) get him up. That was when I decided I should take time off work because I no longer wanted to leave him alone. I was concerned about losing my job, but decided, "It is what it is." Larry was quite irritable during this time, alternately pouting because I wouldn't take on Vallian and being impatient because I wasn't working more on Book III. Then later, while we were watching TV, he would gently rub my back, as if trying to make amends. When I notice I am feeling sorry for myself, I write:

I guess I'm grieving, but looking at our lives, I have a lot less to grieve for than he does. I have been honored and acknowledged; he has been ignored. This is why I feel it is so important for Book III to come into being. My feeling right now is I don't want our life together to end like a cheap novel. I don't know that I had any expectations of how we would end—the romantic going out together on the ice flow, unrealistic and not romantic! I have wanted honor and public acknowledgment for Larry, but that is not for me to determine: Larry has his own karma and perhaps he can't have that.

In Books I and II, he doesn't come out as a very sympathetic character. Indeed, important qualities he has, such as mentoring and teaching, are only dimly visible. Thus the reason for Book III is to bring out his strengths and courage, and especially the caring that I seem to be the major recipient of. And it will also build on the brilliance of his mind. I can do that ... but will he let me? I know from past experience that he can derail me, but when something is important enough, like my doctorate, I keep going regardless.

So my path is laid down. I only hope he will join me.

Later in November, I came to the realization that I was very angry at Vallian, the project not the man. Why?—For messing up our life, for putting and keeping us in debt, but most of all because Vallian was his "mistress," and I often felt abandoned because he cared more about it than he did me. Of course, and fortunately so, I did realize that it was my "spoiled little girl" talking and I knew that, for my own wellbeing, I must find a way to forgive Vallian. (It wasn't until almost two years after Larry's death that I experienced the rage I had for Vallian and for Larry. I then was able to begin healing.) But the hits were coming with increased velocity. I had an occurrence that greatly disturbed me.

I was doing a visualization about my ideal life five years from now; I would be 80 and Larry 90. My ideal was an A-frame on the primary dunes in Long Beach, Washington. It had front windows looking out at the ocean and side windows looking off to the trees. The bathroom was huge and had a large hot tub; my office looked out at the trees as I wrote and edited for others.

When I told Larry about this ideal life image, he suggested, "On one level," and I hastily agreed. But then I realized with a jolt that my ideal life five years from now did not include Larry. I hurt to think that I might live beyond him— that A-frame had been a mutual dream. But I see an alternative interpretation: Larry is there but he is so much a part of me that I don't differentiate space for him and me. And I don't see him so crippled that he can't go upstairs to the loft. But, I think I am offering myself this alternative to soften the pain, that I am, as such, denying the seriousness of his present condition. I'm optimistic he will get better, and it is important that we both stay upbeat while we deal with his current limitations. Love Larry in the present!

On Thanksgiving, we had dinner with our friends; Larry was very quiet. Two days later on November 24th, I requested a formal leave of absence from VA until after the first of the year. On December 2, Larry was hospitalized for two days with chest pain, which was determined to be due to decreased oxygen to the heart muscle—no change of treatment. On December 11th, I wrote in my journal

I just mailed my Christmas letter, full of gratitude and optimism, but I don't feel that way tonight. I feel like next year's letter will read, "Larry died on Christmas day of a broken heart because he could never get any external acknowledgement of the gift he wanted to give the world." In truth, he didn't get that acknowledgement from his family either, me included. Oh, I helped when I could, but never with much enthusiasm.

I feel like I've lost him already; I nag him to eat, to go upstairs to the bathroom, to get cleaned up. I think if I quit nagging him, he would just fade away. But I do need to remember that he was only loaned to me for whatever time he wished to remain; if he wants to leave, it is not up to me to force him to stay—as much as I want to.

Around this time, I began doing his physical care for him; I always had washed his hair. We had a ritual where he would sit on the toilet seat and put his arms around my waist while I soaped and rinsed his hair. I knew I was losing him when he no longer did that. But now, I helped him in the shower, and when he was too weak to shower, I would give him a sponge bath. I also helped him get dressed; this was the nurse in action. But there was also a strange intimacy borne of my giving of myself to his most basic needs. It became a time that we both treasured and made the other concerns more bearable. I still remember the love that flowed between us during the simple act of washing his feet.

On December 14, Larry and I were sitting in Doctor Young's examining room. I had been talking to Larry when I abruptly noticed that he was no longer responsive. I gave him a hard whack on the chest while screaming for the nurse. Dr. Young looked in, but before he could even check Larry, the tiny room was filled with about five, very large men who attended to him with practiced skills. I think my "whack" might have had an effect because Larry seemed to "come back" right away. But nevertheless, he was carted off to Peninsula where we stayed for two weeks, which of course included Christmas. During this time, Larry was seen by no less than ten different doctors, including Dr. Young and Dr. Cohen, who managed his care with various specialists and house doctors. Dr. Cohen gave us hope by putting Larry on a special cardiac stimulant drug; Larry did show some improvement, especially in strength and walking, but tired easily if too many activities occurred at once.

As I had done during the previous hospitalization, I stayed with Larry and did most of his care, which we both enjoyed. I had hoped that we would be home for Christmas but that wasn't going to happen. While I wanted him home, I knew that his opportunity to have more years would only be enhanced by where he was now. I wrote:

I alternate between despair (he'll never get better) and optimism (look to next Christmas). This is tough for Larry because he is trying to understand the significance of this illness. Sometimes he says this is payback for all the awful stuff he did. I'm trying to convince him he has already paid back for everything—in spades! I'm going to make him watch "It's a wonderful Life." 12/25—I have no sense that this is Christmas, that it is different from any other day. But hey, if we have to be here, we might as well bring Christmas here. So we did! The music was just right and we enjoyed opening our presents. I even went to a nearby Walgreens and got some decorations.

During this hospitalization, Larry started developing some new symptoms that seemed like his old migraines: headache behind one eye, visual auras, nausea, shakiness. As measured by weight gain, the drugs were not getting rid of his excess fluid; I reasoned that with extra sequestered fluid, he might also be having some cerebral edema that could cause his symptoms. But with the new cardiac drug improving his heart function, his kidney function was also showing improvement—the abnormal values had been very high before the treatment was started. However, on the day before we were to go home, Dr. Cohen told us that the drug had reached the maximum dosage and that, although Larry was stronger than when he had come in, his condition would probably deteriorate. He wanted to get Larry into home care and even mentioned the H (hospice) word. I'm sure the doctor wanted me to be prepared. "But we can't count Larry out. He may be 85 with a weak heart, but he still has a strong will," I reminded Dr. Cohen.

But Larry did deteriorate. I wrote, *It is amazing how lonely it is when Larry has a bad day. Even though he is here, his body is so involved with conserving energy, he is very distant, doesn't interact much. Is this how someone who is slowly dying behaves?*

During the first part of January 2013, he retained fluid to the point that his swollen, blistered legs couldn't get rid of the fluid any other way, so it leaked out of the pores of the skin. By now we had a home health nurse who visited several days a week and helped me find ways to keep his legs from leaking all over the recliner chair or bed. When heavy dressings no longer retained the liquid, we put towels and plastic wrap over the dressings; we used a lot of towels every day. We were also given a home health aide who came once a week to shower Larry—to give me a little relief, they said. I resisted at first because I wanted to continue doing all his care. Friends wanted to come over and give me a day away, but I really didn't know what I would do with a day away. I didn't want to be separated from Larry very long. I think I sensed we didn't have much time left.

I did have feelings of being overwhelmed off and on during those months.

I was having difficulty dealing with his symptoms. As the uremia levels worsened, so did his fluid retention, shakiness, itching (red, raised rash all over his back and on his bottom), and his lack of involvement with his environment, including me. He would get mad at me when I got tired and cranky. One night, in utter exhaustion, I slept through his bell ringing from downstairs and was awakened when the neighbors in the adjacent apartment heard his yelling and came over to help. Larry had slid out of the recliner and couldn't get up. I was so embarrassed.

And I got angry with him when he began using what little energy he had on the Vallian project. He was going to get Martin back to redo the code or sell it on E-bay. I even had some feelings, quickly suppressed, that it might be easier if he would just die. But just when it was getting intolerable for both of us, a "savior" arrived.

On January 7th, I took him back to Peninsula with chest pain and the terrible state of his legs from all the weeping serum. He stayed in the ER only long enough for the attending to call in a kidney specialist and secure Larry a bed in the hospital. We were there for nine days while they drained off gallons of fluid via renal dialysis. That was the savior because there was marked improvement in Larry's affect as well as his physical functioning. Dr. Cohen had recommended against dialysis, telling us that, once it was started, there was no going back. But because of his rapid improvement, Larry and I together made the decision to go that route. When the doctors were assured that his condition had stabilized, Larry went back home and started outpatient dialysis the next day.

Hemodialysis is a procedure to replace abnormal kidney function by removing excess fluid and the unwanted substances usually excreted in the urine, such as urea, and by correcting electrolyte imbalances. This is accomplished by connecting the patient to a dialyzing machine by means of intravenous catheters in an artery and a vein. The patient's blood is then in contact, through a semi-permeable membrane, with a carefully balanced solution (dialysate) where, using diffusion, selected substances are filtered out while others are retained. For many people with chronic kidney failure, these 4-hour treatments, three times a week are their only way to stay alive.

Larry did well for the first two weeks, not minding the dietary and schedule changes, even let me began measuring out a limited amount of water for him to drink throughout the day. Larry never had been a heavy water drinker, but now he seemed to crave it. Was it because he couldn't have it whenever he wanted, or was it the changes in his biochemistry? But water restriction was so important because, since his kidneys were producing only small amounts of urine, every pint of water consumed resulted in an extra pound of retained fluid.

Three days a week I drove Larry to and from the dialysis center, ten miles away in San Mateo, and stayed with him part of the time; the staff always had a chair ready for me. Some days I would go to the nearby Hillsdale shopping center to get some supplies or to Barnes and Noble to read free books on my Nook. I was in the process of getting new equipment, believing he would now be around for much longer than I had envisioned in early January. We had bought a new bed, actually two new beds, that enabled the head and feet to be elevated, because Larry needed to sleep with his head elevated and I preferred lying flat. But now, because we had two Tempur-pedic twins instead of one king bed, I had to get new bed linens. We also selected a new recliner—his old one was too slippery, making it hard for him to get out of it, and occasionally it dumped him on the floor.

On Valentine's Day, I gave Larry a cup I had found in the gift shop, on our last visit at Peninsula Hospital. Its message resonated with Larry, as though it said what he wanted to say to me. As we read it, front and back, Larry commented on the truth of the almost hidden message, residing on the inside back lip that read: "Our bonds are everlasting." I hold in my heart the love he conveyed in noticing what I had missed.

The Valentine's Day Cup

I enjoyed sitting with him during part of his dialysis; we would talk or sometimes watch TV together. It seemed to comfort him to have me there. We even discussed going to Long Beach, Washington for Christmas with our kids; I talked with the staff about how to find dialysis centers on our route up so we could plan our trip around treatments. We intended to be in this for the long haul.

Larry was always cold. I assumed that the cool dialysate running through his blood vessels was the culprit; I noticed that most of the other clients at the center were bundled up with blankets, so I brought one of his favorites from home. Generally, Larry felt better without all of that excess fluid. His legs healed, his rash went away, he could breathe more easily. However, he still did not have much energy for extra activities, other than to walk from the chair to the stairs and haul himself up to the bathroom and bedroom, with the rope he fashioned as a support, attached from the upper to the lower stair railing. He tried the new bed a couple of times, but unfortunately it was a little high and its smaller size made him feel claustrophobic. I fixed up his large office chair in the bedroom with blankets so we could at least sleep more or less together. Besides, he was so unsteady I didn't want him going anywhere without me. Fortunately, I'm usually a light sleeper.

All went smoothly for a while, but gradually he became more resistant to the lack of salt in his food, the restrictions on what he could eat (low protein, low dairy products, low potassium), and the coup de grâce, the limited water. One morning he angrily refused to eat his eggs because I had put Mrs. Dash on them instead of salt. Nothing tasted very good to him—people with renal disease often have a metallic taste in their mouths—but he did enjoy the fruits he could have (those with less potassium) and ice cream, which even that I had to limit. Our friend Pat would come to visit and bring several boxes of allowed fruit: strawberries, blackberries, blueberries, raspberries. Her husband had been a dialysis patient, so she knew the rules. To help the unpleasant taste in his mouth plus the chronic dryness, I bought bags of sugar-free candies and water-substitutes that had been recommended. Nothing worked.

As he became more tired and irritable, so did I. I had periods of resentment because we couldn't go anywhere, and I had difficulty getting very much sleep because of his needs; he slept very little. I also became discouraged because he balked at doing any walking that he felt was unnecessary, except for dialysis; that certainly included going outside. I tried taking him out to a restaurant for dinner, but that was not enjoyed by either of us. To my supreme shame, I got so mad at him because I thought he needed to get more exercise and he wouldn't cooperate, I threatened to send him to a nursing home if he didn't start walking more. I can't believe I did such a horrible thing to him; I guess I was at my proverbial "wits end."

When I think back about those last few months, I cringe to remember how mean I was much of the time. I was often in my nurse "Minnette" mode, insisting that he follow "the rules" absolutely. It really wasn't necessary. With the dialysis, his electrolytes were normalized so restricting all the foods he loved wasn't that important. And so what if he gained a few pounds from drinking water between sessions—they could just take it off the next time. And why didn't I get him a large, heavy blanket instead of the flimsy one I brought from home? I can only presume that I had treated the man I had loved for many years so badly was because I was terribly stressed, not in my right mind. And *I* resorted to magical thinking: if we followed the rules to the extreme, he could live a few more years. I didn't think about the quality of those years for him. It will be some time before I can fully forgive me.

Late Sunday night, February 17th, Larry complained of severe chest pain, and I called an ambulance that took him to the Stanford Emergency Room. We stayed in the ER until the next morning when they finally found a bed for him on the renal dialysis unit. His legs had started weeping fluid again.

On February 18th, I wrote in my journal:

I feel today as though I've lost Larry already—his mind and spirit. Maybe he has had a psychotic break. Last night I came home from Stanford at 9 pm with the intention of cleaning up the house and getting some needed sleep. That was a big mistake!

I didn't care much for his night nurse, Christopher; I should have heeded my intuition. He alternated between abrupt and rude and super polite, more like obsequious; he seemed to resent my presence. After I had asked for more supplies to change Larry's dressings—the weepy blisters were exposed—and none were forthcoming, I finally borrowed his scissors and did it myself with the inadequate few dressings left by the day nurse, who had forgotten to change the dressings. I suppose he was annoyed by my interference. I do get persistent when it comes to Larry's care, but felt it was justified since the too busy nurses had forgotten several things.

But finally I did go home. I had been asleep for about 20 minutes when Larry called and begged me to come back; he said he was scared. I had taken two sleeping pills and my vision was double by then—what a danger I was driving! Then when I got there, Larry said he was upset because he couldn't sleep. Christopher ignored us both; the vibes were not good. I stayed the night. Stanford did not have the accommodations for family as Peninsula did, so I slept in Larry's bed since he insisted he slept better sitting up.

At about 3am, I awoke and found Larry very agitated. He didn't know where he was—thought he was at "Central Station Post Office," and there was a gambling conspiracy going on. He latched onto two pieces of junk on the floor (a paper straw cover and a tag from an IV tubing) as part of the " wrong-doing" going on. I suggested it was a dream, but he became more agitated and said we were in danger. When I tried to reorient him, he got a sly smile that implied I was part of the conspiracy. Later on in the morning, he again became agitated and insisted that I hear his story, which was much the same as the 3am one. I listened, but made no comment. As the morning progressed, he kept looking around with a "deer in the headlights" look; then as they started dialysis, he withdrew and wouldn't look at me, or the doctors.

I now think that the combination of Christopher's barely veiled antagonism, the chemical and fluid imbalances, and the strange sleeping medication they had given him caused him to relive CIA events when he was very afraid and played possum to protect himself. I'm not sure what to do. I'm afraid I've lost him long before he dies.

Later, when I come back, he had been on dialysis for an hour and he greeted me with smiles, saying how good he was now that I was back. He seemed almost like he had been at outpatient dialysis—though weaker, and still not quite right … After dialysis, he was ready to take a nap when in came the occupational (OT) and physical therapists (PT), who ran him through extensive tests. He did well, but when the PT asked him where he was, Larry said he was in "some sort of an extension of …" He dodged the question but then read "Stanford" off the OT's shirt and admitted that he had done that. When pressed about "what kind of place?" he could not produce hospital, but quickly agreed when the PT said it.

Was this our usual aged nominal aphasia or did he truly not know. Later I asked him, and he said he didn't remember getting here and it looked like some Stanford off-site building. After Peninsula, I had to agree! I wondered if his responses weren't just fatigue or even the slowness of processing that occurs in stressed older people when pressured. Later Larry chewed me out for not believing him that his nurse Christopher was running a gambling scam.

Now at 2130, he is bright and alert, and we are analyzing the pictures on TV together. His speech is a little strained, but he says he feels so much better. "And," he says, "put that Christmas trip to Long Beach on our agenda." See, don't count him out just yet; live day-by-day!

We went home on the afternoon of the 19th. Larry had lost 3 kilograms or 9.86 pounds of fluid from the dialysis at Stanford. But he seemed to have lost more than that—he seemed enervated and dispirited. Although I still read to him, his level of interest was limited. Usually he just wanted to watch TV—the NASA station was a long-time favorite and continued to be his first choice.

Since we planned on dialysis being a long-term process—he had turned down the recommended hospice—we made an appointment to meet with a specialist who was to evaluate his blood vessels for the insertion of a permanent internal, arterio-venous (AV) shunt. Rather than putting needles into the two catheters that had been temporarily placed in an artery and a vein, an internal AV shunt would be created by surgically connecting (anastomosing) a side-by-side artery and vein that would result in a large vessel that, with an inserted cannula, created an easy access for dialysis. The permanent AV shunt was considered less invasive with a decreased risk for infection or obstruction by a clot. (Miller and Keane, 1987).

Despite Larry's fatigue, we made the trip up to that doctor's office and sat in a crowded waiting room for at least a half hour, waiting for the doctor to do the evaluation. He was skeptical about the quality of Larry's vessels, but scheduled the surgery for a week later.

On the afternoon of February 26th, we had an appointment with our long-time cardiologist Dr. Cohen. While Larry was elaborating on how good he felt in general but how difficult the dialysis was for him, especially being cold and thirsty all the time (Dr. Cohen had recommended against it), Dr. Cohen listened solemnly. Then abruptly he said, "What are you going to do if your heart stops suddenly when you are at home?"

Flustered, I stuttered that of course, as a health professional, I would do CPR (cardiopulmonary resuscitation). Larry nodded agreement. With a hug to both of us, Dr. Cohen suggested we think about it.

That evening after dinner, I asked Larry if, even though he wanted CPR, did he want more invasive procedures such as intubation and a ventilator to keep him breathing. He firmly said he did not. Thus I had my instructions. And a little later, without thinking, I said to him, "Honey, if this is all too much, the dialysis and all, it is OK for you to let go." He nodded, understanding.

Over the previous few days, Larry had been trying to make his large tesseract model more sturdy by gluing the rod-shaped pieces into the small round balls designed for them. On this night, I sat with him to help for a while, but when he indicated he was going to stay up longer, a tired me went to bed. I had a hair cut the next day, and Phoebe, the home health aide, was coming to give him a shower. I was annoyed with him because the day's events had been tiring and I wanted him to get some rest, but his mind was doggedly focused on fixing his tesseract.

The next morning when I went downstairs, I found Larry looking dejectedly at the pieces of his model strewn across the table where he had been working. Just as Einstein had asked for a pencil and note pad the day he died so he could continue his work (Halpern, 2015), so did Larry stay up all night, trying to put his tesseract back together. Not understanding and still annoyed with him, I helped him to his chair upstairs where he could wait for Phoebe. Then I left for my hair appointment.

When I got home, Larry was in his upstairs chair, but now clean and dressed. I commented, in an almost impersonal, nurse way, "You had a nice shower from Phoebe." And in a very soft voice, he retorted, "Not as nice as yours." I still hold that comment close to my heart. I hugged him and reminded him it was time to go to dialysis. I helped him downstairs, sat him in my recliner (we had not yet received his new one), and went out to get the car.

Over the past two months of dialysis treatments, we had developed a pattern. While I would get the car, Larry would use his walker and come to the front door. Then I would assist him into the car, store the walker in the backseat, and off we would go. That was the plan for this afternoon, but when I pulled up to the front door, I could see through the screen door that he was still in the chair. Impatiently getting out of the car, I walked in the front door ... and then I saw him ... "Oh no, Larry, oh no, no!"

I was in shock, but I had to do something! I ran to him and tried to hit him in the chest, hoping to restart his heart, but it seemed to have no effect. I grabbed the phone and called 911, telling the operator that he was nonresponsive. She asked where he was, and when I said in a recliner chair, she said to get him on the floor. "But he's too heavy." I said as I was feebly trying to do compressions. "Just get him on the floor," she repeated. So I pulled him out of the chair, and he landed on the floor with a loud thump. I was sure that I had probably broken every bone in his body. I restarted heart compressions only to have gentle hands pull me away and take over—the EMTs, who had picked Larry up off the floor a couple of times before, had arrived. Soon the room was full of very busy people shouting orders at each other. Another pair of gentle hands delivered me to my neighbors who were waiting outside. Even with all the chaos, I managed to yell, "He doesn't want intubation." Was I prescient when I asked him about that last night? But then, I also gave him permission to die, didn't I ...

I stood outside, shivering, surrounded and held by my neighbors and friends. I recognized the second pair of gentle hands: he was a small, caring EMT who had comforted me the last time we had called 911. In a relatively short time, they had Larry's heart beating again, but he had not regained consciousness. The ambulance took Larry to the Stanford Emergency Room, and my neighbor Sandra followed with me. As she turned me over to the ER staff, she gave them her cell phone number and said to call when I was ready to come home.

I don't know now who all of those wonderful people were who talked to me and held me as we watched a crew of doctors struggle to bring Larry back to life. They worked so hard to save him for me, but after a half hour, recognized that he was gone. Before they turned off the life support, they asked me one more time if they should intubate him, and I said "No." I had remained quiet and dry-eyed throughout all of the rescue activities, but as we were watching the final efforts, a tall young man, one of our EMTs, enfolded me in his arms, and finally I cried.

While the nurses prepared Larry for final viewing, a kindly woman, probably the social worker, sat with me in the hall outside the room. She asked me about my family, and I said I would call our children later tonight. Then another woman came along and quietly inquired if Larry would be an organ donor; I affirmed that he would. I was brought coffee—I had not even asked—and the social worker then wanted to know if I wanted a minister or a priest. I said no, but asked if they had a Buddhist monk—a Buddhist nun had visited us at a hospitalization years earlier, but she was no longer there. Then it dawned on me: the Buddhist was for me; Larry had been studying Kabbalah for several years. We needed a Rabbi. The on-site Rabbi was summoned, and Larry and I were now in the care of this kind, sensitive woman.

The Rabbi asked me if I would like for us to pray over Larry, so I told her about Larry reciting the Tree of Life every night before retiring to bed. She said she had a perfect prayer. She took me into the room of the now peaceful-looking Larry and softly sang the Tree of Life over his body. Then she asked me to join her in this ceremony, and singing together, we were able to give Larry the most beautiful spiritual send-off possible; his soul would find peace.

The next few weeks were as though I were in an alternate existence—nothing seemed real. But I did write, the words piercing my fog of denial to give me something to remember of that time. I won't include all of them—that's for my next book—but I find the March 1st entry notable.

I didn't want to wake up this morning even though I had about 9 hours of sleep. I am trying to catch up, but it was not good sleep: lots of dreams. The one I remember was someone replaced my bright green soap with something beige; I was very upset because they took my green soap. That one wasn't very hard to read: they took my bright and pretty life and left a drab one. Who were they? The Cosmos.

I also woke up with a headache. Now I notice I'm feeling some anger at Larry—why did he leave me now? "If not now, when?" I must set aside the guilt about the time I let loose and excoriated him because we couldn't go anywhere or do anything; now I can go anywhere and do anything ... but what for?

I think (actually I'm sure) Larry knew his body was damaged enough that it wouldn't get any better despite his optimistic projections. Life for him would be misery: just one round after another of cold and fatigue, of weakness and inability to do what he wanted, especially the project and the book. At one point, after a very tiring day of dialysis, Larry looked at me and poignantly said, "Is this my karma?" And also he could see the effect on me. Perhaps he knew it wasn't the physical burden that hurt me, it was the loss of the pleasurable things we did together. Just trips to the grocery store and to Barnes and Noble didn't cut it. He knew me and knew that the pressure and losses would cause me to be crankier, but also I would be prodding him more to follow the restrictive medical regimen. Our quality of life would deteriorate further. So, in effect, he was freeing me, but he was also subtly pushing me to live my life, not depend on him for my happiness or pleasure. I have been very dependent on him, as we have been on each other.

Although I don't want to think about it, I will need to accept that I must find my own way, and for now it will be very lukewarm, drab like the soap, but necessary. His love for me was very beautiful and, in many ways, unselfish. He did try to get me involved in his geometry project, but I think that was because he wanted me to be a partner in what was very much an important part of him. I was dependent on him as a friend who accepted me unconditionally, even though I feel I disappointed him by not becoming more involved with Vallian. He would encourage me and even push me to do things I felt incapable of doing (like the doctorate and being an editor). I usually would do them my own way, but I would move forward.

Larry died the way he did—in our home, in my chair, with neighbors close by—to make it easier for me. All his life, he paved the way for me to grow and become the best person I could be. That kind of love and commitment is not easy to come by. Larry's greatest gift to me was his love, which will nourish me for the rest of my life.

EPILOGUE

The fine-toothed comb of time
marches on through the scalp of life.
—*Dr Seuss*

The next few months were a blur. I don't know how I would have survived them had it not been for my friends and neighbors: Tereza, Judy, Margo, Mike, Pat, Annie and Dave, Sandra, Ursula, Marty, Duc Vu, Kevin. And I will never forget the outpouring of caring and love for Larry and me: the cards and emails and gifts and donations. Even the three EMTs gave me a beautiful plant. The following is just a sample of the "gifts" I received during those difficult months.

Tereza took me to a funeral home the day after Larry's death so I could arrange for the cremation. She offered her home for a memorial and was a wonderful hostess. She checked on me daily and offered food and support. She continues to be a caring friend, helping me find and do things, encouraging me as I try to arrange a new life.

Judy was almost as devastated by Larry's death as I was. Her response reminded me that I had to stay strong and support the people who loved him. She helped with the memorial, brought lots of wine, and frequently kept me company, taking me places I wouldn't have gone to alone.

Margo spent a whole day with me, touring the shops in Half Moon Bay; I wasn't very good company. She was the MC at the memorial, and much later, she and Richie helped me clean out Larry's very packed, cluttered home office. She brought wine for the memorial.

Mike designed the flyer announcing Larry's death and the memorial. He helped me to send it out via email as well as providing copies for mailing. During the memorial, he acted as our photographer, providing me with a lasting catalog of pictures.

Pat left a beautiful bouquet of flowers on my front porch (She tried to be anonymous, but I figured it out). Then she dropped in frequently with soup and fruit and wise suggestions. She had been doing that during Larry's last few months, as well. She helped out Tereza at the memorial. She continues to support me through my grieving and takes me to the theatre.

Annie and David sent loving messages and poems, and David gave the eulogy at the memorial. They will be the publishers of this third book.

Sandra had also been very actively helping both Larry and I (husband Ian lifted Larry off the floor when he slipped out of the chair) by offering to shop and bringing food. She is the one who followed the ambulance, taking me to the emergency room at Stanford and bringing me home later that evening. She brought flowers to the memorial.

Ursula also provided neighborly services for us, but a most special one occurred during the memorial when she had her beautiful, five-year-old daughter Claire present me with a lovely bouquet of lilies. It was a poignant moment I will never forget.

Marty transported me to a number of Stanford hospital visits with Larry when I was too tired or stressed to drive. When she learned about Larry's death the day after, she came over and sat with me while I told *the* story, the first of many times.

Duc Vu, the printer who had helped me get the first book published, did all of the materials Mike and I created for the memorial and refused payment for his very professional work.

Kevin, as a "newly-minted lawyer," provided thousands of dollars of legal services, not charging me a cent. I gave him two bottles of wine for a new will, advanced directives, and power of attorney.

And finally, my beloved children Eric, Jill, and Tim came to Menlo Park and stayed with me for a week, supporting me amidst their own grief. After the memorial, we went down to the beach at Davenport (near Santa Cruz, CA) and scattered Larry's ashes into the ocean he loved so much.

There is no way that I can really thank all of these folks who made this painful period more palatable, but I will always love them.

Larry had often said that he didn't want people blubbering over him at a funeral; he wanted a good old-fashioned Irish wake! I'm not sure that the memorial we had was up to the standards of an Irish wake, but we had it on St. Patrick's day, March 17th, and it was lively despite being a purportedly somber occasion. As I mentioned above, Tereza and Peter hosted the memorial, Margo MC'd, and David gave a numinous eulogy. But his wasn't the only eulogy: many people who knew Larry well, even his children, spontaneously shared their memories. But the most memorable happening was when Judy challenged me to "do the Elephant, Sharon!"

I stood up, and to everyone's surprise and enjoyment, I did the Elephant and they did it with me. Thus we sent Larry off with humor and style.

Now I rest in Larry's love.

The Family: Eric, Larry, Sharon, Jill, Tim. Sometime in 2000.

The last word: I wanted Larry to have it.

While firmly believing I am a re-creation of Leonardo Di Vinci, I take little pride in the fact. I am reading a book now that indicates that most of the things "discovered" in the 1400's actually came from China, much earlier. Whether this is true or not, makes little difference to me, because everything I learned this lifetime, I spent many hours educating myself from multiple sources. None of it was automatic, and most of it was simply absorbed from the many thousands of learned men who have gone before me.

I love life, and I love all of the experiences I have had, even the bad ones, or perhaps the bad even more than the good ones. We are all here to learn. That is a certainty, and I do my best almost every day. Just as I was able to receive instruction from Loomis, I have a pantheon of scholars that I know and love both for what they managed to do, as well as for all the trouble they had and the failures they experienced.

As the years have rolled by, I have discovered that my gifts have consisted of about an even number of successes and failures, and that down at the bottom, there is not a hell of a lot of difference between these supposed opposites. Given the horrible example of "The Bonfire of the Vanities," I could see the difficulty, if not the impossibility, of having a guarantee that anything would be left behind, except what might have happened accidentally. I believe that we either get better and better, or we get worse. And whatever that supposedly FINAL decision or report card is, we take it with us to the next classroom, the next series of experiences – the next lifetime. LXV

And I'll see you next lifetime, Larry love!

Unspeakable losses ...

These are the moments when life slams you between the eyes.

You collapse into pieces, unsure when or if you will pick up those pieces again.

They [the losses] pick you up and casually drop you off the nearest cliff.

You sit up blinking with no idea where to go next.

Suzanne Falter, *upon the death of her daughter*
Life Ties: The California Organ Donor Network

The Song of the River
by William Randolph Hurst

The snow melts on the mountain
And the water runs down to the spring.
And the spring in a turbulent fountain,
With a song of youth to sing,
Runs down to the riotous river,
And the river flows to the sea,
And the water again
Goes back in rain
To the hills where it used to be.
And I wonder if life's deep mystery
Isn't much like the rain and the snow
Returning through all eternity
To the places it used to know.
For life was born on the lofty heights
And flows in a laughing stream,
To the river below
Whose onward flow
Ends in a peaceful dream.
And so at last,
When our life has passed
And the river has run its course,
It again goes back,
O're the selfsame track,
To the mountain that was its source.

So why prize life
Or why fear death,
Or dread what is to be?
The river ran
Its allotted span
Till it reached the silent sea.
Then the water harked back
To the mountain-top
To begin its course once more
So we shall run
The course begun
Till we reach the silent shore
Then revisit earth
In a pure rebirth
From the heart of the virgin snow.
So don't ask why
We live or die,
Or whither, or when we go,
Or wonder about the mysteries
That only God may know.

References

Front Matter
Green, B. (July/Aug 2013). *Mind over matter.* Smithsonian, 303, 4, p.27.

H. D. (2011). *Never more will the wind.* In *She walks in beauty*, C. Kennedy, Ed. New York: Grand Central Publishing.

Wahl, L. E. and Wahl, S (2011). *The Vallian trilogy: An inventive life. Part I: The engineer.* Menlo Park, CA: CreateSpace.

Chapter 2
Loomis, A. (1944). *Figure drawing for all it's worth.* New York: Viking Press.

Wahl, L. E. (2012). *The Vallian trilogy: An inventive life. Part II: The learner.* Felton, CA: River Sanctuary Publishing.

Musing 102
Gardner, H. (1983). *Frames of mind: The theory of multiple intelligences.* New York: Basic Books.

Chapter 3
Ehrmann, M. (1927). *Desiderata: A poem for a way of life.* New York: Crown Publishers.

Chapter 5
Myers, I. B. (1998). *Introduction to type,* 6th Ed. Mt. View, CA: CPP

Musing 105
Gibran, K. (1958). *The prophet.* New York: Knopf

Chapter 6
Steinbeck, J. (1939). *The grapes of wrath*. New York: Penguin Classics.

Theory 201
Wahl, L. (2011). *The elephant in the room*. Menlo Park, CA: Speedy Printing.

Chapter 7
Friedman, M and Rosenman, R. H. (1974). *Type A behavior and your heart*. New York: Knopf.

Wahl, S. (Jan 1989). *Septic shock: How to detect it early*. Nursing 89, 19, 1, p. 52-60.

Chapter 8
Sabini, N. (2013). Personal Communication.

Chapter 9
Capra, F. (2013). *Learning from Leonardo: Decoding the notebooks of a genius*. San Francisco: Berrett-Koehler Publishers.

Gardner, H. (1983). *Frames of mind: The theory of multiple intelligences*. New York: Basic Books.

Lykken, D. (1998). *The genetics of genius*. In Stepton, A. Ed. *Genius and the mind: Studies of creativity and temperament*. London: Oxford Press.

Chapter 10
Gibran, K. (1958). *The prophet*. New York: Knopf

Chapter 11
Gagne, R. M. and Briggs, L. J. (1979). *Principles of instructional design*. New York: Holt, Rinehart, and Winston.

Wahl, S. (1992). *A Computer-assisted Instructional Software Program in Mathematical Problem-solving Skills for Medication Administration for Beginning Baccalaureate Nursing Students at San Jose State University.* Major Applied Research Project (Dissertation) for Ed.D degree, Nova University, August. UMI Dissertation Abstracts, 1995.

Chapter 12
D'Sousa, K. (2015, Mar 31). *Mother of all demos on stage.* San Mateo County Times, pp. 1,10.

Gladwell, M. (2011, Nov.14). *The tweaker: The real genius of Steve Jobs.* In The New Yorker Annals of Technology.

Green, B. (2015, Jan). *Hanging by a string.* Smithsonian, 45, 9, pp. 21–27, 88-90.

Isaacson, W. (2011). *Steve Jobs.* New York: Simon and Schuster

Wahl, S. (2011). *Chasing the tesseract: The history of the Vallian Coordinates.* Menlo Park, CA: Speedy Printing.

Chapter 15
Kurtz, E. and Ketcham, K. (1992). *The spirituality of imperfection: Storytelling and the search for meaning.* New York: Bantam Books

Chapter 16
Berg, Y (2004). *The power of the Kabbalah: Technology for the soul.* New York: The Kabbalah Center.

Chapter 17
Halpern, P. (2015). *Einstein's dice and Schrodinger's cat.* New York: Basic Books.

Kubler-Ross, E. and Kessler, D. (2005). *On grief and grieving: Finding the meaning of grief through the five stages of loss.* New York: Scribner

Kurtz, E. and Ketcham, K. (1992). *The spirituality of imperfection: Storytelling and the search for meaning.* New York: Bantam Books.

Miller, B. F. and Keane, C. B. (1987). *Saunders encyclopedia and dictionary of medicine, nursing, and allied health.* Philadelphia: Saunders.

About the Author

Dr. Sharon Wahl has had a 55-year career as a professional nurse and educator, which has been interspersed with her love of writing and helping others to write. She started writing at nine years old with a four page "newspaper" and hasn't quit yet. In between, she has published numerous articles and book chapters, mostly in her favorite field of medicine, pathophysiology. This latest editing and writing project has spanned nine years as she assisted her husband to organize and publish the first two books of his unusual autobiography—The Vallian Trilogy—only to be left to complete the third book of the series after his death. She will continue the story with an upcoming book titled, *A Journey without Larry: Suffering and Surviving.*

After living all of her life on the West Coast, Sharon now lives in Colorado Springs, Colorado, with her cantankerous tortoiseshell cat Pauline and near her daughter and son-in law Jill and Tim Grove. Son Eric Wahl currently lives in Eugene, Oregon.

www.ingramcontent.com/pod-product-compliance
Lightning Source LLC
Chambersburg PA
CBHW060241100426

42742CB00011B/1600